THE RELATE GUIDE
TO SEX IN LOVING RELATIONSHIPS

By the same author

The Working Mother,
A Practical Handbook
The Relate Guide To Better Relationships

THE
RELATE GUIDE
TO SEX IN LOVING
RELATIONSHIPS

Sarah Litvinoff

VERMILION
London

Published in 1992 by Vermilion
an imprint of Ebury Press
Random Century House
20 Vauxhall Bridge Road
London SW1V 2SA

Catalogue record for this book is available from the British Library

ISBN 0 09175294 9

Designed by Bob Vickers
Illustrations by Kathy Wyatt and Peter M Gardiner

Typeset by Saxon Printing Limited, Derby

Printed and bound in Great Britain by Butler and Tanner Ltd, Frome and London

CONTENTS

Acknowledgements

This book has been based on the sensitive, tactful and compassionate work of RELATE sex therapists and counsellors, many of whom gave their time to talk about their clients and their work. Marj Thoburn, Head of RELATE Sex Therapy, was involved in the book from the beginning, and read and commented on it while it was being written, ensuring it was in line with RELATE's approach. Alison Clegg, former Head of RELATE Sex Therapy, gave many hours to talk about sex therapy generally and specifically, and made useful suggestions on the manuscript. Zelda West-Meads, RELATE's Press Officer, also gave her time and encouragement during the writing of the book.

The following counsellors and sex therapists helped by talking about the experiences of many clients: Kathie Burton, Carol Carsley, Paula Carter, Julia Cole, Sue Davies, Elizabeth Lawrence, Peggie Manning, Joan Melling, Norma Moore, Dennis Nash, Joan Rayson, Christina Robinson, Catherine Roblett, Rebecca Sparks, Janice Trivett, Sandra Tucker. The experiences of many other counsellors and sex therapists have also contributed, through the interviews they gave for *The RELATE Guide to Better Relationships* and the work in progress, *The RELATE Guide to Starting Again*.

Thanks also to Peter McCabe, the Director of Fund-Raising for National RELATE, and Steve Hodgson, the Publications Manager.

Case histories

All the case histories in this book are based on real people. However, all names and distinguishing details have been changed so that the couples are unrecognisable.

WHAT IS SEX THERAPY?

Sex therapy is for couples who need help in coping with a sexual problem. The sex therapists are fully trained and experienced RELATE counsellors – men and women who are chosen for their ability to share people's problems sympathetically and who have had further specialized training to help couples overcome sexual difficulties.

Everything couples say is treated confidentially. Therapists realise that sexual problems are difficult to talk about and know how to put couples at their ease. They also know that couples are often unable to discuss their difficulties together and will help them do so.

The sessions with the therapist involve talking in explicit ways about sexual matters, and the therapist offering a great deal of information. During the course of therapy couples are often asked to carry out specific sexual tasks tailored to their needs. These are carried out in the privacy of their own homes, and never with the therapist present.

The sessions talking to the therapist, which last about an hour, take place in private rooms at RELATE centres. The number of sessions varies, but most couples attend on average between twelve and fourteen times.

To find your nearest RELATE sex therapist, contact your local RELATE centre by looking in the telephone directory under 'RELATE' or 'Marriage Guidance'. The national office is at Herbert Gray College, Little Church Street, Rugby CV21 3AP; Tel: 0788 573241.

INTRODUCTION

Sex is part of a loving relationship. At its best, when there is openness, trust and friendship as well as love, sex can be everything you ever hoped for – and even better. But sex with someone you love can also be as routine and dull as brushing your teeth. It can be a cause of shame and misery. It can be painful and disturbing. Sex with someone you love can be something that you avoid at all costs.

How can doing something so intimate and potentially good with the one you love also be the cause of such disappointment, even pain? On the one hand it is the most natural thing in the world, a logical result of romantic love, the physical expression of a more symbolic union. On the other hand, just because it is natural doesn't mean that it is simple. Talking is 'natural', but there is a great difference between a four-year-old child who has the vocabulary and grammar to get by in life and an adult who is able to express complicated ideas and the subtleties of emotions. To use words is natural, but to become an articulate adult involves work, education and practice. Sex is similar. It is a basic drive, and most healthy couples will manage sexual intercourse. But sex that is good and satisfying is more than that, and it doesn't just happen. Loving someone is not enough to guarantee a happy sex life. This book tells you what else you need to know to improve your sex life.

There is probably more written and talked about sex than any other aspect of a loving relationship. In some ways this is good, but it is also part of the problem. Many people have recognised that good sex needs time and technique, and this has helped some towards a more rewarding sex life. But, along the way, this focusing on the mechanics of sex has caused a distortion that increases unhappiness.

Sex has become both separated and elevated in our time. The most obvious result of this is the complete separation of sex from love. It is no longer considered unusual for sex to come before love – one of the first acts of a new relationship – or as an end in itself, something you do with a stranger, like a game of tennis. The emphasis in recreational sex without love is on performance – being 'good' at it, and on gratification measured in orgasms.

Perhaps because of this, sex in a loving relationship has also come to be to be viewed as separate from the rest of your lives together. But sex in a loving relationship *is* different. Sex in this case is also an expression of the way you feel about each other, and as such it can be much more rewarding, varied and subtle than sex with someone you scarcely know. Loving sex can be more sensual than sex without love. Discovering sensual sex brings the revelation that penetration and even orgasms are not essential to joyful and satisfying sex. But, as sex in a committed relationship reflects the way you feel about each other, about yourselves and about the state of your life, it can also have its difficult times.

The concentration on the 'joy' the 'magic', the erotic highs and the technical expertise of sex as sport has also had an impact on sex in loving relationships. Your sex life can suffer from too high expectations or too low expectations – sometimes both at the same time. The high expectations consist of a belief that sex always has to be intensely exciting and passionate, that you should be swept away by desire that culminates in a peak experience physically and emotionally. The low expectations develop when your experience of sex is not what you have been led to believe it should be; it is disappointing or worse, and you don't think there is anything that you can do about it.

One of the main aims of this book is to place sex in its proper place in your relationship: an important part of a much larger whole. It depends on your general feelings for each other and has an effect on them. Good sex is not a cure-all for relationship problems, though if you are giving each other sexual pleasure it will help you to feel good about each other. Unsatisfying sex might have a purely physical cause, but it is just as likely to be a symptom of other things that are not satisfying in your relationship. Sex in a loving relationship is better than sex without love because of the quality that trust, tenderness and affection bring to it. But if you are going through a difficult patch these loving elements will go from your sex life too.

Sex in a continuing relationship ebbs and flows, as do all other aspects of your relationship. Sometimes it can be a peak experience, but not always; neither need it get to the point that it is never pleasurable or is only a hasty and rare occurrence.

What you need to know to make your sex life better is contained in this book. Some of it might come as a surprise: improving your sex life is not a question of learning new positions – though if that appeals to you both, there are recommendations here. Gaining more pleasure from your sex life depends on much more simple and ordinary elements: plenty of time and the right conditions are two of the most important, and just getting these right can make all the difference.

More challenging, and ultimately the most essential element, is increased knowledge and understanding about yourselves. On one level this means knowing your bodies and how they work. Many people think that they know all there is to know about the mechanics of sex and how their bodies work sexually but, in reality, few people have a proper understanding of this. RELATE sex therapists always explain this in detail to the couples they counsel, and say that almost everyone learns something that they did not know before. Doctors who, after all, are trained in the working of the human body, can be just as ignorant about many of the details of arousal and what is necessary for satisfying sex – so it is unsurprising that the rest of us know even less. By the time we are sexually active adults most of us have read or heard so much about sex that we can believe there is very little left to learn. But although we know many of the ingredients, we might not know the essential recipe.

One counsellor talked of a couple who were very much in love, but for whom sex had never been good. Carol had been a virgin and Gerald's experience had been limited to casual sex with short-term girlfriends. Both of them felt that it was his responsibility to make sex good for them both. 'Suppose I led you into the kitchen,' the counsellor said to Gerald, 'and showed you a packet of flour, some eggs, sugar, margarine and dried fruit. Then I said, 'I want you to produce a fruit cake for me in three hours time.' What would you do?' 'Panic!' said Gerald. The counsellor commented that without directions he would probably fail – but that he wouldn't be ashamed to admit that he didn't know what to do, or to ask for help or consult a recipe. Sex, she told them, was in some ways similar and a good deal more complicated. The 'master recipe', which she could give them, involves a proper understanding of how bodies work best together sexually. But, just as there are variations in cake recipes, so there are individual variations in sexual preferences. If sex was to be really good between them they would have to discover these variations for themselves and tell each other clearly what they were – and continue this sexual dialogue through the years.

This is a very important point. Most people who buy sex books are looking for an expert to tell them what to do. One of the main messages of this book is that *you* are the expert when it comes to your own sex life. You will find guidance on general matters and on the specifics that work for some people, but there is no substitute for exploring your own feelings and finding out your unique physical likes and dislikes. Good sex in a loving relationship can be better than the most passionate casual encounter because over time you develop a depth of understanding about yourselves and each other which allows you to sustain quality and satisfaction. As your body and needs change over the years you can explore new aspects of your sexuality – if you have developed the habit of listening to your body and sharing your understanding with each other. Sex in a long-term relationship, however loving, is likely to deteriorate if you miss out these vital elements of self-understanding and communication.

Understanding yourself goes beyond knowing what sexual touching you need, however. Your sexuality – by which we mean what you like about sex, what turns you on, how you feel about yourself as a sexual being, what sex means to you – is the most complex ingredient in your sex life. The sex act is physical, but your sexuality is largely emotional and intellectual. To understand your sexual needs it is useful to understand how you have become the sexual person you are.

To do this, you have to look beyond the relationship you are in now. You need to look back at your childhood and upbringing, your parents, and all the other experiences that have shaped you. Some couples come to RELATE with a sexual problem assuming that they are doing something wrong. In quite a few cases the real cause of the problem has its roots in the past. Until these are tackled, no amount of sexual training in techniques is going to solve it. An obvious example, increasingly seen by RELATE, is sexual abuse in childhood. If you were abused, this can have a fundamental effect on your developing sexuality. Sex becomes connected to misuse of power, unhappiness, anger and guilt. Any future sexual relationship as an adult, however loving, will activate these confused feelings, which will then get in the way of trust and satisfaction. Pinpointing what it was in the past that has made you feel as you do in the present can help you towards a more conscious assessment of your feelings. It can also help you come to terms with or transform them.

Similarly, some people's problems with sex can be traced to ideas about it being dirty or bad, which they learnt from their parents or their religion. Recognising that these beliefs have made it difficult for you to enjoy sex can allow you to challenge them and, as an adult, to modify them. The first section of this book is devoted to helping you see in what ways your upbringing has affected your sexuality. With this awareness you can go on to tackle problems and increase your satisfaction with more success.

If both of you read this book and so learn more about yourselves and each other, you are laying the foundations for a good sex life. Even so, sex will have its highs and lows. You must remember that this is the same for everyone. No one gets it right all the time. Sometimes you will both be feeling very passionate, sometimes sex will be the last thing on your mind. Sometimes, indeed, you might find a sexual problem emerges. Sex, after all, is a normal part of normal life, and problems are normal too. What you can also learn from this book is that every sexual problem has a solution if you are both prepared to be creative and resourceful, and when the love and will is there.

There are, however, some sexual difficulties that a book can't cure, though it can help you start the healing process. Sex therapy, on the other hand, has a high rate of success. If you find that you reach a point from which you can go no further on your own, you will be reassured to know that most RELATE centres have a sex therapist. No problem surprises or shocks sex therapists, and their trained professionalism can help you move forward faster and further than you would believe possible. Choosing therapy is an expression of loving commitment, and that can only benefit your relationship.

PART ONE
YOU AND SEX

1

YOU AND SEX

The age you become aware of your sexuality varies – for many people it is when they first become romantically attracted to someone. But most people don't realize that your sexuality develops long before this, even before you begin to think or fantasize about sex. Your sexuality is related to emotions and ideas that seem to have nothing to do with sex. Indeed, your earliest experiences of life contribute eventually to the way you react sexually and how you feel about sex – just as they also affect the total human being that you become. An example is a child who is given a lot of enjoyable cuddles and affection will very likely turn into an adult who is a cuddly and affectionate lover.

It is hard to credit the fact that even things you don't remember, such as being born and your first few months of life, affect how you feel today, but it is true. It is easier to connect later experiences, which you do remember, to the way you feel now, particularly if they were unpleasant or hurtful. It is important to take a complete look at your early life to understand your sexuality. It is the accumulation of all your experiences that makes you behave and think as you do – and that is why all of us are different sexually, just as we differ in our thoughts and feelings from everyone else.

Gaining a greater understanding of the past allows you to do more than say, 'That's why I'm the way I am.' You can use the knowledge to make changes, approach problems with more chance of success and build a better sex life. Suppose you were a child who was never cuddled and was treated strictly. As a lover you might find more playful and affectionate sensual touching awkward or threatening. Recognizing why you feel like this gives you the opportunity to decide to change it. You can make the effort to learn how to relax and enjoy this sensuality and add a new dimension to your sex life.

Some early experiences affect you in ways that are much harder to change, however. Making the connection to them and the way you feel now won't effect a miracle cure but, if you feel strong enough to deal with them, improvement is possible. Even if this is difficult, telling your sympathetic partner about it and explaining why it has affected you sexually allows you both to adapt your sex life to accommodate the way you feel. Some problems in relating together sexually become acute precisely because the causes are never talked about.

For instance, one woman always leapt up after sex to scrub herself clean. Her man felt that this was a rejection of him and that she found sex with him disgusting. This caused rows and continuing bad feeling between them. During sex therapy it emerged that her mother was neurotic about cleanliness and had passed this on to her daughter. The woman could not change her need to wash thoroughly after sex, but when both of them understood it better the rows stopped. Her man knew not to take it personally. They developed a routine of showering together after sex and returning to bed for a cuddle. Sharing the problem allowed them to reach a solution that suited them both.

This chapter is a chance for you to look at your early life carefully and assess the impact it has had on you. It will help you to trace elements of your developing sexuality and also see how experiences in former relationships might have reinforced any difficulties and problems. Later in the book you will take a similar close look at the relationship you are in now, the progress and nature of which you will be able to understand better.

Your relationship with your parents, from your babyhood on, is one of the most important elements in how you feel about yourself and how you live your life. This includes you as a sexual being, too. The first thing to do is cast your mind back to your earliest memories of your parents and how you felt with them.

YOUR PARENTS AND YOU

A few people have clear memories of the time when they were babies, before they could speak, but this is quite rare. Most people can date their first real memories to the time when they were toddlers, or older. It doesn't matter when your memories start: the kind of atmosphere and emotions that attach to them will give you some idea of the period that came before you can remember. There may well be family stories about your birth and your early babyhood that will give you some idea of what it must have been like for you. For instance, if you hear that your birth was difficult, or made your mother ill, or that you were an unsettled baby who cried a lot or were in other ways hard to handle, the early experiences that you can't remember might well have been mixed ones and, in some ways, not happy.

Very broadly, if you experienced your parents as loving towards you and kind and affectionate, you will have started to build good feelings about yourself at an early age, even though you have no actual memories of this time. A baby who receives just the sort of love and attention that he or she needs experiences this as an inner conviction that he or she is good and lovable. These very early feelings, which are not logical and rarely put into words, are likely to produce an adult who has these same feelings inside. What this means is that the adult finds it easy to trust the love that someone offers and is not frightened of being intimate. Trust, and an ability to be intimate, are two of the most important ingredients in being a loving adult and in a healthy sexuality. Someone with these good feelings inside has an ability to bounce back even from disappointments in love or from a relationship that has caused pain.

Sometimes a baby can feel frightened and unloved or that his or her parents are stern and remote even when they were good and loving people. Through no fault of their own – perhaps there was illness or difficult financial circumstances or a family tragedy – your parents might have had problems that meant they couldn't give you the attention that a baby needs. As a baby and young child you have no understanding of these outside problems. What happens instead is that at a very deep level you feel somehow at fault, not worthy to be treated lovingly and well.

This feeling is so deep that you can have no idea where it came from. You just 'know' that you are not really good enough, or sometimes that you are plain 'bad'.

If you felt regularly rejected by your parents, or frightened of them, or even hated them, this can result in a belief that love is not reliable, or that it can be painful to attach yourself to someone because there is the likelihood that if you do so you will be made unhappy. Because of this, later on, as an adult, you can find intimate communication threatening and difficult, even when you feel yourself to be deeply in love.

Really opening up to someone makes you vulnerable, gives them power over you, and your early experiences have left you with the feeling that this is dangerous and leads to misery.

Any hurtful experiences with love later on can make you even more convinced that you can't trust anyone to love you, and even more cautious about opening up. If you don't dare take the risk, your loving relationships will suffer, as will your sex life. It is impossible to hold back some parts of yourself and not others. You might well have vigorous, active and intense sexual experiences without ever achieving true closeness and satisfaction from sex. These more profound elements require trust, an ability to let go, the confidence to be selfish and the will to be generous.

It might seem that closeness and true sexual satisfaction are beyond your reach if you were unlucky in your early childhood. But while it is true that the feelings that developed before you were three (as well as what comes later) will have set a pattern, this *can* be broken. Sometimes this happens because after a difficult start your life settles down into a much more secure and loving phase, which does a lot to restore your faith in yourself, other people and life. But even if this doesn't happen, you can still make the changes as an adult. It is difficult, and requires courage, to challenge these deep feelings, but people do manage it. The best place to do so is within a loving relationship. Both counsellors and sex therapists have seen individuals and couples slowly reap the rewards of learning to trust in love, which usually starts by learning to value and love yourself.

It can be difficult to remember how you felt about your parents when you were very young, even if you have quite clear memories of events. This process can be blocked by a number of things. For instance, if you were very unhappy or frightened you might have suppressed the feelings because they were too hard to bear. When you try to remember how you felt, nothing comes to you. Or your own memories might have become super-imposed with what you have been told by your parents and others. Parents seem powerful and all-knowing to a young child, and if they have told you that you felt or thought a certain thing, you can come to believe that they must be right. Similarly, when we are young we all have a need to feel that our parents are wonderful, so it can seem more bearable to remember yourself as having been bad than to feel that they ever did anything wrong or cruel.

Sometimes it is easier to remember negative feelings about your parents if you don't get on with them now. But if you love and respect them it can seem an act of betrayal to remember feelings that reflect badly on them, particularly if you know how hard they tried to do their best for you. You must remember that it doesn't have to mean that they knowingly or purposely tried to hurt you. Perhaps you were ill as a young child and had to stay in hospital. All you will have understood is that you were separated from the people you loved and needed most, and that can feel like rejection by them even though it wasn't. The effect on you can be the same as real rejection by an unloving parent.

Similarly, if one of your parents dies when you are a child, you can feel as if you have been left in the lurch. The feelings of lack of trust become part of you, even though, as a mature and logical adult, you know that it had nothing to do with how much you were loved. Other less dramatic happenings can also affect your feelings of lovableness and security. With the best will in the world parents sometimes get things wrong – unfortunately, even when they believe they have their children's best interests at heart. If you have children yourself you might recognise the truth in this, because of your experience of making mistakes with them.

Don't worry if you can't remember early feelings. However, if you often feel worthless, you need to accept that this feeling is unhelpful and wrong. If you find loving someone difficult or frightening then you need to understand that the fear is likely to be inappropriate and more to do with you than with the other person. Making these changes in yourself is possible – by finding ways to increase your confidence, and with the help of a loving and concerned partner.

❛ ════════ Talking point ════════

My first memory

Take it in turns to describe to each other your earliest memory. Was it happy or sad? Your very first memory often sums up the atmosphere of early childhood. **❜**

Your mother

Your first and closest relationship is with your mother. If that was experienced by you as loving and happy you are more likely to feel good about yourself, even if other people or events were less helpful. But if, for example, she was depressed, she will not have been able to give you the warm, free loving you needed all the time, and that can result in you not feeling good enough – either in yourself, or for other people.

Your mother is also your first model of femininity, and the kind of person she was has a profound effect on your ideas about women and your own sexuality, whether you are a man or a woman.

As a woman, you will have been unconsciously modelling yourself on her from the time you were a little girl. Even if, as an adult, you don't admire the kind of woman she is, at a much deeper level you will have made yourself partly like her. For instance, if she seemed happy about herself and relaxed about all the elements of being a woman, including menstruation, it will be much easier for you to feel good about your own female body. But if she was in bad health, or complained about 'women's troubles' you are more likely to feel suspicious about your own body and less happy about being a woman.

Similarly, if you are a man, the way your mother was is your first intimate picture of what women are like, and some part of you will come to expect other women to be like her. If she obviously found being a woman difficult, it might give you a distrust of women, or you might find yourself drawn to women who are similarly uncomfortable about themselves, even if you believe you are consciously looking for someone who is very different.

For both men and women, every aspect of their mother's life – and how she behaved as a mother and a wife – has some bearing on their ideas about women: whether she was a housewife or worked outside the home, whether she was gentle or angry, happy or depressed, downtrodden or powerful. These feelings about her will colour very basic ideas you have about women, and how mothers and wives should behave – or are likely to behave.

! ========================= *Task* =========================

My Mother

On a sheet of paper sum up your thoughts about your mother during your childhood, under the following headings. You can write sentences or list words that most aptly describe how she appeared to you.

- **Personality**
- **Her feelings about herself**
- **Her feelings about being a woman**
- **Her feelings about being a mother**
- **Her feelings about being a wife/partner**
- **Her health**
- **Her feelings about work/lack of work**
- **Her feelings about the home**
- **Her way of dealing with anger**
- **Her way of showing love**

Encourage your partner to do the same, and then talk about what you both have written.

!

Your father

Most people have a less intense relationship with their fathers when they are young children. In the early days he is more on the fringe of your life, though this can change as you get older. But the way you saw him still has an important effect on you, your ideas about men, and your developing sexuality, whether you are a man or woman.

Your father's attitude to himself and his maleness affects the way you are (if you are a man) or what you think about men (if you are a woman). A boy will be affected if his father held his emotions in control, only ever showing anger or 'acceptable' male emotions, finding it hard to be gentle or loving. The boy might believe that he must work hard to suppress these 'feminine' emotions and develop the manly ones. Some fathers and mothers openly encourage him to do so. What this means is that later on he can find it hard to get in touch with these suppressed emotions – which are precisely what he needs to develop an intimate, loving relationship. These feelings are also necessary to a fully rounded sexuality.

A girl brought up with a father like this will also assume that it is a natural way for men to be. She might find it hard to be attracted to men who are more in touch with their full range of emotions, or suspicious of them – even if she yearns for the kind of intimate relationship these men can offer.

A girl who felt that she didn't receive enough love from her father might feel unsure that she can expect it from other men. A boy who felt the same might also question his own ability to be a loving person.

Just as your mother provides your most deeply entrenched ideas about women, so your father does about men. His feelings about work (or the lack of it), his effectiveness as a husband and father, his life outside the home, his moods, his health, and, indeed, everything else in his life, shape your feelings about how men behave as individuals and as husbands and fathers.

!_____ *Task* ═════════

My Father

On a sheet of paper sum up your thoughts about your father during your childhood, under the following headings. You can write sentences or list words that most aptly describe how he appeared to you.

- **Personality**
- **His feelings about himself**
- **His feelings about being a man**
- **His feelings about being a father**
- **His feelings about being a father/partner**
- **His health**
- **His feelings about work/lack of work**
- **His feelings about the home**
- **His way of dealing with anger**
- **His way of showing love**

Encourage your partner to do the same, and then talk about what you both have written.

!

Identifying with your parents

It is usual to identify most closely with your same-sex parent, and in certain ways become like him or her. However, some children identify more strongly with the parents of the other sex, and model themselves on them. This can happen when the relationship with the other parent is most close and loving, but it is even more likely when the same-sex parent provides a model that you can't respect or like – is disturbed, unhappy, victimized, threatening or in other ways living in a way that, as a child, you find off-putting or frightening. This can lead to conscious or unconscious attempts to be more like the parent of the other sex. Sometimes this can lead to confusion in relationships later, or ambivalence and uncertainty about your own sexuality.

‘———— Talking point ————

That's where I get it from

Take it in turns to describe to each other aspects of your personality and ways of behaving that you identify as being like your parents'. From whom did you get what? Are these things you like – or not?

’

Your parents' expectations of you

As you become older, you also become more aware of what your parents think of you, what they expect of you and what they want from you. To a degree, their ideas become your ideas. If your parents seemed to think highly of you and respect you, you will have these same feelings about yourself – even if, sometimes, the rest of the world disagrees. These feelings give you confidence.

If, on the other hand, your parents don't appear to think you are worth very much it can be hard for you to think of yourself as someone who will do well. Some people go on to fulfil this prophecy – even unwittingly causing themselves to fail, when in reality they have the aptitude to succeed. Sometimes, however, this gives you an 'I'll show you!' attitude, and because of this you go on to succeed; even so, there remains a part of you that thinks failure might be inevitable, and continues to fear it, against all signs to the contrary.

The expectations of some parents get in the way of the love they offer. If they want or need you to be good and do well they might be more loving and accepting when you do, and unloving and rejecting when you don't. This makes you feel that you are not lovable for yourself – warts and all – but only when you are good or successful. This can continue to trouble you within relationships, where you feel that you must hide what you see as the bad and unlovable side of yourself for fear your partner will go off you. Sometimes this need to do everything well to gain love can also transfer itself to your sex life, in which you also need to be 'good' and 'achieve'. For men, 'achievement' in sex often means penetrating and ejaculating within the partner, and other sorts of sex can seem like a waste of time.

! ──────────────── *Task* ────────────────

Labels

Make a list of ways that your parents 'labelled' you. Were you considered good, bad, difficult, easy, good-looking, plain, intelligent, clever, resourceful, clingy? Write down what they used to say that sticks in your mind. Any sentences that began, 'You're always...', 'You never...', 'You're so...', 'You are the ..... one' will remind you what those labels were.

Discuss these with your partner. Do you think they were right or wrong? Do you find yourself continuing to think of yourself in these ways? Which were helpful and which were unhelpful?

!

Lack of parents

A few people experience the loss of their parents at an early age, either through death or perhaps because they were put into care. If you had no strong mother and father substitutes this can make you feel insecure and unsure about yourself, your lovableness or your ability to love. Developing more positive feelings becomes something that you need to do as an adult, just as people who had unhappy experiences with their parents have to.

Adoptive parents

If you were adopted at birth, then to all intents and purposes your experiences will be the same as those of children of biological parents, good or bad. But if you were adopted later in your babyhood or childhood, some of your earliest experiences will have been affected by the disruption of being transferred from your first carers. Sustained and reliable loving from your adoptive parents can do a lot to make up for this, as it can for any child who has had difficulties early on.

Divorced/separated parents

If your parents divorce or separate, this has an effect on you, whatever age you are when it happens. The unhappiness of the parent you stay with and your changed circumstances are powerful experiences for you, which will be dealt with in detail later on in this chapter.

Physical attention

The aspect of your relationship with your parents that has the most obvious effect on your sexuality is the quality of the physical affection you received. As we have already said, if you had an abundance of cuddles and kisses you are likely to end up as an affectionate cuddly person – as a lover, and also perhaps as a parent.

The kind of touching you received also includes the way you were handled as a baby, whether you were breastfed or held closely during feeding, how you were bathed and your nappy was changed. If all this seemed to be done with warmth and pleasure, your earliest feelings about your body will be similarly warm and pleasurable. These feelings about your body are very important in making you the lover you are. If you like your body you will be a more responsive lover. If you find your body ugly or disgusting it will dampen your sexual feelings, because you feel shame and self-dislike – or because you can't believe that anyone else really finds you attractive.

Early experiences that can start to make you feel uncomfortable about your body include your carer finding changing your nappy distasteful, difficulties with potty training, being made to feel bad about touching parts of your body, particularly your genitals, and frequent physical punishment.

The worst experience, as far as your developing sexuality goes, is sexual abuse in childhood. This is looked at later in the chapter under **Traumatic Sexual Experiences**.

' —————————— Talking point ——————

Cuddles and smacks

Describe to each other your cosiest memories of being cuddled and kissed by your parents, if you have any. How did it make you feel? When did it stop? What did you feel about it stopping? Then go on to talk about what you remember of physical punishment, if any. How did it make you feel? When did it stop?

'

YOUR PARENTS AND EACH OTHER

It is not just the way that parents behave towards you that affects you. Their relationship with each other is also very important to your development. It provides your clearest and most detailed picture of how two people behave in a close relationship and therefore has an effect on your own behaviour in future relationships, whether heterosexual or homosexual.

If their relationship was close, loving, respectful and equal, your expectations of the kind of relationship you are going to develop for yourself will contain those elements. Similarly, if they seemed broadly happy together, enjoyed each other's company, showed each other affection both physically and in the way they talked to each other, you develop the idea that this sort of relationship is possible, and the confidence to try to form a similar relationship yourself.

This is the best sort of relationship, and not as common as it should be. Most children see a far less balanced relationship between their parents – and even a basically happy couple will inevitably go through times when problems make them unhappy or angry with each other.

If your experience of your parents' relationship was less than good it makes it harder for you to know how to develop a good relationship yourself. You might build up your own picture of what an ideal relationship is like and vow that's what you will have. But the trouble is that you do not have the experience or understanding of how to make that happen on a day-to-day basis. What this means is that you might start off full of good intentions when you first fall in love, but when you meet any one of the usual problems that happen in relationships you don't know what to do.

This is when you are most likely to fall back into what you have learnt and do know – the unhelpful way your parents behaved with each other. Much of relationship counselling involves helping a couple to realize what patterns they might be reproducing from their early home life and consciously setting out to do it differently and more helpfully.

If the relationship between your own parents was unhappy, you might either settle for an unhappy relationship yourself because it feels 'normal' or leave any relationship that threatens to be unhappy. What you did not learn from your parents was that there is another way to deal with this: which is to work together to tackle the root of the unhappiness and make changes to increase happiness.

You also gain some ideas about your parents' sex life, even when you are too young to know what sex is, and even if they never talked about it. Small clues in the way they touch at other times, locked bedroom doors, innuendos and jokes will build up a picture of whether it is frequent and happy, or rare and a source of contention. These ideas have a way of transferring themselves to your own long-term sexual relationships, particularly if you marry.

Expectations that sex doesn't happen between a couple who have been together for a long time, or that one is demanding while the other is reluctant, or that cuddles are for children and not for adults, can mean that you allow your own sex life to follow that pattern later – even if it started off well and happily. But if your parents showed all the signs of sexual satisfaction, and were cuddly and affectionate with each other, you will enter a long-term relationship with an expectation that you will behave in the same way yourself.

The balance of power in your parents' relationship is another important element. One parent might be very obviously controlling and in charge. Whether this is your father or your mother, it gives you the idea that it is a normal pattern in relationships. A part of you might either feel it is your fate to be like the same-sex parent in a relationship of your own, or you might strive to be different.

If you have a relationship with someone who is naturally inclined to take the other role, you will have a similar power balance to your parents. If, on the other hand, you meet someone who feels the need to take the same role as you there could be a power struggle, rather than an equal sharing. If both of you take the 'victim' role you might cling together in fear or seek to force the other to take more charge, or blame each other for anything that goes wrong. These ways of behaving together might work for a time, but they are much less helpful and happy than a relationship that is equally balanced and where partners share responsibility.

Similarly, the way in which one or other of your parents got their way – by nagging, crying, shouting, threatening, sulking or other manipulative behaviour – can affect your own relationship. You might try these ways yourself, or resign yourself to similar behaviour from your partner because you believe it is the way people conduct negotiations. If you were made profoundly unhappy or frightened by the way your parents behaved together you might shut off from a partner who behaves the same way, or leave the relationship, rather than working to improve matters.

In the same way, it is relevant if your parents' relationship included violence. As a child, what you are learning is that the way to handle anger is through violence. This includes violent, aggressive language in rows, throwing things, as well as actual physical attack. This can make you very frightened of anger – your own and other people's. Perhaps you control it until it bursts out, or control it so well that you are only ever aware of feeling sad or depressed instead.

On the other hand, it can also lead you to become violent in your own relationships, or tolerate violence from your partner – even though you hate or fear it. Sometimes you tolerate or welcome violence because your early experiences have caused you to connect it to love. This unbalanced attitude to anger can also develop when your parents are not violent and do not argue – but when you can sense the anger or dislike underneath this. You either fear anger even more because you have no idea what terrible things would happen if it were to be unleashed or you become more openly angry in your own relationship because it seems better than holding it in.

Either way, you have no direct experience of anger that is not in some way bad. What this amounts to is that you have not learnt effective ways of dealing with anger so that it is positive and constructive. Everyone feels angry from time to time, but not dealing with the emotion safely or at all can have a bad effect on loving relationships. Many sexual problems also have their root in angry feelings that are left to fester.

Chloë and Steve illustrate how your parents' relationship can ultimately affect your sexuality. They were in their late twenties, and had a three-year-old daughter. Ever since the child's birth they had felt they were drifting apart. They got on well together, almost like casual flatmates, but they hadn't had sex for over two years. They came for counselling to see how they could become close again.

When Chloë started to talk about her early life, she was still consumed with anger at her father. He was a domineering 'man's man', who was not interested in Chloë. He obviously preferred her brother and showed it; he thought women and girls were inferior beings, beneath his notice. Chloë resented her father's treatment of her, but she was much more deeply affected by her father's treatment of her mother. He bullied her relentlessly and was often violent. There was no love lost between them. Chloë's mother was frightened of her husband and would bend over backwards to do just as he wanted; she was very unhappy and would often cry.

Chloë loved her mother and was desperately upset for her. But she also despised her and feared becoming like her. She hated her father, who seemed to enjoy his life at the expense of her mother's happiness. While he indulged her brother and egged him on with his girlfriends, he ignored Chloë and under-valued her.

The result of this was that Chloë was determined not to be like her mother. Being a woman meant too much unbearable pain. Despite hating her father, she modelled herself on him – she knew no other way to be different from her mother. She was a very pretty teenager and she used this to wreak vengeance on boys, despising them as her father despised women. The only way she knew to bolster her self-esteem was to get power over someone else.

She became sexually active young, and went through boys very quickly. When she met Steve she warned him that she had a male sexuality and wasn't interested in anything lovey-dovey.

Their sex life was all right to begin with. Sex happened at Chloë's instigation and the way she wanted it. Steve came from a close, almost suffocating family. He had been so over-protected that he was unable to make decisions on his own and was a fearful person. Chloë's strength and decisiveness were therefore very attractive to him. Both of them liked her to be in control.

When Nina was born all this changed. Steve was determined to be present at the birth, but Chloë did not want him there. However, he was backed up by the hospital staff and stayed with Chloë. Chloë was angry and distressed that he should have seen her so vulnerable and out of control. It made her fear that she would lose her power in the relationship. It was after this that Chloë went off sex. She didn't feel it was possible to be a mother and a sexual woman – you had to be one or the other. Although she was unaware of the reason, it was because she identified much more closely with her own mother when she became a mother herself.

During counselling they were helped to address the question of their lack of closeness. To become close and intimate Chloë would have to relinquish power, allow Steve to get to know her – insecurities and all – which would mean also letting her vulnerability show. This was too horrifying for Chloë to contemplate. She feared that in doing this she would suffer like her mother.

Chloë and Steve were keen to bypass the relationship counselling and go straight on to sex therapy to deal with Chloë's lack of interest, but the counsellor felt this would fail if they could not get their relationship in better shape.

However, she did help them to explore the reasons behind Chloë's loss of interest. It was inexplicable to Chloë, who had always wanted and needed a lot of sex, but working with the counsellor produced an astounding revelation. When she began to think in careful detail about her sex life she had to admit that she had never enjoyed the physical act of sex itself. The power over the men was the only exciting element, something Chloë had never realised before.

This emerged because the counsellor asked Chloë to remember sexual occasions when she had enjoyed herself in the past. What conditions or sexual acts contributed to her pleasure then that could be re-introduced now? Back they went into Chloë's past with her dozens of lovers, and as she reassessed each sexual experience she was forced to conclude that, without exception, the sex had done nothing for her. Being wanted had made her feel good, discarding the men had made her feel even better; the thrill of the chase was the best bit of all. But the sex itself was a non-event.

This was painful for Chloë to realize, even shocking. She wanted to be able to enjoy sex, and she and Steve insisted they were ready for sex therapy. The counsellor was reluctant, but felt she had to give them a chance. She started them on the first, gentle task of exploring each other's bodies in a non-sexual way. But, as she had guessed, this proved too much for Chloë. She hated it, said it was a useless thing to do – it made her very angry. This task requires you to get in touch with your feelings, physical and emotional, and for Chloë this was just too dangerous.

Until Chloë was able to dare to let down her guard it was hard for any sort of counselling or sex therapy to help them. Chloë and Steve stopped coming for counselling, but they knew that the door was open should Chloë feel strong enough to try again.

❛━━━━━━━ Talking point ━━━━━━━

My parents together

Tell each other the nicest memory you have of your parents as a couple, if any. Then describe the most disagreeable memory, if any. Which was most usual?

Talk about what you believe their feelings were for each other – did they like each other? Did they love each other? Did they show affection? How did they deal with disagreements? Did you feel they had a sex life?

❜

YOU AND THE REST OF YOUR FAMILY

The relationships you have with other members of your family might be significant, particularly if your family is close. For instance, loving grandparents whom you saw regularly as a child might have helped to offset more difficult and strained relationships with your parents. A good relationship with an aunt or uncle might do the same. Seeing at close quarters a loving relationship between couples of relatives helps widen your experience of how people relate together and provides alternative models for you.

On the other hand, a member of the extended family might sometimes be a sexual abuser, which can be as traumatic for you as if the abuser were a parent. Or your parents might still be in awe of their own parents, who continue to wield power within the family.

Brothers and sisters

The most significant family members for you, after parents, are likely to be any brothers and sisters you have. Siblings can be allies and friends, or enemies and rivals – sometimes your relationships with them change from good to bad and then back again over the years.

Broadly, relationships with brothers and sisters teach you lessons about sharing – of love, possessions and personal space. They teach you ways of handling anger and unfairness for good or ill. If parents were difficult in some way siblings can sometimes help share the burden and support each other. The better and happier your sibling relationships were the more confident you feel about relationships in general – and the reverse is also true.

Only children sometimes feel lonely, particularly if they do not have access to an extended family of close grandparents, uncles, aunts and cousins. They can feel excluded from their parents' relationship, or alternatively too closely involved with one or other of them, or feel over-responsible for their parents' happiness. They can find dealing with the unfairness of other children difficult. All these feelings can be transferred to the relationships they make as adults.

❛━━━━━━━━━ Talking point ━━━━━━━━━

My family

Share memories of your family with your partner. Which members did you like and love? Which members did you not get on with? ❜

YOUR POSITION IN THE FAMILY

When you were born also counts towards the way you feel about yourself and can later affect the kind of relationships you make. For instance, eldest children – if they were used to feeling important and controlling where younger brothers and sisters were concerned – can go on to make relationships in which they continue this pattern. Sometimes their partners turn out to have been younger brothers or sisters in other families. Youngest children tend to have little experience of having to take responsibility, and might be babied or bullied by the rest of their family. They are more likely to go on to make relationships in which they continue to be looked after. Children in between can suffer from not feeling special enough, and this feeling can continue to haunt them in relationships later. Only children are often like eldest children in their attitudes and the relationships they make later. However, if they were over-protected or cossetted they might be more like youngest children.

Frances is a good example of how position in the family is able to affect sexual development. She and her husband, Tom, came for sex therapy because they wanted to have a baby. Frances, however, suffered from vaginismus, which means that the muscles of her vagina would go into involuntary spasm so that Tom was unable to penetrate her. They were both twenty-six years old.

Frances was the youngest of three daughters. The elder two were born very close together and Frances came along ten years later. Three years after she was born her parents divorced. Throughout Frances's childhood her mother had made a few unsuccessful attempts at other relationships. Each time these failed, she was plunged into depression for months.

The other sisters were teenagers when this was happening and were caught up with boyfriends and concerns of their own. Frances became her mother's solace. She looked to Frances for emotional support, and needed her to be her 'joy'. This was difficult for Frances, but she did her best. She adored her sisters and longed to be close to them. But while they loved her and petted her, she was too young to be of any interest to them. She felt excluded and thrown together with her mother even more.

Frances's mother did not like her to have boyfriends. She disapproved of one boy whom Frances had liked a lot. She could never understand why he suddenly stopped seeing her, and she half suspected that her mother might have intervened.

When Frances was twenty her mother finally made a good relationship and married the man. A year later Frances met Tom, and this time there was no resistance from her mother. They were married shortly afterwards, but her mother continued to lean on her 'little girl'. They spoke on the phone three or four times a day, and Frances and Tom visited her every weekend.

Frances was reluctant to talk about her family when she saw the sex therapist alone. She was particularly prickly on the subject of her mother. She didn't have a word of criticism to say, and was defensive when she thought the therapist seemed critical. She was able to say that she still felt isolated from her sisters – that she felt she could never 'catch up', and she was feeling this particularly poignantly because they had children and her problem meant that she was unable to. The therapist was struck by the fact that she looked and dressed like a little girl.

Tom was more forthcoming about Frances's mother. When he saw the sex therapist alone he said he was sure she had something to do with the problem. Frances's life still revolved around her.

The therapist believed that apart from the sex difficulty they had a good, solid and loving relationship – and she told them so when she discussed the therapy with them together. Sex therapy involves 'homework', for which the couple regularly have to set aside undisturbed time to do the sexual tasks. The therapist told them that for this to work, Frances must be prepared to take the phone off the hook, so that there was no chance of being interrupted by one of her mother's calls.

Frances was aghast, and rather angry. When they came back the next week, they reported that Frances would not take the phone off the hook, and they had been unable to start the tasks.

The therapist was not accusing, but she gently pointed out that matters were unlikely to improve until Frances was able to take that step. She said, 'If you want to catch up with your sisters and have a family you have to be able to be sexual, and allow yourself to grow up.'

This conversation had a profound effect on Frances. It was as if she had only just realized that she had subconsciously colluded with her mother to stay a little girl for her mother's sake. When they returned the next week, Frances reported that she had felt quite all right about taking the phone off the hook. Not only that, she had told her mother she was only going to phone her once a week. She further said that they would not be visiting every weekend, but would do so once a month. It turned out that in the course of the conversation she had also asked her mother if she had had anything to do with her first boyfriend dropping her so suddenly. Yes, her mother admitted, she had warned him off. For the first time Frances was able to allow herself to feel angry at her mother. It was the most obvious example of her mother's interference and desire to keep her young, even at the expense of her happiness. The anger did not last long, but it fuelled her determination to stick to what she had resolved.

The therapist says the change was extraordinary and sudden. 'It was as if the blue touchpaper had been lit.' Frances loved the sexual tasks and almost immediately got in touch with her repressed sexuality. She bought new clothes and restyled her hair. Each week she looked more sophisticated, mature and happy. She had always felt fearful outside the home, but now she found herself a job. Her conscious decision to grow up released her sexuality: little girls don't have sex, but women do.

Very quickly Frances was able to get over her vaginismus. Her relationship with her mother took a new turn. There was more normal contact, and she felt that it gained in quality; nothing was lost.

Frances and Tom were very happy. The issue of having a baby became less urgent. Sex itself was so good that they wanted to have time to enjoy it. When Frances last saw the therapist she said, 'We've decided to give ourselves a year without worrying. If I'm not pregnant after that, we'll see a doctor.'

Favourites and scapegoats

In some families there are very obvious favourites or scapegoats. Sometimes just one parent favours a particular child, or picks on another. This has an impact on you, whether it was you or one of your siblings.

If another child was the favourite it is easy to see that you are likely to have been jealous and have had doubts about your own lovableness.

However, if you were the favourite, you are also likely to have had mixed feelings. While it is nice to be made to feel special, you can suffer from the resentment of the others. Or the special attention might make you feel guilty. Oddly enough, it might also make you feel insecure about the reliability of love because more is given to you than the others – the supply is not constant, so you might fear it can be switched off.

If you were designated the 'bad one' in the family, you will believe it is true. You have no way of understanding that a scapegoat is often created by your *parents'* behaviour and expectations. One counsellor told of a woman who had been brought up to believe that all boys were difficult and bad. Without realizing it, she pushed her bright and active son into difficult behaviour by her treatment of him. She rarely cuddled or praised him. She was inconsistent about what he was and wasn't allowed to do, so he never knew where he was until she exploded with rage. Although she came for counselling about her relationship with her husband, the counsellor also worked on ways to help her make a better relationship with her son. Within weeks the boy became much easier and no longer a problem. Children who are scapegoats in the family find it difficult to make good, loving relationships later because they feel unlovable and can't believe in the love they are given.

❛ ════════════ Talking point ════════════

'It's always you!'
Talk together about whether there were any favourites or scapegoats in your family. Were you one of them? If so, how did you feel about the different attention you received?

❜

Traumatic experiences

Any traumatic experiences in your childhood affect your development, particularly those that include close family, such as brothers and sisters.

An obvious example is the death of one of your siblings. The death of someone you love when you are young causes natural grief. The pain makes you feel that loving someone is likely to be painful because they can be taken away from you. This can make you hold back in adult relationships. Sometimes your feelings are complicated by any jealousy or rivalry you felt towards the sibling who died. A child who sometimes felt anger or hate towards a brother or sister who later dies can fear that their own feelings caused the death. Even though, as an adult, you know it was not your fault, part of you can still feel fearful of your destructive powers, which can make it hard for you to love fully. The impact on your parents also affects you. Their grief for your dead sibling can make you feel isolated, or give you the impression that the other child was loved more than you.

Sexual abuse by a sibling is also traumatic. This is different from innocent sexual exploration and games with a brother or sister very near you in age, which is quite common among children under seven. (Even this, however, can make you feel guilty when you remember it as an adult.) It is sexual abuse if one child is much older and uses this power to make the other do as he or she wants. In this case it can affect sexuality in some of the ways described later.

You can also be affected by knowing about any difficult sexual experiences one of your brothers and sisters had; for instance, sexual abuse or an early, unwanted pregnancy. The reaction of your sibling or of other members of your family can be upsetting for you. It can also mean that you begin to connect sex with fear, problems and upheavals.

❛ ——————— Talking point ———————

A death in the family

Describe to each other an early experience that upset you. Did somebody who was important to you die when you were a child? You can include an animal in this. How did you feel, and how was the death handled? Were there any other incidents that were profoundly upsetting?

❜

LIFE AT HOME

The atmosphere in your family home is affected by many things. Your parents' financial circumstances are important, particularly if money is a problem – in which case there might be difficulties and unhappiness in the home or tension between your parents (though this is not always the case).

These are some of the other issues or events that can affect your home life, and ultimately your sexual and other development:

• **Frequently moving house.** To a young child the world and the people in it often seem unpredictable and therefore sometimes frightening. Familiar surroundings are particularly comforting at these times. Children make a relationship with the home in which they live, which is similar to the relationships they make with people, but much less demanding and changeable.

Moving is stressful for adults, and even more so for young children. If you moved home a lot, either because of a parent's job, or because your family was going up or down in the world it will have been difficult for you. Learning your way around a new home, a new bedroom; leaving friends and having to make new ones; changing schools – all these require great resilience from a child. If everything is going well between the child and the parents, and the parents and each other, then these changes are easier to handle. But if there are other difficulties then moving will increase the child's insecurity.

• **Religious influences.** Strong religious faith can be a great source of comfort. But sometimes the way religion is taught to a young child can cause problems later. An over-emphasis on sin and consequent punishment can be very frightening, and lead to repression of perfectly normal impulses and emotions. Children who lived under a cloud of fear about what might happen to them, and are ashamed of their thoughts and actions, can turn into adults who are fearful or quite out of touch with some aspects of themselves.

This has special impact on sexual development. When sex is presented as sinful and the body as an unruly enemy, it is difficult for the adult to experience a healthy, uninhibited sexual relationship. This causes difficulties even within marriage and with straightforward sexual intercourse. In women it can cause vaginismus or an inability to experience orgasm, and men can experience difficulty with erections or find it difficult to ejaculate.

For instance, Maria came for sex therapy because she was unable to have sexual intercourse. She was forty-three and had never married, but had recently met a man she liked a lot. They had gone in for some heavy petting, but he was becoming impatient, and she was hoping to try to do something about her sexual problem.

She worked with the sex therapist on a self-focus programme, learning to find out how to touch herself sexually in ways that she liked, so that she could eventually help her man friend to do the same. This was very difficult for her. Her religious upbringing had stressed that your body should not be touched, or even looked at. As is usual in sex therapy, at an early stage Maria was shown some sexually explicit material by the therapist during an information session. Maria was disgusted and frightened by pictures of female genitalia, so much so that it took weeks before she was able to look at them with a degree of comfort.

During her self-focus programme she would do anything rather than look at her own body, even after she could bring herself to touch it. In the bath she would float flannels on the water so that she would not see herself. Sex therapy proceeded very slowly, and although she was eventually able to have sexual intercourse with her partner, the taboos from Maria's background were too strong for her to feel free and uninhibited about sex.

❛————————— Talking point —————————

Faith

Talk about your religious education, if any. Has it had any effect on your ideas about life or sex? Has it been a source of strength or fear?

❜

Separation or divorce

The childhood experience of living through your parents' separation or divorce is in a special category. It is always difficult for a child of any age. It is an upheaval that affects the parents' emotional states, sometimes the financial and living circumstances, and, most importantly, disrupts the child's closest relationships and living patterns. These are some of the issues in more detail:

● **Losing a parent.** When your parents separate you lose the daily contact with the one who leaves. Sometimes contact ceases altogether. This is painful for you, even if it is not your favourite parent who goes. Very young children can fear that the other parent will leave too, which increases insecurity and worry. Young children do not understand that it is the parents who have split up, however carefully it is explained to them. As far as they are concerned *they* have been left, and this can make them feel that they are at fault – were too naughty or not lovable enough for the parent to want to stay around. Even older children, who understand the reason for the break-up, can feel this. That the parent can leave them, no matter what the circumstances, can seem like proof that they just weren't loved enough.

These are very hard feelings to deal with. The lessons you learn are that love can end, and however strongly you love someone they will still leave you. These lessons can blight your healthy sexual development as a child and make it difficult to trust in loving relationships when you become an adult.

● **Continuing bitterness between parents.** The worse the relationship between your parents after the break-up, the more difficult it will have been for you. Contrary to the belief that divorce and separation mean an end to bad feelings and rows, they often continue worse than before. If you were caught in the middle of bitterness you will probably end up taking sides. This might be pleasing for the parent you opt for, but it does you no good. Children are very aware that they are made up of 'half mum and half dad', and if they learn to hate or despise one parent, they also begin to hate and despise aspects of themselves. Sometimes children change sides when they are older and go on to reject the other parent.

If you are caught between your parents for a long time the lesson you learn is not only that love can die, but that it can become an enduring hatred. This makes it even harder for you to enter into a loving relationship without deep reservations when you become an adult.

If your parents handled the break-up with sensitivity and concern for you, and neither tried to turn you against the other, then you will have been better able to come to terms with the separation eventually.

● **Changed financial circumstances.** There is often less money around after a break-up, and perhaps you had to move. Children – who find it hard to understand the world of feelings – are very likely to focus their anger and sadness on the results of these changes. When life is more of a struggle, and you can no longer expect the standard of living you had become used to, you are likely, as a child, to feel cheated as well as unhappy.

● **Emotional state of parents.** As a child you are affected by your parents' emotional states of mind. Both your parents are likely to have experienced a turbulent time around the separation, but it is the mood of the parent you stayed with that will have mattered most. That parent's grief, anger and depression will have had an impact on you. A very distressed parent can have found it difficult to give you the loving and attention you needed, so that you felt less sure of his or her love. If you were very young, you might have felt you were the cause of the sorrow or anger.

Sometimes the parent reacts by clinging very tightly to you, or lets you know that you are vital to his or her wellbeing. This is a heavy burden for a child. The distress of the absent parent, which you might have experienced on the days of access, can make you feel torn and unhappy. These experiences can result in you feeling helpless and angry.

All these strong emotions, experienced before you have the maturity to cope with them, can make you frightened of feelings and wish to be able to shut them off. If you succeed, it is not just the negative emotions that are shut down, but many of the spontaneous, loving ones, too. It can be hard to turn them on again later, when you want to, in a loving relationship.

- **The impact on emotional and sexual development.** The combination of these issues make all aspects of loving more difficult when you are older. As we have said, you find it harder to trust in love, which can make you hold back – and when you hold back emotionally your sexual relationships also lose the quality of emotional as well as physical union.

Many adults who lived through their parents' separation when they were young are determined to do better in their own relationships. They tend to imagine for themselves perfect relationships without the difficulties that their parents experienced. Of course, this is unrealistic. Every relationship goes through difficult patches, but if you haven't seen your own parents handle such patches and survive them, it is hard for you to find the will and the ways to do so yourself. Children of separated parents are statistically more likely to go on to separate from their own partners. Of course, there is no need to add to the statistics yourself. Usually this means learning to trust yourself and others in love when you become an adult. It also means finding ways to work through difficulties in relationships so that you learn from them and use the lessons to make a better relationship.

It can be hard to remember your unhappiness as a child, or how distressed you were by events. However, there are certain physical symptoms or habits that are linked to stress in children, and if you remember having any of these, it is likely that you suffered emotionally, too, even if you don't remember doing so. Some of the obvious ones are nail-biting and late bed-wetting. Continuing to suck your thumb way beyond the age when it is appropriate or being over-attached to a childhood comfort item until a similarly late age are also signs of stress, as are nervous habits and tics. Certain illnesses, too, are usually considered to be stress-related, particularly eczema and asthma.

An unhappy or difficult home life when you are young, vulnerable and not in control of circumstances, means that similar feelings later on cause you to feel anxious and afraid. It can make it hard for you to make the final commitment to a loving relationship. This always means opening up to your partner and risking a degree of vulnerability which you might find frightening. These feelings of insecurity can also make you long for a stable relationship where you will be sheltered and safe. This can lead you to jump too quickly into commitments without taking the time to test them properly.

6 ————————— **Talking point** —————————

Separate ways

If your parents divorced or separated, talk about how it affected you. What were your feelings about the absent parent, and did these change? What were your feelings about the parent you remained with, and did these change?

If you were brought up by a single parent, talk about how you felt about this, and your feelings for the absent parent. *9*

————————— **LEARNING ABOUT SEX** —————————

So far we have been talking about elements that affected your sexual development which might seem unconnected to sex. But you are also likely to have received much more direct lessons about the subject as you were growing up. Interestingly, these lessons can have less impact on your sexuality than the unspoken lessons we have already covered. This is because the lessons you absorbed unconsciously are harder for you to challenge, because they go so much deeper and because they have become part of you.

More obvious sexual attitudes and lessons are important in how they match up to the unspoken ones. They will either reinforce the others or be confusingly different.

Attitudes in your family

The attitude to sex within your family will, to some degree, determine your own. This is probably first apparent to you over the question of nudity: whether your parents were open and casual about it, or whether bodies were always covered up.

Their attitude will also have been made clear to you by the way they handled your questions about sex while you were growing up. Questions such as 'Where do babies come from?' might either be answered clearly and without embarrassment or dealt with uncomfortably, or you might have been fobbed off with jokes or untruths. In some cases you might have been told off for asking the questions or told that it was none of your business. Perhaps the television was switched off if a programme contained sex scenes. If talking about sex was obviously difficult or taboo in your family, you will have learnt not to ask questions or talk about it yourself. This can give you the impression that sex is some kind of dark secret, or something to snigger about with other children.

Sometimes the ban on talking about sex is so total that you don't even talk to other children and might know very little about it until you first become sexually active yourself. Less common are the households in which sex is inappropriately and too frequently stressed. This can be disturbing or threatening to young children. The right balance is when sex can be talked about naturally and without embarrassment, but is not forced as a topic on the children.

Some women who have had bad or disappointing experiences with sex pass on the information that sex is a chore or worse to their daughters.

' ————————— Talking point ————————

Not in front of the children?

Discuss your families' attitudes to sex. Who told you about sex, if anyone? How was it handled? What do you think your parents' views on sex were (whether it was discussed or not)?

'

Sexual experimenting

Innocent sexual games between children of the same age are quite common. These include 'doctors and nurses' and looking at each other's genitals. Boys examine each other, as do girls, as well as liking to look at and touch the genitals of children of the opposite sex. The interest in these sorts of games usually passes by about six or seven years old, and is part of your general curiosity about the world.

These games usually have little impact on your developing sexuality. The exception is if you were found playing the games by an adult who was very shocked or upset. If you were punished or made to feel wicked, the guilt might continue to attach itself in your mind to sex.

Sexual activity in others

As a child you also become aware of other people's sex lives. This can be through stories and jokes told to you by children, or through films, sex magazines or television programmes. These sources might have been disturbing or exciting, and all will add to your ideas about sex.

You can also become aware of other people's sex lives because you witnessed sexual activity between them. Perhaps you came into the room when your parents were making love, or saw siblings with their partners, or older friends petting. Depending on your age and sensitivity these sort of experiences can have varying effects on you. A young child who sees parents making love can perceive it as a struggle and therefore frightening, and can misinterpret passionate noises as expressions of pain or fear.

Sex education

Most people receive some sort of sex education at school, even if they received little at home. Some parents who are reluctant to talk about sex sometimes force themselves to give warnings about pregnancy when their children become older – though it is often confined to telling a boy to 'be careful' and a girl that she 'shouldn't get into trouble'.

If the ideas you have formed about sex are negative then sex education at school might seem distasteful or shocking. Sometimes, however, it is a relief to have it explained in a calm factual way. In either case, the information is usually very basic and biological, and not as helpful as it might be about how bodies react sensually and sexually.

❛ ——————— Talking point ———————

Doctors and nurses

Tell each other about any sexual games you played when you were young, either with brothers and sisters or friends of your own sex or the opposite sex. How did they make you feel? Were you ever discovered doing so? How was this handled? How did it make you feel?

❜

YOU AND YOUR BODY

As a child you start to build up ideas about your body according to the way you were handled as a baby, how loved you felt, whether you were cuddled and other factors. It is also usual for children to touch their genitals and enjoy the sensations this produces – unless they have been stopped from doing so or punished. But none of this is connected to sexual matters except very vaguely, until you reach puberty.

At puberty your body starts to develop, and you start to have feelings you recognize as specifically sexual.

The hormone activity necessary to cause the changes which turn you into a physical adult also have a powerful effect on your emotions. Wild mood swings are common, from elation to despair, and these emotions become connected to your feelings about yourself, your body and your sexuality.

Generally, the more comfortable with yourself and happy you were before puberty, the easier it will have been for you to handle all these changes, though it is difficult for everyone. The less happy you were, and the less good you felt about yourself, the harder it will have been for you. If your experiences of sex or the ideas you developed about it were bad, the more uneasy and ashamed you will have been about your newly awakened sexuality and changing body.

Your age at puberty

The age you were when puberty started can also be important. Broadly, if it happened to you at roughly the same age as your friends, you will have found it easier. If, however, you were much younger or much older than your friends it could well have caused you anxiety. For instance, a girl who develops breasts much earlier than her friends can feel awkward and ashamed, or a boy who develops much later than others can feel inadequate. Your own fears about being different and strange, at a time when children need to be as like each other as possible, will often have been compounded by the attitudes of others. At a time when most of your age group are feeling churned up and insecure in themselves, it is common for them to bolster themselves up by ganging up on others who are different.

These feelings about being different and awkward in your body can persist long afterwards.

The experience of puberty is in some ways different for men and women, so we will look at them separately here.

Puberty for women

The body makes many changes as a girl grows into a woman. The most significant for you, however, are likely to have been developing breasts and the onset of menstruation.

Girls who have had good feelings about being female and like and admire their mothers or other close women can be proud and pleased about their developing breasts. Girls with more mixed feelings might find them embarrassing or distasteful. Most women have some reservations about their breasts, thinking they are too large, too small, too floppy, or in other ways not 'perfect'. These feelings often begin in adolescence, when these worries are usually more acute. Girls with large breasts might be teased or receive unwelcome attention from boys or men. Girls with small breasts might also be teased and feel inadequate. Support and reassurance from parents can help, but at this age it is what your friends think that counts most. These worries can make you feel uncomfortable about your body – a feeling that can endure and make it harder for you to feel good about sex.

The first menstrual period is also significant. Girls who have been well-prepared for this happening, and whose mothers are relaxed about their own periods, can feel perfectly relaxed – even pleased – when their own periods start. But girls who are not comfortable about being female or don't feel ready to grow up, can be unhappy about it.

Sex therapists see many women who were told nothing about menstruation, and for whom their first period was a great shock. Usually they come from families in which sex was never mentioned, and sex was already surrounded by negative associations. Some think they are bleeding to death – a very frightening experience – and when they discover that it is a normal part of being a woman, and will happen every month for years, it is very distressing. The fear, and then the disgust, can have a bad effect on their sexuality later.

An example of this is Eileen, who came for relationship counselling with Joe, her husband, when she was forty-eight. The counselling went so well that they went on to sex therapy, to try to sort out why sex had never been good for them, and how they could improve it.

Eileen had been a repressed child. Everything she had ever been told about being female was negative and bad. Sexuality didn't exist. The only sex education she was given was that 'nice girls don't'.

She was shy and inhibited about herself and her body. No one had thought to tell her about menstruation. One day a man followed her home from school 'talking dirty'. He came up close and grabbed her breasts. She broke free and ran home. She went to the bathroom and to her horror she found blood on her knickers. She believed it had happened because of the frightening sexual attentions of the man. This traumatic start reinforced everything she had ever learnt about sex being bad, and dirty – and her own female body being disgusting.

Joe was a loving and kind man, and marrying him made her happy. But she was petrified on her wedding night. He had never done more than kiss her cheek before. Eileen had no idea what was going to happen, except that she knew it was something awful. She was repulsed and frightened when he tried to make love to her, despite the fact that he was very gentle. It took weeks before they could manage intercourse. They eventually went on to have three children.

Joe continued to be very gentle over the years, but Eileen found intimacy impossible and sex uncomfortable. Joe also suffered from premature ejaculation – but, he said ruefully, he had never tried to do anything about it because from Eileen's point of view the quicker it was over with the better.

The sex therapy programme made a lot of difference to them. Eileen learnt to enjoy the more sensual touching of the programme, and she had her first orgasm. But she still could not fully enjoy penetrative sex, even when Joe learnt to control his ejaculatory function and last longer. Eileen also had difficulty touching Joe's penis, which she saw as dirty – though, logically, she knew he was very clean.

They also found that Eileen felt better when she initiated sex, and she was able to do so occasionally, now that she enjoyed it more. They increased the amount of cuddling and other affectionate behaviour, which they both liked. Their sex life suited them both for the first time, but it had been hard work to overcome Eileen's childhood lessons and her trauma at puberty.

Your parents' reactions to the changes

Your parents' attitudes to you often begin to change as you show signs of maturing. The most helpful attitudes are interest and pleasure in what is happening to you, and a recognition that you are growing up and perhaps need more privacy and the space to be allowed to develop some responsibility and independence.

But it can be difficult for parents, too. Some parents become more protective as their daughters start to look more like women, worried about boyfriends and fearful of pregnancy. Some fathers become more heavy-handed, and also less comfortable about affectionate contact. Some mothers resent their daughters blossoming and slap down any signs of flirtatious or provocative behaviour. If your parents were unduly disturbed by the changes you were making at puberty, it can add to your own uncertain and uncomfortable feelings.

‘ ========= Talking point =========

Becoming a woman

Tell your partner how you felt when puberty started. Were you early, late or average? How did this make you feel? How did you feel about your breasts developing? How did you feel about starting your period? Were you well prepared for these changes?

,

Puberty for men

The changes boys go through at puberty are equally complex. The most significant ones, however, tend to be growing taller and more manly in physique, growing body hair and beard, and the voice breaking. The onset of 'wet dreams', when you ejaculate while asleep, is also an important stage.

Many boys find that the attitude of the outside world to them changes quite radically when they go through the ungainly phase of becoming used to their new, larger bodies. Strangers are more suspicious and intolerant of them, particularly as this stage is often accompanied by loud and anti-social behaviour when they are with their friends. It is sometimes a shock for a boy who was previously treated kindly as a child to experience this change in attitude. A boy who was very much taller or shorter than other boys can also feel bad, as can a boy who is physically much weaker.

Wet dreams can also be a cause of anxiety and shame. Boys can go to great lengths to cover up the signs of this, and some are made to feel worse by the shocked or disgusted reactions of their mothers.

Pubescent boys are also plagued by inconvenient erections, which can be a cause of worry and shame, particularly if they have learnt that sex is wrong and dirty. Being unable to control their bodies can be disturbing. At a time when sex is on their minds a lot, traumatic episodes can have considerable impact.

An extreme example is Gareth, who came for sex therapy aged twenty-eight, suffering from impotence. This was traced back to his mother's death in a car crash when he was fourteen. He remembered himself as being 'sex obsessed' at the time, and he was also arguing a lot with his mother. Although his sexual feelings and problems with his mother were quite unconnected with his mother's death, somehow they became mixed up in his mind. It was also as if he had told himself that becoming too close to women was dangerous.

Your parents' reactions to the changes

Parents can also change their attitudes to boys who are developing. The most helpful attitude is to welcome the changes and respect the need for the boy to grow up and test himself, but also to recognize that he might be less mature inside than he looks outside, and still need love and attention. Sometimes, though, this is when the cuddles stop for boys, and anything that might seem 'babyish' or 'girlish' is dinned out of them. Fathers sometimes feel competitive with a boy who is becoming big and strong. At this fragile time emotionally, when a boy is likely to be insecure anyway about his masculinity, these sort of reactions push him to become more 'manly' and suppress much of his more gentle, emotional side.

' ================= Talking point ================

Becoming a man

Tell your partner how you felt when puberty started. Were you early, late or average? How did this make you feel? How did you feel about changes in height and strength? What did you feel when your voice broke? What was your reaction to wet dreams, if any? Were you well prepared for these? Did you suffer from inconvenient erections? How did you cope?

'

Masturbation

Most boys masturbate at puberty and so do many girls. Your attitude to this is likely to have been governed by the feelings you developed about sex in general. If sex was taboo or in other ways bad, you might well have felt guilty about masturbating. If you were discovered doing so and punished, or the person who discovered you was shocked or disgusted, this will have added to your negative feelings.

If you felt bad about it you will probably have tried to make yourself 'grow out of it'. But masturbation is a perfectly normal sexual activity and can continue to be an important part of your sex life, either alone or with your partner. Through masturbation you learn how your body responds sexually, and what caresses or fantasies are necessary to make you excited and produce an orgasm. This knowledge can be particularly useful for women, whose arousal system is more complex. In sex therapy a woman is encouraged to show her partner what she likes, rather than hope that this will be discovered by a hit-and-miss method and that he will know what gives her pleasure without being told. Before she can tell him, she must know her own needs and responses herself.

Guilt about masturbation can cause sexual problems later. This is most obvious in men, who might suffer from retarded ejaculation (when they can't come), especially if religious instruction has taught them that 'spilling the seed' is wrong. Men can also suffer from premature ejaculation (coming too quickly for their own and their partner's satisfaction), sometimes a result of guilty, hasty masturbation.

This was the case with Robert, who suffered from premature ejaculation, often climaxing before he could penetrate his wife, Moira. This was causing rows between them, and Moira felt frustrated and unloved.

Robert was brought up in a strict religious family. He had learnt at an early age that he must not touch his private parts. One of his earliest memories was naptime at a religious nursery school, where all the children had to sleep with their arms crossed over their chests above the blankets. Robert was three at the time and he assumed that it was because he would then be in the right position if he died in his sleep. Later he realized that it was to stop the children touching their genitals.

Sex was scarcely mentioned except when awful warnings were handed out. He tried very hard not to masturbate when he was a teenager, but sometimes the urges were too strong, so he would do it quickly and feel deeply disgusted with himself and guilty.

Until he married Moira he tried to control his sexual impulses, but 'fell' once or twice with other girls when he was younger. He managed not only to suppress his sexuality, but most of his other feelings as well. When he first entered therapy he was unable to express his emotions at all.

Moira, on the other hand, was angry. She was particularly angry about the sexual problem. She had come from a similarly strict family, which showed no affection. Sex was also taboo when she was growing up. Her first period came as a shock to her, and her first sexual experience was painful. At first they fitted together well. Both were uneasy about sex, and neither was good at expressing intimate feelings. Robert's premature ejaculation didn't seem to matter to begin with. Moira minded more after their baby was born. Before that they had had a little more time for sex. If Robert came too fast they could always try again. This wasn't so possible with a demanding baby. Sex was now over in a few minutes, and it was the only time they touched and showed affection. Neither of them had any idea that there was more to love-making than penetration. When Robert's erection went, that was the end of it.

Sex therapy changed many things for them. They learnt that it was necessary to talk about feelings and show affection for each other. But the real revelation for them was the part that masturbation played in the therapy. Both of them had to learn to touch themselves and each other. Robert had to learn to masturbate again – but this time to take it slowly until he could recognize the point of 'no return' before he ejaculated – the key to control. This took time, because his problem was severe and it was a while before he was able to do it without feeling guilty. Moira, too, would masturbate Robert, and he had to indicate when she should slow up and stop before he ejaculated. In this way Robert learnt that he could wait a longer time before ejaculating, and that it was now under his control during sexual intercourse, too. They also learnt that penetration and thrusting were not the be-all and end-all of sex and that there were many other ways for them to give each other pleasure.

However, it can happen that masturbation during puberty causes problems for other reasons. Some lonely or unhappy children turn to masturbation for comfort, and later find that it has become compulsive, even when they are in a loving relationship. It is quite normal to continue to masturbate from time to time when you are in a committed sexual relationship but, if it is very frequent and affects your sex life with your partner, it can be a problem.

This was the case with Harry, who was married to Vanessa. He was thirty-two, and she was two years older. They had been married for ten years and had two children.

When they married, Vanessa was the sexually experienced one. Harry was a virgin. She had enjoyed initiating him to begin with, but over the past few years sex had become very infrequent. Harry was always too tired. Vanessa had found herself assessing other men, and felt that if they didn't do something about their relationship she was going to have an affair.

When Harry saw the therapist alone, he admitted that he was a compulsive masturbator, up to ten or twelve times a day. He didn't feel guilty about it, but it made him tired and he wanted to be able to stop. He had been a lonely child, brought up in a correct, unemotional family. He never had many friends or any girlfriends. He didn't think he was worth much, and masturbation was a great comfort to him. It was not just sexual thoughts that would set him off. He had discovered that if he was frightened or under pressure, masturbating would make him feel better. Even now that he was married to Vanessa, it was the only way he knew to cope with the problems of life. Sex was something quite different: masturbation brought physical and emotional relief and was over quite quickly. It was more like an addiction to drink or drugs.

Once the therapist had talked to them in detail about their relationship she discovered that there were many other problems between them, causing stress and difficulties. She judged that sex therapy would not be right for them at that time. They needed to do more work on their general relationship, and on emotions and closeness. She referred them to a relationship counsellor instead, with the proviso that they could come back later for sex therapy if they needed it. She later heard that the counselling was underway and progressing well. Harry had cut down on his masturbating, though it still occurred two or three times a day. Their sex life was improving, and it did not look as if they would need therapy.

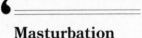 ———————— Talking point ————————

Masturbation

Discuss with your partner what you had heard about masturbation when you were growing up, if anything. When did you start to masturbate, if ever? How did you feel about this?

EARLY RELATIONSHIPS

When you make your first emotional and sexual relationships, all the lessons you have learnt up to this point will be put into practice. For although this seems like a beginning for you, you are not starting with a clean slate. Somehow or other you tend to be attracted to people who are likely to reinforce the ideas you have built up about relationships and sex. For instance, a girl who has grown up feeling unlovable and let down by the people she loved, often finds herself attracted to a boy who is a bit of a rat and will treat her badly. She just can't seem to fancy the nice boy who is interested in her and will treat her well. When she is let down by her boyfriend she will believe even more that she is inadequate and feel she is right not to trust a partner in a relationship.

The people you fancy

You are most aware of the physical attractions of people you fancy. In some ways they are likely to remind you in looks of other people you have felt strongly about. Sometimes they will look vaguely like members of your family, or even yourself. Usually you are unaware of the less obvious ways in which they are like people from your past – but there is often something in their personality and behaviour that reinforces your in-built ideas about relationships. When these are good and healthy you are more likely to find yourself attracted to someone who will be good for you. If these were distorted in some of the many ways mentioned in this chapter, you are likely to find yourself attracted to people who are not so good for you. Of course, this is not a strict rule – but it happens often enough to be unsurprising to counsellors. The people you make the longest relationships with are much more likely to fit the pattern of your early days, even if that pattern made you unhappy and you were convinced you were not going to repeat it.

Crushes

Your first emotional attachments tend to take the form of crushes: great longing for people at a distance. These can be all sorts of people, including people of your own age, teachers, famous people. They can be the same sex as you, as well as the opposite sex. A 'same-sex' crush does not necessarily mean you are likely to have homosexual feelings later. A crush is the safe way of trying out strong emotions without the reality of a relationship. Even these will give you a good idea of the kind of partners and relationships your upbringing has caused you to be ready for. Some will have crushes on good and worthwhile people, others will feel passionately about difficult or downright unpleasant people.

Sometimes these crushes tell you as much about the sort of person you yearn to be yourself as well as the kind of person you are attracted to.

Early sexual relationships

Your first sexual relationships – which means relationships that include any sort of petting and touching, not only full sexual intercourse – are important for a number of reasons.

Good experiences in early relationships will give you the confidence to continue to seek good relationships when you are making your permanent choice. Unhelpful relationships, especially those that reinforce early disappointments and difficulties, will make you more scared and untrusting in the future.

Pleasant sexual experiences will build your sexual confidence and ability to maintain good sexual relationships later. Disturbing, unpleasant or otherwise disappointing sexual experiences will make sex more difficult for you.

Homosexual/lesbian relationships in adolescence

Sometimes your first emotional or sexual relationship is with someone of your own sex. For some people this confirms what they had begun to suspect: that their natural tendency is to be a homosexual or lesbian. For others it is just a stage, and they later find they prefer partners of the opposite sex. Sometimes these people feel guilty about their homosexual relationship and fear that they are not normal. But people have varying degrees of attraction to their own sex. Some are not attracted to their own sex at all, some are only attracted to their own sex. Many others are in-between – with a stronger tendency towards one or the other. All these variations are normal, in that they happen. The fact that you had a homosexual relationship in the past doesn't necessarily make you homosexual, neither do occasional feelings of attraction towards a member of your own sex.

❛ ═══════ Talking point ═══════

First love

Take it in turns to describe to each other the first time you thought you were in love, whether it was a crush, someone of your own sex or the opposite sex. What was he or she like? How intense was the experience? Were the feelings painful or pleasurable?

❜

Difficult early relationships

Particularly difficult experiences in early relationships can over-shadow the relationships you go on to make later. This was the case with Marianne, who was married to Gary. They came for relationship counselling because their sex life had ceased. Marianne would not let Gary make love to her anymore.

Gary was a copy-editor for a publishing firm, who worked from home. This gave him a lot of freedom. Marianne did not have a job, but looked after their five-year-old son, Sam. Gary helped quite a bit in the home and with Sam. At first the counsellor thought that perhaps they were together too much, and Marianne had created space for herself in rather a negative way by refusing sex.

But after a number of sessions Marianne asked to see the counsellor alone. She wanted to talk about her first boyfriend, a relationship she had finished over twelve years ago, but which still haunted her.

Matt had been almost like two people. The young man her parents knew was charming and well-behaved. They approved of him heartily. But over the months with Marianne he had exerted a sinister power over her. He never became violent, but she sensed violence in him. He would pick up knives and stroke them while looking at her. He never raised his voice but when he was annoyed he would become hard and cold and she sensed that the consequences might be terrible if she didn't do what he wanted. They became engaged, despite Marianne's fear. She didn't dare break up with him. They had sex fairly frequently. Marianne didn't mind it, but never enjoyed it. Her overwhelming sense was that she was doing it to keep him sweet. He was certainly at his nicest when he wanted sex and after.

She might even have married him, if she hadn't accidentally discovered that he was being unfaithful. This gave her a way out. She told her parents, and was able to get their support to break off the engagement. Matt left the area shortly afterwards, but Marianne continued to be terrified of him. She dreamt that he would come back one day and kill her for her betrayal. Even now, twelve years later, she was frightened that he might reappear in her life.

Gary was totally different. Their marriage was happy and Marianne said that she had enjoyed sex at the beginning. But after Sam was born she went off sex for a while, as many women do after the birth of a baby.

The less Marianne wanted to make love, the more Gary pestered her. This made matters worse. On the one hand, she saw him as a lovely, kind and caring partner. But when he was pushing for sex it reminded her horribly of Matt. The connection of sex to violence and cooperating out of fear made what might have been a temporary problem a more permanent one. She didn't want this other 'horrible Gary' spoiling their cosy little family life. Why couldn't he just forget about sex?

The problems this had caused between them were affecting other parts of their relationship. But they were both very motivated to respond to counselling, and after some weeks their relationship was so much better that Marianne desperately wanted to re-start their sex life. Gary now knew the root of the problem and his contribution to it, and was prepared to make changes. Marianne still found that this was not enough, however, so the counsellor referred them to a sex therapist. She was sure that the improvement in the couple's understanding of their problem, as well as their willingness to tackle it, would mean that the outcome would be successful.

TRAUMATIC SEXUAL EXPERIENCES

Sexual abuse
Sexual abuse during childhood is traumatic, particularly if a parent is involved. This affects every part of your developing personality and can be the cause of lifelong difficulties in relationships. However, for the purpose of this book, it is the impact on your sex life that is relevant.

Since the subject has become more openly discussed it is known that sexual abuse in childhood is much more common than was previously realised, and that very young children – even babies – have been subjected to it. Boys can be abused as well as girls, and although sexual abusers are usually men, some women abuse children, too.

Being touched sexually when you are too young, or being made to perform sexual acts, or being hurt by penetration before your body is physically ready – all these are damaging. Although your sexuality starts developing from the moment you are born, and you can experience sexual sensations very early, a child's sexuality is completely different from an adult's. Being made aware of adult sex before it is natural, and before you have the emotional maturity to cope with it, makes for an unhealthy sexuality. Violent and painful sexual abuse will obviously create difficulties, but even more gentle awakening of sexual feelings too early can cause problems later.

Even more important than the physical act itself is the emotions that are attached to even mild sexual abuse. Being touched sexually by a parent feels very different to being cuddled and kissed when there is no sexual feeling. Even a child who doesn't understand what is happening senses this. A sexually excited or guilty adult looks, sounds and behaves differently. The child, however young, knows that something is wrong. Any sexual contact between an adult in a parental or responsible role and a younger person, even if he or she is at the age of sexual maturity, will create powerful negative emotions that will get in the way of healthy, joyous sexuality later.

What all abused children have in common is great difficulty in experiencing sex as a true expression of loving commitment when they become adults. Even if they can get physical pleasure from sex, they have trouble feeling the emotions of warmth, generosity and trust that need to accompany the most intimate and loving sexual relationships.

These are the main issues and emotions that are stirred up by sexual abuse, which can have a continuing impact on your sexuality:

● **Abuse of power.** When an adult uses a child's body for sexual reasons, the child's trust is betrayed. The closer the adult the worse this betrayal is. It is an abuse of power because the adult exploits the child's loving trust, or uses the child's fear to get what he or she wants. This effects the child's sexuality in a number of ways, but the most obvious is that sex becomes connected with power rather than love. As an adult, sexual feelings may still be connected to power struggles, and be triggered by similarly unloving and unhealthy relationships.

The adult who has been sexually abused as a child is likely to be suspicious of the motives behind any sexual attention. The adult is also more likely to give in to unwanted sexual attentions, because of this early lesson that doing so is a fact of life.

The adult victims of child sexual abuse sometimes go on to abuse their own children – either because it is the situation that is connected with arousal, or because the boundary between what is acceptable contact between parent and child was broken down for them so that they have difficulty understanding it when they become parents.

They are also more likely to find themselves compatible with other adults who are similarly confused, some of whom might have been abused as children, or who are abusers themselves.

● **Fear, anger and guilt.** Many abused children feel fear. Sometimes this is because the abuse is painful, or because a loved adult is different and frightening during the abuse. Sometimes it is because they feel afraid that they will lose the adult's love if they don't do what is wanted of them. The younger the child the more important this love is to them – losing it seems worse than the abuse.

Fear is also felt if the adult swears them to secrecy or threatens them with the consequences of exposure. They might fear that they will be punished, or that the family will be broken up, or that the abuser will go on to abuse a younger brother or sister.

This fear affects sexual development. Sex can continue to be frightening for them. Or they might need to feel fearful of a sexual partner to become aroused.

Abused children can feel bitterly angry, although these feelings might not surface until they are much older and look back on what happened to them.

Abused children often feel guilty. Sometimes they are told by the adult that it is their fault: that they behaved enticingly or that they wanted it to happen. Or they can feel guilty because they feel they could or should have stopped the abuse.

This guilt affects self respect, which means that they can become adults with little self-worth. This can lead to promiscuity later – taking many sexual partners, even when they feel little or no desire.

● **Shame, disgust and sorrow.** Shame is connected to guilt. But children can also feel ashamed if the abuse caused them to become aroused. Arousal is a natural physical consequence of being touched in certain ways, lovingly or not. A child has no control over this.

This can affect their sexuality in two main ways. Either the adults find they are most easily turned on by sex that is in some way shaming, or they develop a control over the arousal process so that they never allow themselves to feel aroused again.

Shame is also felt because the child feels no one else has suffered this experience, that other parents treat their children normally. They can feel shame on behalf of the parent, not wanting to tell a soul for fear of letting the family down.

Whether the child felt aroused or not, the sexual attentions of an adult can cause disgust. Being touched can seem disgusting, and feeling aroused can seem equally disgusting.

Sex can continue to appear disgusting once the child has grown up – either so disgusting that it should be avoided at all costs, or there can be a need for it to be disgusting and dirty to be arousing.

Being sexually abused can cause great sorrow, which continues to be felt when the children grow up.

● **Forgetting.** For some children the experience of being sexually abused was so horrifying, or caused them to feel such grief, anger and other frightening emotions, that they block out the experience from their memories. Some erase it entirely. Others only remember snatches of what happened, or the memories come back to them later. Some counsellors and sex therapists see people who are showing symptoms of damage caused by child sex abuse, but these people cannot remember anything, or are unable to think or talk about it.

It is understandable when you realise that, as adults, they have usually carried the burden of the secret for many years. Not talking about it, or even thinking about it, has helped them cope with life, and it is extremely hard for them to let down the barriers which might make coping more difficult again temporarily.

But although it can be almost as painful to remember the occasions of abuse as it was to experience them, talking about it with a sympathetic loving partner, a counsellor, or in a group with other victims of sexual abuse, can start the healing process. When the memories are first confronted again they can cause you to feel the same emotions as the child you were – raw and childlike. But expressing your anger and working through the other emotions, gradually allows them to lose their power over you. Most people who are able to talk about what happened say that they feel relieved of a burden.

The experience of Sandra and Clive is an example of how sexual abuse can affect sexuality, relationships, and the next generation of children.

They came for counselling because their marriage was in trouble. There was very little sex: Sandra said Clive didn't wash enough; he was upset by her sexual rejection of him, and was intensely jealous and convinced that she was having an affair.

Before the counsellor could help them with their current problem she had to find out more about them. Sandra had been abused by her father between the ages of eight and thirteen. She had felt unable to tell her mother, who was unloving and rejecting and had always made Sandra feel that she was a horrible person. At thirteen, however, she rebelled and would have screaming rows with her father. Her parents couldn't control her and she went to live with an aunt. Away from home Sandra calmed down; however, she felt very bad about herself – the effect of her mother's attitude and the sexual abuse. She returned home when she was fifteen, and although her father never touched her again, she fell into a pattern of indiscriminate sex with lots of boys. At seventeen she became pregnant and she married the father.

The marriage didn't last long. Sandra had another child, and then embarked on an affair. When her husband found out they split up.

Sandra was twenty, and for the next few years she brought her children up on her own. She was a good and caring mother to her children, but her relationships were disastrous. She had countless affairs, and she was usually the one who finished the relationship to move on to the next man. She liked and needed sex, but her early experiences made it impossible for her to be intimate with anyone. Her longest relationship was an affair with a married man. This suited her because his circumstances meant that they could never achieve a truly close, intimate relationship.

That relationship ended when the man moved from the area, and soon afterwards she met Clive. He had also been married and was in the process of divorcing his wife, who was having an affair. Clive needed the relationship because he wanted to be part of a family again. It suited Sandra because Clive was a weak man who made few emotional demands on her, and because she liked to feel needed.

Clive, too, had been abused by his uncle. The man was large and powerful, and Clive had been very frightened by him. But he had also been sexually excited by the abuse, which had made him feel guilty. This guilt made him unable to tell his parents, despite the fact that he had a good relationship with his mother. After the abuse stopped, Clive discovered masturbation, which recreated the same feelings of excitement and guilt.

The way that the abuse affected Clive was to make him feel ambivalent about sex. Intense sexual pleasure made him feel bad, but he loved the kind of gentle, sensual foreplay that reminded him of being cuddled and loved by his mother. Sandra had a horror of any tenderness and intimacy – she had never known any, and stroking and sensual touching reminded her of the furtive attentions of her father. She wanted straight sex with as little touching as possible. She liked it often and quick, and she had orgasms easily.

It is not surprising that sex went wrong between them. Sandra didn't like sex the way Clive wanted it and she lost interest in him sexually. Clive thought it was because she was having an affair – he knew how essential sex was to Sandra. She said that it was because he didn't wash and smelt of cigarettes, but the real reason was more fundamental. They came for counselling for six weeks, until Sandra said that it wasn't working and they would be better off trying to solve the problem themselves.

Two years later they were back. This time they had been referred by a social worker: Clive was abusing one of Sandra's daughters. She had told a teacher and the authorities had been informed.

Sandra was offered assistance if she wanted to leave Clive, but she decided to stay with him. She said that she was sure that it would never happen again. They were told to seek outside help, so they came to RELATE again.

It might seem difficult to credit that Sandra could stay with a man who had abused her child, when she had been made so unhappy by abuse herself. But it is not unusual. One of the effects of Sandra continuing to feel so 'bad' inside was that she was always expecting to be punished. Clive's behaviour seemed like a punishment on herself. She felt responsible for Clive's behaviour because she had sexually rejected him. This echoed the guilt she felt about the abuse from her father: part of her assumed it was her fault, because she was so bad. She wanted the best for her children, but her own experiences of not being protected by her mother seemed to make her unable to protect her own daughter. In a strange way, because she had been abused herself, it somehow felt natural for her daughter to have the same experience. All of this combined to make her feel that the best thing she could do was to stay with Clive and make him feel so much better that he wouldn't do it again.

For a while things improved. Clive and Sandra started to have sex intermittently. Clive talked about the abuse: his response to sexual rejection was a childlike fear and rage. He couldn't make a grown woman do what he wanted, so he turned to a young teenager, whom he could touch and make touch him in the ways he liked. His own guilt and fear during the abuse he had suffered hardened him to the girl's guilt and fear – and because those feelings were so intimately connected to sexual excitement for him, it also made the abuse feel, in some ways, 'right'.

In the event, Clive went on to abuse Sandra's daughter again, and this time Sandra found the strength and anger to leave him. Through counselling she was able to resolve some of her mixed feelings about sex and relationships, and understand her own patterns better.

Dealing with having been abused

Coming to terms with having been abused usually means building your self-worth, which also means understanding that you were an innocent victim of what happened and should carry no guilt or shame. Even if there was some sexual arousal or cooperation, it is not your fault. Adults are in charge of relationships with children, and it is their duty not to let any sexual content enter into these relationships.

Talking about what happened with someone who loves you, or a sympathetic professional, can help you to help yourself. If you fear telling your partner, through shame, or because you don't know how your partner will react, then counselling is a good idea. The counsellor can help you in the telling and also help both of you to come to terms with what happened.

Loving a partner who was abused as a child

It can be disturbing to discover that your partner was sexually abused as a child. Sometimes finding out about it can make you feel even worse than your partner, who has had to live with the knowledge. Sometimes, however, it is a relief to find out that any sexual problems you might have are not your fault, and understanding where they stem from can help you deal with them.

Some people feel rage against the abusers. Some blame their abused partners for having 'allowed' the abuse to happen, or, if their sex life together is difficult, feel that their partners let the abusers have the sexual contact which is now denied to them.

These feelings are unreasonable, however natural. Counselling can help you be realistic about what happened and also help you both deal with the issues that have been raised.

The most helpful attitude is loving sympathy. Patience in your sex life is also important. Knowing about the abuse might explain why your partner does not like certain aspects of sex, and respecting this is important.

Some adult victims of child sexual abuse are haunted by their memories. During sex they might have vivid recollections of events that happened to them, which can turn off their sexual feelings or cause them to feel misery or anger. At these times your partner will need love and reassurance and no more sex for the time being. Forcing sex on someone who had to submit to it as a child will only reinforce his or her negative feelings about sex.

! ══════════════ *Task* ══════════════

Not my fault

If you were sexually abused, you might find it very hard to talk about – even to think about. One way to start is to write about it. This can be difficult too. On the first occasion it is enough to write '[*name of person*] sexually abused me'. Acknowledging it is important. As you feel able, write more of what you remember, even if it is painful. Put down events that you can remember, what happened and how you felt. You could also write what you wish you had said or done, or what you would like to do or say now to the person concerned, even if that person is now dead.

You can keep these writings private if you wish. But when you are ready it is good to share them with a sympathetic partner. Again, take it slowly, at your own pace. You might like to talk about it a little at a time, especially if your partner finds it disturbing too.

If it is your partner who is telling you about sexual abuse, just listen. Don't comment. Show sympathy and love, but don't press your partner to talk more than he or she wants to.

!

Rape and other sexual abuse

You might remember other sexual experiences which were unpleasant. We have already dealt with sexual abuse within the family and extended family, but you might also have been sexually abused by someone you knew less well, or witnessed a flasher who scared you. If you remember early experiences that were traumatic, then sex possibly becomes connected with fear, shame and anger.

If your parents knew about the experience, then the way they handled it is also relevant. Careful and sensitive treatment can go a long way to helping you come to terms with what happened. But if they blamed you or were unduly distressed on their own account, the experience can stand out as being even more traumatic for you.

Rape is in a special category, and this experience can affect your sexuality badly. Women are more likely to be raped than men, but men are raped, too. For either sex the experience is humiliating and frightening as well as painful, but men are often deeply ashamed too. Both sexes might find it difficult to talk about, but men are less likely to report it than women. Whatever age it happens to you, the experience is profoundly disturbing. Talking about it to a counsellor helps, and it usually helps to tell later sexual partners about it as well.

Fiona's experience shows how rape can affect your sex life in many ways. When she was raped at the age of eighteen it was her first sexual experience of any kind. She was a trainee nurse, living away from home. She was a timid girl who had been brought up very strictly. The man had offered her a lift home after a party and had taken her back to his place instead. The rape had been prolonged and quite violent, and had included forcing her to perform oral sex on him. Although Fiona had not told her parents, she had told a friend, who had urged her to go to the police.

From that time on, Fiona was very frightened of sex. She avoided friendships with men until she was in her middle-thirties, when she met a widower, Paul, an older man who was very kind. Fiona felt safe with him, and able to let herself become attached to him. They had started a tentative sexual relationship, but because of the rape Fiona felt unable to let him make love to her fully.

She came for sex therapy on her own, wanting to be helped to deal with the problem, as she hoped that they might marry. She told the therapist about her sex life with Paul, none of which she enjoyed, but she endured it for his sake. One important aspect was that because she wouldn't allow him to penetrate her she felt obliged to satisfy him in other ways. This included oral sex, which disgusted and frightened her, linked as it was in her mind with the rape. Afterwards she would have to go to the bathroom and scrub her mouth out, and try to stop herself being sick.

The therapist worked with her over a period of time, helping her to get in touch with her sexual feelings safely. But an important part of the programme was for her to realise that her own sexual needs and preferences were as important as Paul's. She needed to be more assertive with him, and to make it clear what she didn't like, as well as what she did. This, of course, included explaining to him how she felt about oral sex. The rape had made her feel worthless and sub-standard. Once she had worked through these feelings it became possible for her to enjoy sex more and recognise her right to feel as she did.

Pre–marital pregnancies, terminations and miscarriages

Accidental pregnancies from early relationships can also affect the course of your sex life later, particularly if there were emotional or physical difficulties resulting from terminations, miscarriages or having to give the child away.

This was the experience of Helen, who was forced by her father to have an abortion when she was eighteen. It was one of a series of difficult and disastrous experiences for her connected with sex. When she and William came for counselling she was forty-five and was adamant that she never wanted sex again. They had been married for seventeen years and had three children.

Helen's father was consistently violent to her and gave her no love. She was one in a large family, and her harrassed mother did not have the time or energy to make up for her father's treatment of her. At thirteen Helen became sexually active. Part of her hoped that by giving boys sex she would get love back.

Helen soon got a 'reputation'. Boys queued up. But sex was all that they were interested in, and none of them stayed around long. Helen enjoyed the sex, she was very quickly aroused and had orgasms easily. During sex she fantasized that she was being loved, but gradually she came to understand that it had nothing to do with love at all. The boys had no respect for her, called her a slag, and were contemptuous of the fact that she liked sex. After all, they were agreed, nice girls don't.

When she became pregnant she was desperate to keep the child – at last someone who would love her – but her father insisted that she had an abortion. Before Helen met William she had other disastrous relationships, and was also raped.

William was a kind and gentle man, who fell deeply in love with Helen. He found her very attractive from the beginning, and still did. Helen was happy with him, but could never really believe that he loved her for herself or that he was attracted by *her*. When he wanted to make love to her she just thought he wanted sex – and as his wife she was the obvious choice.

Throughout their marriage Helen had been the dominant partner. She treated William almost like her child. He needed her to be the way she was. She was his anchor.

Their sex life suited them both for years. Then two years before coming for counselling, Helen sharply cut it down to once a month. By the time they came for counselling she said that she didn't want it at all.

One of the complicating factors was that Helen still got enormous sexual pleasure from making love. During sex she was very noisy, and was turned on by sexual swear words. She liked William to be rough and act as if she were a prostitute. She would have two or three very intense orgasms. But immediately it was over she felt vile and dirty. She felt used by William, insisting that all he wanted was sex and he wouldn't have cared who it was with. For her, sex was loveless. She found herself disgusting for enjoying it. It made her feel out of control.

Another complicating factor was that while William wanted and needed sex with Helen, he was also a little frightened by her over-the-top pleasure when she did agree. He also worried that he would not be able to satisfy her. When he pushed her for sex she would reject him most of the time. Even when the counsellor pointed this out, and suggested he backed off a bit, he couldn't. It was as if pursuing her also kept her at a safe distance.

The counsellor suggested a sexual contract, in which they would agree a day and time for sex. The idea was that they would both participate fully during that time, but that William would not push Helen for sex the rest of the time. Although they agreed to this, they never tried to make it work. When the counsellor suggested that they did further work with a sex therapist, Helen refused. 'I don't want sex,' she said. 'Why should I do anything I don't want to do?' Helen was prepared to give up something she enjoyed intensely because it also made her feel so bad.

It was an unsatisfactory end to the counselling. Helen had agreed to come to shut William up. But in reality neither of them was prepared to make necessary changes. The counsellor felt that they would stay together, and continue to fight about sex.

Helen's experience is a particularly clear example that physical pleasure in sex is only one element in the sexual experience. When sex becomes divorced from love it is not ultimately satisfying. The pursuit of the orgasm without attention to the emotional side denies the more profound pleasure that only sex in truly loving relationships can offer.

The following quiz can be helpful to clarify the issues that have been raised by reading this chapter and talking to your partner about them. The intention is to identify how these might have affected your developing sexuality, and therefore where you might have difficulty in your sex life now.

It is divided into three sections. In the first two sections you have to range your feelings on a number of issues between 1, GOOD and 5, BAD; 3 in the middle is OK. Circle the number you choose. What counts here is what *you* felt, not what anyone else tells you was right, wrong, or what you ought to have felt. In the third section you are asked to choose words to describe various sexual ideas or experiences.

?_____ Quiz _____

Your sexual profile

PART ONE	GOOD		OK		BAD
HOW I FELT ABOUT...					
...myself as a small child	1	2	3	4	5
...how much my mother loved me	1	2	3	4	5
...how much my father loved me	1	2	3	4	5
...how much love I deserved	1	2	3	4	5
...how happy my home was	1	2	3	4	5
...my relationship with brothers or sisters	1	2	3	4	5

...my parents' relationship with each other	1	2	3	4	5
...how anger was expressed in my family	1	2	3	4	5
...how love was expressed in my family	1	2	3	4	5
...how respected I was	1	2	3	4	5
...how liked I was	1	2	3	4	5
...how understood I was	1	2	3	4	5
...my friendships with other children	1	2	3	4	5
...my ability to get on with people	1	2	3	4	5
...the loss by death or separation of a person or animal I loved	1	2	3	4	5

These feelings relate to how well or easily you find it to be intimate with someone. If most of your answers are 1, 2 or 3, then this is probably not too hard for you. If many or most of your answers are 4 or 5 then becoming close to someone is probably more difficult for you, or makes you feel anxious, vulnerable and open to pain. This can make it harder for you to trust that your partner loves you and wants to stay with you, however often you are reassured that this is so. Sexually, this can make it difficult for you to 'let go', or to tell your partner about your deepest desires, or to feel free to be healthily selfish in taking what you need sexually.

Recognizing that this is a problem for you is a helpful start. You can begin to notice when you 'pull back' emotionally in a sexual or other situation. You can tell your partner about your difficulties. You should also allow yourself plenty of time to become comfortable with tasks in this book that increase intimacy.

PART TWO	GOOD		OK		BAD
HOW I FELT ABOUT...					
...the way I looked as a small child	1	2	3	4	5
...the idea of sex as a small child	1	2	3	4	5
...my body at puberty	1	2	3	4	5
...my attractiveness as a teenager	1	2	3	4	5
...the idea of sex as a teenager	1	2	3	4	5
...the amount of physical affection I received	1	2	3	4	5
...the amount of physical punishment I received	1	2	3	4	5
...sex play with other children	1	2	3	4	5
...the way I learnt about sex	1	2	3	4	5

HOW I FELT ABOUT...

...sexual contact in the family	1	2	3	4	5
...early sexual experiences	1	2	3	4	5
...masturbation	1	2	3	4	5
...the sexuality of others	1	2	3	4	5

These feelings relate to how positively you feel about your own body and the physical aspects of sex. If most of your answers are 1, 2 or 3 then these are not likely to be too much of a problem for you. However, if many or most of your answers are 4 or 5 they can present difficulties. If you are not at ease with your body, making love can feel embarrassing or awkward, or it can be hard to believe that your partner finds you attractive. Bad feelings about sex generally – or because of early experiences – can make the physical act of love-making appear threatening, dirty or unwelcome, even if the sex is pleasurable.

Recognizing that you have these feelings is important in overcoming them. Explaining them to your partner also helps. However, it means that you must both be patient when it comes to improving your sex life, or dealing with problems. Talking about sex freely is likely to be difficult for you, as is feeling comfortable with certain aspects of love-making. Make changes slowly, and concentrate on the tasks that make you feel good about yourself and your relationship.

PART THREE

WORD CHOICE

exciting	threatening	unifying
erotic	frightening	memorable
intense	sordid	generous
animal	warm	emotional
energetic	cosy	religious
thrilling	intimate	magical
ecstatic	happy	boring
passionate	fun	uncomfortable
urgent	relaxing	depressing
primitive	sensual	tiring
disgusting	friendly	silly
embarrassing	gentle	annoying
rude	reassuring	pointless
dirty	romantic	routine
alarming	loving	immature
painful	mystical	mundane
angry	satisfying	

Choose as many words as you like, but at least three, to describe the following:
1) What you thought sex was like as a child
2) What you thought sex was like as a teenager
3) Your first sexual experience
4) What sex should be like
5) What you need sex to be like to be turned on

It is interesting to think about your lists, as they further define your sexuality. Your answers to questions 1 and 2 might be different to what you think now, but those ideas still lurk somewhere in your mind. If you are conscious of this, you might be able to see how they still affect you.

Your answer to question 3 is also important. If this was a distressing experience for you it can still affect your feelings about sex. Powerful early experiences shape your reactions, especially unpleasant ones – so what turns you on might be something that reminds you of this, even though you would rather this was not so. It is best if these feelings are acknowledged, even if they are not acted upon. They can illuminate why you might have problems with desire or arousal.

Questions 4 and 5 show what you know about yourself sexually, and how you would like things to be. There might be discrepancies in the words you choose to represent what sex *should* be like and what turns you on. This shows possible areas of conflict in you, if they are very different. These mixed feelings can also cause problems with desire and arousal or with your reactions to aspects of love-making. What turns you on is likely to be fairly consistent, and needs to be integrated in your view of sex.

Talking about your own words and comparing them with your partner's words can also show you areas of potential agreement or problems.

?

You should by now have a better idea of which aspects of your early experiences have shaped your personal sexuality. But there is another strong influence on your ideas about sex, which is shared by everyone in our society. This is the way sex is portrayed in the media – and it is the subject of the next chapter.

PART TWO

SEX IN LOVING RELATIONSHIPS

2

SEX, LIES AND VIDEOTAPE

Never before has so much information about sex been available so widely. It would be impossible to avoid the subject, even if you wanted to, without cutting yourself off from television, books, newspapers, magazines and films.

The way sex is shown is often interesting, fun, thought-provoking or erotic. But it is rarely *realistic*. Sex as it happens on screen or in books bears little relation to sex as it is. Yet most people base their theories and beliefs about sex on what they see and read. In the fantasyland of sex there are mythical 'facts' about men and women – and the sex they have together – that are so common that people now believe they are true.

This matters because these manufactured myths create misunderstandings, which cause unnecessary unhappiness and stand in the way of a couple who want to develop a good sex life.

Among the myths about sex are some old ones. These, sometimes, are opposite to the modern myths prevalent in the media – but both are often wrong and harmful. It is important to look closely at the myths – old and new – to see how they affect you, and what the truth really is.

These are the most common myths – and what RELATE sex therapists have to say about them:

MYTHS ABOUT MEN

The myths about men have remained fairly constant. Many of the old ones are being re-peddled in a new guise. But just because they have remained the same, it doesn't mean that they are true.

● **The old myth: 'MEN ALWAYS WANT, AND ARE READY FOR, SEX'**
This, and its variations, is still around. The myth is that a 'real' man gets an erection in any situation involving an attractive woman and always wants more sex than a woman is prepared to give him. A refinement of this myth is that a 'real' man can maintain an erection until he brings a

woman to orgasm by thrusting alone, and that he will be ready for sex again within a short time of ejaculating.

This image of male sexuality is the *only* one used in the description of an attractive and worthwhile man in literature and on screen. The same image is used in material aimed at both men and women. It is also perpetuated by men talking to each other about sex, who routinely exaggerate and boast. They rarely say (truthful) things such as, 'I haven't been interested in sex for months', 'I couldn't get it up last night', 'I always come within three minutes of thrusting', or 'My wife is always nagging that she wants more sex'.

What the sex therapists say

This myth makes most normal men feel inadequate. But the truth is that only very young men become erect so indiscriminately, or are able to make love more than once within a short time. The majority of women will *not* come to orgasm through thrusting alone, however long a man is able to maintain his erection. Libido varies: a man can be attractive and a good lover but not want sex very often. Libido also varies according to outside circumstances: if something is going wrong in your life or your relationship you are unlikely to be very interested in sex. But while a man might be well aware that his experience is very different from the machine-like functioning of the myth, he has no way of telling what other men are experiencing. He blames himself; he blames his partner. What he doesn't blame is the nonsensical idea that the fictional man is real.

Women, who believe this myth as much as men do, can also feel disappointed when their men deviate from this supposed norm. A woman might feel that she is not attractive enough to excite her man, or that there is something wrong with him if he doesn't want sex all the time or as often as she does.

● **The new myth: 'A REAL MAN KNOWS HOW TO PLEASE A WOMAN'**

This is similar in spirit to the old myth. The idea is not only that men are constantly on the hunt for sex, but whenever they get a woman into bed they will magically know exactly how to turn her on. Behind this lies the belief that men should be in charge of the sexual experience, and that it is wrong for a woman to share responsibility or to indicate what she likes – if she does so it means the man has done something wrong. This implies that sex for a man is a performance – and he can pass or fail.

This telepathic man is everywhere in fiction. It's not just that he instinctively knows how to please a willing woman – he has equal success with an unwilling woman, and women who don't even like him. Within seconds of getting his hands on a woman who was his enemy moments before, he has kissed and touched her in such a way that she is putty in his hands. When they make love – wordlessly – she has orgasm after orgasm.

What the sex therapists say
This myth leads men and women to believe that it is possible for a man instinctively to arrange a sexual encounter with complete sexual satisfaction for the woman, as well as himself. Not only is it believed possible – it is thought that it *should* happen. But the truth is that it cannot. Everyone is different sexually – starting from what ideas and images excite you, to where and how you like to be touched, and the atmosphere and conditions before, after and during sex that make the experience good for you. Not only is it almost impossible for a man to get this right on a first encounter – if it is left solely up to him, he will *never* get it right, even for a partner he has been with for years. Good sex can only happen when both people involved take joint responsibility and let each other know through words, actions and experimentation what suits them both best.

This myth makes both men and women feel that if sex isn't good it must be the man's fault. If he can't 'get it right', she is going to feel disappointed, but she won't make efforts to bring about an improvement herself.

It also fosters the wrong idea that there is a standard pattern for turning a woman on: a man who has followed the manuals and concentrated on various erogenous zones, but finds the woman is not excited, can conclude that there is something wrong with *her*. After all, he believes he 'did it right'!

● **The old myth:** 'A REAL MAN IS TOUGH, AND IN CONTROL OF HIS FEELINGS'
This myth promotes the idea that the best kind of man is the traditional hard man, who is as strong emotionally as physically. This man, when roused, can become violent and aggressive, but he never, ever, feels weakness, fear or helplessness. He certainly never cries. He is a rock for his partner.

The idea of this man has always been around, and he still crops up as a modern hero. In material aimed at men there is no crack in this hardness. The softest emotions he can feel are a fierce love and passion for his partner and a fierce protective tenderness for the weak. In material aimed at women this man is very similar. However, when he falls in love with 'the' woman, he reveals, to her alone, a gentle romantic side, too.

What the sex therapists say
The effects of this myth start young. It is dinned into boys that 'big boys don't cry'. Boys and men reinforce it, being scornful of others who are more successfully in touch with the whole range of human feelings.

This produces men who strive to be like the men in the myth. The problem is that they *can* succeed. But succeeding means ignoring and controlling unacceptable 'feminine' emotions. These emotions – which everyone feels – don't go away, but become stifled. The main result is that the man can lose touch with all his feelings. The other result is that the stifled feelings, needing an outlet, emerge as anger.

In sexual situations, men who have lost touch with their feelings are at a disadvantage. Enjoyment includes experiencing emotions and being able to let go. If you watch and control yourself, it stands to reason that you can't let go. A man who denies feelings of fear, sadness, hurt – yet gets angry instead, can also find his sex drive affected: angry feelings are often found to be the cause of loss of interest in sex.

Women, who are attracted by the image of the mythical hard man, can be disappointed by the reality. Denying certain feelings might give a man the impression of strength, but a woman soon finds it mainly means a problem with communication. The woman who expects a gentle romantic to emerge from her hard man (as in the books) usually finds that the two images are incompatible.

●   **The new myth:** 'A "NEW MAN", WHO IS EMOTIONAL AND CARING, IS BEST'.
At first sight, the 'new man' appears to be a very different creature from the tough 'real man'. But he is only a modification, allowed a few acceptable feelings. This myth attracts women rather than men. The new man has his soft and tender side. He is good with children and does his share, he communicates about his feelings with his partner. He will cry when he is very moved. But he *still* doesn't feel frightened or powerless, or look to his partner for support or help. He is a rock – but with feelings.

The new man was born in women's magazines of the 1980s. As women learnt about relationships it became clear that communication was important. The strong, silent 'real man' was not going to talk about feelings, or the relationship, so women started looking for the 'new man', in touch with his 'feminine' side.

What the sex therapists say
The idea of the new man met a backlash. Some women who had found new men – or converted their old ones – were saying that they didn't find them sexually attractive, or couldn't respect them. These women

thought they wanted an equal relationship, but were unable to cope with it.

The reason is that although some women welcomed the increase in communication, it was only up to a point. Communication that meant talking positively about feelings for each other was fine, as was a man revealing sentimental, so-called 'feminine' emotions. But not when the feelings were negative, or when the men exposed fears and insecurities and appeared weak and in need of support.

The myth of the new man who is still a rock therefore creates even more tension in relationships, and makes them unbalanced. Communication is about accepting and attempting to understand *all* your partner's feelings, even the ones you find disturbing. This is what creates real intimacy – which provides the basis for the best sex life.

• **The old myth:** 'TO HAVE SEX, THE MAN MUST HAVE AN ERECTION' The idea behind this is that sex is only sex when there is penetration. Other sorts of touching – however satisfying – are second best. This myth has three main unfortunate effects on your sex life. The first is that many men, when they are aroused with a strong erection, are eager to start penetrating as quickly as possible. Women are often slower to arouse than men, and a woman who is penetrated before she is ready might be uncomfortable and is unlikely to reach the heights of arousal or have an orgasm, however long and enthusiastically the man thrusts. The second effect of this myth is that if the man comes quickly or loses his erection for any reason, love-making stops – whether both partners are satisfied or not. Lastly, some couples never make love unless the man is aroused enough to have an erection. At difficult times it can be months or years before he becomes spontaneously aroused, and all intimate love-play stops.

What sex therapists say:
Penetration is an aspect of sex, but by no means all of it. Other sex play, 'petting', is much more varied and can be even more exciting. To become fully aroused, most women need love-play that encompasses the whole body, and the stimulating variety of sensations caused by imaginative use of hands and mouth. Both men and women find the tenderness and intimacy created by this kind of love-making makes sex much more satisfying. A man who has trouble getting or sustaining an erection can find that taking time to make 'whole body' love helps.

The idea that this sort of sex is 'foreplay', leading up to the 'real' event of penetration is also misguided. Even without penetration, or an erection, this experience can be deeply satisfying for both partners. Many couples find that continuing with caressing after the man has come is just as important. Some women need further direct stimulation with hands or mouth if they are to reach orgasm, even if they have enjoyed the sensations of thrusting. Continuing to touch and enjoy each other's bodies, even after orgasm, shows affection and warmth – ingredients that make sex memorable and emotionally satisfying.

Love-making that revolves around a man's erection is likely to be over in a matter of minutes. Love-making that consists of giving and receiving sensual pleasure can go on for as long as you please. You also need to understand that just as a woman can be turned on by sensual touching when previously unaroused, so can a man. Love-making can start even if he has no erection. As he enjoys the experience, he may also become erect. But sex like this can be pleasurable and satisfying even if he doesn't, or if neither of you wants or happens to come to orgasm.

● **The new myth:** 'A BIG PENIS GIVES MORE PLEASURE THAN A SMALL ONE'
The new myth adds pressure to the old: it implies that not only is 'real' sex about penetration and thrusting, but a big penis gives maximum sexual pleasure. This myth shows a number of misunderstandings about the bodies of men and women. The main one is that sexual satisfaction for women is chiefly gained through penetration and thrusting, whereas this is true only for a minority of women. It also shows a lack of knowledge about women's bodies; the vagina is elastic: it can stretch wide enough to give birth to a baby, yet hold the slimmest tampon in place; its walls mould themselves to the penis, whatever its size. This myth also leads many men to feel insecure about their genitals. The male organ comes in many shapes and sizes, but most men's penises are between five and six inches long when erect, whatever size they look when soft. A small minority are larger or smaller than this, but the difference is only rarely significant enough to be experienced by his partner during penetrative sex.

What the sex therapists say
The main problem with this myth is that by believing that size is important, penetration is once again given too much emphasis in sexual satisfaction. A man who concentrates only on penetration and thrusting will be a disappointing lover, however big his penis is. Some women have preferences for large penises, just as some women prefer smaller ones. Ultimately, however, whether sex is satisfying or the man is a good lover has nothing to do with penis size, and everything to do with the care, time and imagination he brings to love-making – and the equal participation of his lover.

MYTHS ABOUT WOMEN

Ideas about female sexuality have changed radically during this century – at the beginning women were considered to have little interest or pleasure in sex, a view that changed around the middle of the century. Some myths have survived, however.

- **The old myth:** 'TO BE SEXY, A WOMAN MUST BE YOUNG AND BEAUTIFUL WITH A PERFECT BODY'
It's not hard to see where this myth comes from. Romantic, sexy heroines are almost always slim, young and beautiful. But sexiness has very little to do with looks. Some of the world's most gorgeous women have little interest in sex, and although good looks play a part in initial attraction, the effects soon pass if the woman is unpleasant, sexually cold or the relationship between the couple is not good. Even more important is that different people find different things attractive – physically and in other ways. All shapes and sizes of women have their admirers – but it is their personalities and emotional qualities that finally determine how attractive and sexy they are.

What the sex therapists say
This myth has the worst impact on women. No woman believes she measures up to the ideal, and even great beauties will list their imagined defects in great detail. The problem with this is that a woman who feels she has the wrong looks to be attractive will not find *herself* attractive, and this can affect her sex life. In the first place, people who are happy with themselves and 'comfortable' with their bodies are attractive, whatever they look like. Sexual confidence, which is an aura, rather than anything physical, is magnetic. It is often the 'secret' of perfectly ordinary-looking men and women who seem, mysteriously, to attract anyone they want.

But feeling unattractive has an even more direct impact on your sex life. If you don't feel attractive, or are ashamed of your body, it is difficult to let yourself go during sex, and this stands in the way of full enjoyment. Sadly, some women still feel the same even when their partners tell them that they find them sexy and attractive. These women insist that their partners 'don't really mean it', and can go to great lengths to hide parts of their bodies during love-making, or avoid sex altogether.

This myth can also mask the real cause of a sexual problem. If your sex life is going wrong it can be easy to believe that it is 'because' there is something physically off-putting about you. Or your partner might say that it is 'because' of an aspect of your looks that he has lost interest.

But, in reality, when your relationship is going well, even physical imperfections are endearing and attractive.

When there are other problems between you, however, causing dislike and anger, desire goes and faults seem magnified. While the problems remain in the relationship, even a magically improved body won't bring back the good, loving and warm feelings necessary to fuel desire. Similarly, some women say that when they are fat their partners lose desire, but when they are slim desire returns. A little probing reveals that when these women put on weight they become depressed, but when they slim down their confidence returns, which makes them happier and more loving. It is this, rather than the weight, that makes the difference.

● **The new myth:** 'AN OLDER WOMAN CAN BE SEXY – SO LONG AS SHE IS BEAUTIFUL AND HAS A PERFECT BODY'
The emergence of glamorous and sexy-looking forty- and fifty-year-olds in the popular culture of the 1980s has in some ways put paid to the old myth that only young girls are attractive. But it has not done women in general much good. What distinguishes these women is that they look young for their age, are still beautiful, and their bodies show no effects of passing time. Women of the same age, or older, who have not 'hung on' to youthful looks are, according to the myth, past it sexually.

What the sex therapists say
Believing that youth is an essential ingredient in sexiness also makes some women lose sexual confidence as they grow older, when in reality the experience and maturity they have gained can add extra qualities to their love lives. An older woman who accepts her age and her looks with good humour can be even more relaxed and whole-hearted about love-making than an insecure younger woman, or a woman who makes herself unhappy by trying to appear younger than she is.

It is not age that determines how sexy a woman is, but her feelings about herself and her sexual experiences so far. A woman who has been lucky enough to have a pleasurable and fulfilling love-life, will go on enjoying sex and giving enjoyment without regard to outward appearances. Some women will be happily sexual into old age, others will find that after a time they lose interest. One way is not better than the other – and neither has anything to do with the youthfulness of face or body. The woman who enjoys sex will probably like and respect her body, taking care of her health and fitness and the way she looks generally. This is different from worrying about lines on her face or changing body shape, and it gives an energy and confidence that continues to be sexy.

- **The old myth:** 'NICE GIRLS (THE ONES YOU MARRY) DON'T HAVE
SEX BEFORE MARRIAGE'

This myth has been around a very long time. In the old days it was assumed that 'nice' girls didn't have sexual feelings, so they certainly wouldn't have sex before marriage. Then the myth evolved: 'nice' girls might be turned on sexually, but they wouldn't have sex – to preserve their reputations as well as their virginities. The myth survived the sexual revolution of the 1960s and 1970s, and sexually active young women today are still sometimes looked down on by friends of both sexes.

The problem is that 'nice' girls have the same human instincts and impulses as the rest of humanity, and the sex drive is normal and healthy. It has never been particularly unusual for 'nice' girls to have sex before marriage, but in the past it created much guilt, which in some cases forced couples into marriages that should never have happened. It is also perfectly normal to fall in love more than once before finding the right partner with whom to build a life. The young woman who has sexual relationships with these early loves, so long as contraceptive and safe-sex practices are observed, is no less 'nice' than another young woman who has not felt strongly enough emotionally or sexually about someone to want to have sex.

Alongside this myth goes the idea that what is frowned on for women is all right for men. A man who sleeps around a lot is a bit of a lad, it is said, but the woman who does so is a slut. In fact, sexual promiscuity – taking lots of partners in short-term, meaningless relationships – is a sign of problems, quite apart from the question of sexually transmitted diseases. It is rarely the sex act itself that is the most important element in promiscuity – it is more likely to be complicated emotional needs.

What the sex therapists say:

Many older women today are still suffering from the earliest version of this myth. Brought up to believe that 'nice' girls did not have sexual feelings, they have never had the chance to explore their own. While they and their partners assume that they have no sexual feelings, there has been no need to adapt love-making so that the women have pleasure, too. Some women have deliberately stifled their sexual feelings out of shame, and then find, paradoxically, that their husbands complain about their passivity and lack of enthusiasm. Some couples come for counselling or sex therapy quite late because sex has become an unhappy issue between them. It is not uncommon to find that this myth is what has stood between them developing a good sexual relationship.

The hidden message in this myth lingers on today. If sex is something that 'nice' girls won't take part in, then there must be something not very nice, wrong, or dirty about sex itself. Some people, quite unaware that they have accepted the idea behind this myth, only find illicit, dangerous or in some way 'dirty' sex exciting. For these people, intimate, warm love-making in the context of an ordinary, long-lasting love relationship does not have the same erotic appeal, unless counselling or sex therapy awakens them to its deeper pleasures.

● **The new myth:** 'YOUR WIFE SHOULD HAVE LITTLE SEXUAL EXPERIENCE BEFORE MARRIAGE — BUT BE HIGHLY SEXUAL AFTER'
This is a refinement on the old myth. The idea is that the woman is able to hold her feelings in check until she is married but, despite having no chance to develop her sexuality, will be magically responsive after the wedding.

What the sex therapists say
This myth puts pressure on both partners. For the man, it harks back to the idea that he can and should be able to awaken the sexuality of a woman. For the woman, it implies that sexual feelings can be turned off and on like a tap. For both of them it suggests that so long as the relationship is sanctioned, then sex should automatically be good and free between them.

The truth is that a woman who comes to a relationship with little sexual experience needs time to learn about her desires and needs. If she has had to exercise control over her sexuality it will take a while before she learns to enjoy her body and her sex life. They both need time to learn about each other as well as themselves, and what works sexually between them, because every couple has a unique interaction. When the couple doesn't know this, or both believe that it is the man's responsibility alone to make his partner enjoy sex, in most cases there will be disappointment.

If sex between them does not start off well, and they do not talk about it or try to improve matters, the woman might not receive much pleasure from it. Consequently her desire goes, and over time she might 'give in' to sex to please her husband when she is uninterested. Because they have not discovered what would make sex good for her, she will remain unaroused. Sex like this will be boring or uncomfortable, and she will want it less and less. Sadly, both of them might believe that she is 'frigid', when really the problem is simply one of communication.

● **The old myth:** 'SEX IS FOR MEN — WOMEN JUST HAVE TO LIE BACK'
This has its roots in the 'nice girls don't' myth. It supposes that sexual pleasure for women is irrelevant, and that a woman's sexual role is a passive one. It suggests that men need sex more than women, and that

there is something unfeminine about a woman who takes an active part in love-making.

What the sex therapists say

This myth is a self-fulfilling prophecy, which still affects some older couples today. Couples who have built their sex life around it never take steps to make sex good for both partners. A woman who feels it wrong to take pleasure in sex will deny her sexual feelings until they fade away. The sad consequence is that she will never enjoy sex with her partner and certainly will become merely a passive recipient of his attentions. This makes sex for *both* of them unsatisfactory. The woman will find it a chore, and the man will find that sex with an unresponsive and unwilling partner has little pleasure in it.

• The new myth: 'A WOMAN SHOULD HAVE AT LEAST ONE ORGASM – THE MORE THE BETTER'

With the sexual revolution it was recognized that women do have sexual feelings and can take as much pleasure in sex as men. But once female orgasm was recognized as a fact, and that it was possible for women to have multiple orgasms, this new myth arose. It implies that sex can't be good for a woman unless she has an orgasm, and it is even better if she has more than one.

In films and on television a woman who is enjoying sex routinely has an orgasm – and she is usually shown moaning loudly or shouting as she does so.

What the sex therapists say

It can only be good that women's sexuality is better understood and that female orgasm is accepted. It is also good that couples are working together to make sex pleasurable and satisfying for both partners. The problem arises if the pursuit of the orgasm puts pressure on the couple, and particularly if the man feels that his ability as a lover is called into question if the woman does not have one.

The fact is that sex with orgasm and sex without orgasm are two different experiences, and one is not necessarily better than the other. Sometimes a woman can enjoy love-making without an orgasm, and feel quite fulfilled on that occasion. At other times she might want to proceed to orgasm – sometimes she will do so easily and on other occasions it will take more time. She might want or like to go on to have more than one orgasm, equally she might not. The same woman can feel differently at different times. In a good, loving, sexual relationship, the woman will feel free to enjoy whatever happens, without worrying that certain feelings or physical reactions are expected of her.

But, if the man feels that she hasn't enjoyed sex if she doesn't have an orgasm, or that he has failed as a lover, then both of them are likely to stop just enjoying what they are feeling, and turn the love-making into work – the goal being her orgasm. The woman might feel she must fake it if she is not close to orgasm, just to make her partner feel good.

This has a number of bad effects on the sexual relationship. First of all, good sex is all about learning what each other likes and needs sexually. A woman who fakes orgasm denies her own needs and also gives out wrong information about herself. When she wants to come to orgasm she might discover that their love-making does not create the right conditions, but she can't tell her partner without exposing the fact that she was faking before.

Faking an orgasm can also mean the woman does not feel good about herself. She might feel that if she doesn't have an orgasm she has failed as a woman, or is not sexy, or that she has disappointed her man. She might feel that there is something odd about herself because she enjoys love-making without an orgasm. She might also feel that if she doesn't make a lot of noise when she *does* have an orgasm then it is somehow an inferior experience. These thoughts can make her worried and inhibited about sex, which starts to spoil the experience.

It is not the ability to have an orgasm, or multiple orgasms, or the noise she makes during orgasm, that determines whether a woman is sexy or womanly. Her attitude to herself, her partner and the quality of their love-making are all more relevant.

MYTHS ABOUT SEX

The experience of sex itself is also surrounded by myths – what's right or wrong, and what constitutes good sex.

● **The old myth:** 'ANYTHING OTHER THAN THE MISSIONARY POSITION IS WRONG'

In the past, the missionary position or 'man on top' was considered the decent position for sex. Anything else was perverted or disgusting in some way. In fact, it is only one of many possible positions, none of which are abnormal or unwholesome. In some countries and other cultures it is not even the most common position.

What the sex therapists say
Believing this myth means that some couples feel unable to explore possibilities that might greatly enhance their sex lives. Different positions create different sensations, and allow for more varied ways of

caressing each other during intercourse. Neither is the missionary position always the most practical. For instance, when a woman is pregnant, or after a hip operation, other positions are more comfortable. If a man is having problems with controlling ejaculation, some positions make it easier. Similarly, some women who find penetration uncomfortable or alarming are more relaxed in positions in which they have some measure of control. There is more about different positions later in the book.

● **The new myth:** 'GOOD SEX MEANS LOTS OF DIFFERENT POSITIONS' Through the 1960s and 1970s, sex came to be considered as a performance art, and as a reaction to the old myth that only the missionary position would do, a new myth arose that a changing variety of positions was essential to good sex.

Encompassed in this myth is the idea that sex always has to be passionate, urgent and wild, a wonderful peak experience of spontaneity.

What the sex therapists say
Recognizing that sex can be varied and different is good, and enjoyable experimentation enhances your sex life. But feeling pressured to make variations for the sake of it – turning sex into a performance – can get in the way of the real enjoyment. Couples in a good long-term sexual relationship can find that at times they want to experiment, and at other times they are happy to turn to the position they have discovered suits them best – or alternate two or three favoured positions. For many couples the missionary position is one of these, and if it is enjoyable then it is not second best.

Variety extends to variation in mood. Sometimes it is right for sex just to be cosy and loving, at other times it can be energetic and gymnastic. Spontaneous passion is right for some moods, and a more carefully planned encounter is essential for others.

● **The old myth:** 'SEX IS FINISHED WHEN THE MAN EJACULATES' This is yet another myth that presupposes that penetration is the most important part of sex, and that without an erect penis there is no point to it. It also suggests that the man's satisfaction is the most important element in a sexual encounter.

What the sex therapists say
If both partners feel satisfied after the man has come, that is fine. But sometimes the woman can feel unfulfilled. Perhaps she is highly aroused and near orgasm herself or feels that she wants to continue showing and receiving love in a physical way, and an abrupt ending leaves her

disappointed. Good sex is about give and take, and a loving attitude means that a man is happy to continue love-making in other ways, perhaps after a rest, until the woman too feels ready to stop. Men can discover a different quality in love-making after the urgency and intensity of penetration and ejaculation are over – and the pleasure and intimacy that comes with taking their partners' needs into account.

● **The new myth:** 'COMING TOGETHER IS THE ULTIMATE OF GOOD SEX'

In some ways this is like the old myth in disguise. After all, if both of you come at the same time, there is a natural break in love-making. It also stresses the 'performance' aspect of many of the new myths – that a man should be able to orchestrate his own and his partner's sexual responses to a timetable.

What the sex therapists say

Coming together can be wonderful, but so can having orgasms at different times. During orgasm you are momentarily lost in a world of your own, and while it can add something to know that your partner is having the same experience, it can also be exciting to watch and experience your partner's orgasm while you are fully aware.

This myth also continues the assumption that a woman must have an orgasm every time, when sometimes she might not want or need to. It also puts pressure on the man to sustain his erection when his partner might be much slower to arouse. Believing that simultaneous orgasm is sex at its best leads to unnecessary feelings of failure when it doesn't happen.

● **The old myth:** 'IT'S BAD FOR AN AROUSED MAN NOT TO HAVE SEX'

In the past many women had sex reluctantly under the mistaken belief, shared by men, that it harms men in some way to have strong erections that do not end in intercourse or ejaculation.

What the sex therapists say

It is not dangerous for a man to have an erection without ejaculating. On the contrary, part of sex therapy can involve a man getting a strong erection till he is almost at the point of ejaculating, and then letting it subside – and doing this a few times during a love-making session. Other sex therapy exercises often involve a ban on penetration, however excited the man becomes.

Another assumption of this myth is that a woman is responsible for satisfying a man sexually, whatever her own feelings, which is not the case. In a loving relationship a woman might well decide to participate in sex, even if she is not particularly aroused herself. But equally, a man can control his arousal if his partner is unwilling – or choose to masturbate if he prefers.

● **The new myth:** '**ALL PHYSICAL CONTACT LEADS TO SEX**'
This myth suggests that being physically affectionate inevitably means that you want sex, or that one of you will expect it.

What the sex therapists say
This myth is very widespread, and its effects harm a relationship in fundamental ways, including sexually. When it is accepted by couples it can lead to a breakdown in ordinary loving intimacy once the couple have reached the stage when sex is less central to the relationship.

When you believe that an affectionate kiss or cuddle is a sign that sex comes next, it can mean that you try to avoid this kind of touching if sex is far from your mind. When you love someone you want to be near them and touch them, but when this is reserved for sexual encounters it can slowly lead to a feeling of being distant or unloved for most of the rest of the time.

Some men believe it is unmanly to need to touch or be touched and not want sex. But it is a human need, and men who don't recognise this often demand or instigate sex when really they just want to be reassured that they are loved. Similarly, although a woman is more likely to recognise her need for 'just a cuddle' she might be reluctant to show this for fear that she will give her man 'the wrong idea'.

When this ordinary physical closeness goes, so does much of the warm feeling of intimacy in a relationship, and this affects your sex life. When there is little ordinary physical affection, then your desire level is likely to drop, too. Women sometimes complain about feeling used when they are only kissed or touched as a prelude to sex. Sex itself becomes more separate from your relationship, rather than remaining a natural part of it, and can feel less loving and satisfying as a result. It is not unusual for couples who have been together for a long time to go through a phase when neither is interested in sex. Sometimes this can go on for months. If you don't touch at all during this time, even in a friendly way, you can both feel lonely when perhaps you both most need to feel close.

MYTHS ABOUT HOMOSEXUALITY

Myths about homosexuality have been hard to challenge, since the subject has often been surrounded in secrecy. For much of this century male homosexuality was illegal anyway, and both male and female homosexuality have been long misunderstood.

● **The old myth: 'MARRIAGE CAN "CURE" A HOMOSEXUAL'**
This myth suggests that settling down with a member of the opposite sex will take away same-sex urges. The idea of a 'cure' also implies that homosexuality is an illness or an aberration that can be put right.

In the past, and still today, many homosexuals did marry, and indeed raise families. Homosexuals, male and female, are capable of sex with the opposite sex, but this does not mean that their desires for their own sex fade – even though they might not act upon them.

What the sex therapists say
Homosexuals are at one end of the normal human scale of sexual orientation. At the other end are heterosexuals who have no interest in their own sex. Somewhere in between are people who feel some desire for both sexes. This has always been the case, and is the same all over the world. It is natural, and homosexuality is not an illness. Some homosexuals might remember incidents that 'caused' their sexual preferences; equally, there are many who insist they were born that way.

This myth has caused much unhappiness for people who are already in a situation that creates difficulties because of the attitude of society. Although some homosexuals can make marriages that are happy in many ways, the pressure of their sexual preferences is often against this. A homosexual who hopes to be 'cured' by marrying can feel guilty and depressed when it makes no difference. The partner, who has hoped to change the homosexual, or who has discovered the homosexuality later, can also feel a failure or angry and upset at the situation.

● **The new myth: 'BEING ATTRACTED TO YOUR OWN SEX WHEN YOUNG MEANS YOU ARE GAY'**
This myth can secretly worry people who have had crushes on members of their own sex or had sex-play with them.

What the sex therapists say
A normal part of development includes same-sex crushes and some-times sexual encounters. Some people find that they continue to prefer members of their own sex when they are adults. But in most cases it is a stepping-stone to sexual love with the opposite sex, and many people never again find themselves attracted to their own sex. However, their continuing guilt and shame about childhood and adolescent sex-play can mark their sex lives later. Men, particularly, might feel defensive about their manhood and feel the need to behave like a 'real man' sexually, nervous of love-making that requires gentleness, or in which they are passive.

- **The old myth:** 'ALL HOMOSEXUALS FANCY YOUNG CHILDREN'

This myth perpetuates anti-homosexual feeling, by suggesting that homosexuals are paedophiles – liking sex with children. An extension of this myth is the idea that homosexuals fancy *all* members of their own sex. For instance, a man who might be realistic about his attractiveness to women, can often feel convinced that any homosexual wants to have sex with him!

What the sex therapists say
There is nothing about homosexuality itself that makes homosexuals into paedophiles or have a promiscuous need for sex with any member of their own sex. Most homosexuals, like everyone else, want to have loving and equal relationships. Some homosexuals, however, have emotional or other problems that make them sexually indiscriminate or only sexually attracted to children. Believing that all homosexuals are like this continues to further isolate them and make it even harder for them to live normal and happy lives.

- **The new myth:** 'HOMOSEXUALS CAN'T MAKE STABLE RELATIONSHIPS'

This is a continuation of the old myth. Homosexuals, it is believed, go from partner to partner without ever being able to settle down.

What the sex therapists say
It is harder for homosexuals to settle down in stable relationships – but not because of their sexual preferences. As many people still find the idea of homosexuality wrong or disgusting, a homosexual couple setting up home together – however happy or in love – suffer far more pressures than an equivalent male-female couple. Disapproval can come from their own families, colleagues, neighbours and complete strangers if they are open about their relationship, which can make it harder to sustain when they experience the inevitable problems that every couple faces.

Because homosexuals are in a minority which faces much hostility and prejudice, there has been a tendency to form a sub-culture with its own rules and practices. Promiscuity has been a feature of this, and some homosexuals – needing to fit in – have gone along with this, sometimes against their own inclinations.

Nevertheless, many homosexuals can and do form stable relationships. Sometimes these are much stronger and long-lasting than heterosexual marriages – when the problems they face unite them rather than force them apart. Many more homosexuals would be able to do this if they were accepted as normal and no more or less interesting than anyone else.

• **The old myth:** 'GAY MEN ARE EFFEMINATE AND LESBIANS ARE BUTCH'
The idea behind this myth is that gay men wish they were women and lesbians wish they were men – so they dress and act accordingly.

What the sex therapists say
Most homosexual men and women are quite happy being the sex they are. Homosexuality isn't the same as transsexuality (wanting to be of the other sex, and perhaps having a sex change) or transvestisism (liking to dress up in the clothes of the opposite sex). Homosexual men can be as tough and manly as other men, and homosexual women can be very feminine.

   Some homosexuals, it is true, do behave in ways that make their sexual orientation very clear. It used to be more of a fashion in the homosexual sub-culture to do so. For some homosexuals behaving like a member of the opposite sex is a 'political statement', and they might like to shock or outrage prejudiced people. But there are many homosexuals who show no sign of their sexual preferences and, unless they choose to talk about it, seem no different from anyone else.

• **The new myth:** 'SEX BETWEEN HOMOSEXUALS MEANS ONE ALWAYS BEING PASSIVE, THE OTHER ALWAYS ACTIVE'
An extension of the old myth concerns speculation about the sexual practices of homosexuals. This assumes that sex between them mimics heterosexual sex – that between men one will pretend to be a woman, and between women one will pretend to be a man – perhaps using a false penis to simulate penetration.

What the sex therapists say
Sex between homosexuals is as varied as that between any other couple – sometimes more so. They are likely to be even less bound than a heterosexual couple by the idea that one should be passive while the other is active. Good sex between homosexuals comes down to the same basic formula as good sex between anyone: that the couple should experiment to find out what they like together. As in any loving sexual relationship, the couple are likely to find that this changes all the time, and that mood and circumstance determine who will be active or passive – not pre-set roles.

THE POWER OF MYTH

All of us are, to some degree, affected by these myths. They are so much a part of our lives that it would be hard to escape them. However, they do need challenging if they are not to put unfair pressure on our sex lives. The next chapter looks at what sex is really like for people, and what you can and can't expect.

3

THE REALITY OF SEX

The myths in the last chapter show the stereotyped view of sex. It is much more interesting to look at the reality of sex, because it is infinitely more complex. So what is sex really like for people?

Everyone's experience is different, and what is good for one person won't be good for someone else. This makes it impossible to give one definition of good sex – which might trouble you if you are hoping to read a set of rules with 'dos and don'ts'. In fact, one of the secrets is recognising that there are no hard and fast rules – not even in your own life.

Everyone has sexual needs, just as everyone feels hungry or tired and needs to sleep – it is part of being human and alive. But just as some people need less food and less sleep than others, and get variable pleasure from the experiences of eating and resting, so the sex drive varies, too.

Sex is more important to some people. They might have a higher than average sex drive and find their thoughts turning to sex more often, or feel the need for frequent sex. They might be physical people generally, who need a high level of activity, be it sporting or sexual. For others it is because they enjoy the sensual side of life, liking food and drink, the feel of nice fabrics, and the sensations of the physical world: the wind on their face, scents and sounds – and the experience of touching and being touched. Yet others like a lot of sex because for them there is nothing better than orgasm itself. Some people need sex because in no other situation do they feel so intimate and close to someone, and the physical feelings are secondary. For some, it is a combination of factors that makes sex important to them.

On the other hand, there are people for whom sex is much less important. They might enjoy sex when it happens, but need it rarely or feel no particular need for it. Some people simply find there are other physical activities that give them equal, or more, pleasure. Or they might be people for whom the physical side of life generally holds much less excitement and interest than the world of ideas.

These are all natural variations, which are just different, one being no better than another. Of course, sexual needs for some people are determined by problems. Someone might want a lot of sex because of insecurity, another person might avoid sex because of a fear of intimacy or of the physical act itself.

As time goes on, how much you want and need sex can change. Your sex drive adapts to circumstances; if, for one reason or another, you can't have sex for a long time your sexual appetite will reduce. Your sex drive will adapt to a higher level with frequent and satisfying sex. Just as people who have to live on bread and water will eat simply to stay alive with little pleasure, so people whose sex life is narrow and dull will 'lose their appetites' and need and want less sex. A naturally high sex drive will tend to drop somewhat with age. Most people find this, though a new relationship will usually act as a stimulant for a while.

On the other hand, some people find that their desire for sex becomes stronger later in life. This is usually the case when unhelpful sexual experiences lowered their sex drives, which are then raised by happier and more satisfying sexual relationships.

Just as the frequency with which you want sex is individual, so is the kind of sex that turns you on and which you enjoy. Broadly, some people prefer sex that is energetic and passionate, others like an experience that is warm and gentle. Still others prefer sex to seem rough and dangerous, or find it more exciting if it is dirty, illicit or lewd. While people can like to vary the atmosphere of sex, usually one or other of these is most satisfying to them.

The important thing is to understand the way you are, and not to feel that you must be any different. This doesn't mean that you should do nothing about a sexual problem, or ignore elements that could improve your sex life. But it means accepting your own level of interest in sex and not feeling that it should be higher or lower. In a relationship, it obviously helps if you both feel roughly the same about how much sex you want and the way you like it. But if you don't, it means accepting yourself and each other and finding common ground, so that you both feel free to enjoy your sexuality.

SEX IN A LONG-TERM RELATIONSHIP

While some of your basic attitudes about sex and how important it is to you might not undergo many changes, your sex life within a long-term relationship certainly will. If sex is not good for you it is not necessary to resign yourself to believing 'it will always be like this'. Equally, if your sex life is very good now it still needs attention. While you might not like the idea that a good sex life can deteriorate, it is comforting to know that this can always be reversed. But while individual experiences vary, there are some trends that are common to many long-term relationships.

Sex and romance: in the beginning

The beginning of a relationship, when you are first in love and are feeling very romantic, is often a marvellous time sexually. Desire levels are very high at this time, even for those for whom sex is not very important. It is very easy to get into the mood for sex – sometimes it might seem as if you're in the mood all the time! – and when you start to make love it often takes very little for you to become highly aroused. The sheer pleasure of touching and being touched by someone you think is wonderful, and who thinks the same about you, can be very erotic – even if neither of you has much experience and little sexual technique. At this time sex has a special magic with hardly any effort.

It's not surprising that many people think this sort of experience is what good sex is all about. This is reinforced by sex as portrayed on the screen, which usually involves couples newly, and madly, in love. They can't keep their hands off each other, take no time to 'warm up', and then sex itself is blissful.

The trouble is that wonderful though this is, it is simply a stage, even when it lasts for many months. Indeed, some people miss out on this heady stage altogether for various reasons, most of them discussed in the first chapter.

Whichever is your experience, you can learn from it to maintain a good sex life or to make a less satisfactory one better. Later chapters go into this in more detail. For now, it is important to acknowledge that this is only one kind of sexual experience, and the reality is that it will change and be different later.

Sex as your relationship matures

When you have been together for some time, are still in love but not madly so, the nature of your sex life also changes. However good sex is between you, there is less urgency about making love. When you are living together or married, and plan to remain so, you know that you have plenty of time and opportunity for sex. Usually by the time you have been together for about two years, sometimes sooner than that, the excitement of being in love has quietened down. This is inevitable. Now that you know each other well and being together is more ordinary, you become used to the situation, however happy you are.

In terms of sex this means that simply being in each other's company isn't enough to turn you on. You might find that you are not so often in the mood for sex, or that it takes more specific sexual situations for you to become aroused.

The start of these changes is a testing time for couples. One of you might want sex more than the other, or you might find that you are in the mood at different times. You might find that the sex that seemed so wonderful early on isn't as satisfying now that your desires are not so quick to arouse. This is when your sexual preferences are likely to emerge – those that are natural to you and which are not specifically connected to your partner – and they might turn out to be different from your partner's.

As you can imagine, these issues create difficulties if they are neglected. Some people feel unable to talk about them with their partners. When you react to these changes with disappointment or anger and accept them as a sign that the best has gone, your sexual relationship can go from bad to worse. This doesn't have to happen if you view them as an opportunity to learn more about each other's needs. Adjusting your sex life to the reality of each other can make for more enduring satisfaction than the guesswork during the haze of romantic love. The next chapter helps you sort out some of these issues in a practical way.

For some people this is the first major change in their sexual relationships. More are to come. Sex between you continues to go through highs and lows. When you are happy together and relaxed, sex is likely to be good unless you have other difficulties. At bad times, when you are under stress for any reason, or are not getting on, sex will suffer, too. The more commitments you have the harder it can be just to find time when you are not exhausted to make love without interruptions.

If you never talk in a constructive way about sex, or make the effort to maximise the good times and support each other through the bad times, you might reach a point in your relationship when sex has lost most of the satisfaction it ever had. Fortunately, this doesn't have to be the case if you both decide to challenge it.

Sex after illness or surgery

In some cases your sex life changes because of health problems. A man might have a condition that means he can no longer get an erection or sustain one. A woman might have surgery that affects her feelings about her body – a breast operation because of cancer, or a hysterectomy. Either of you might have surgery, such as a hip replacement, which makes some positions uncomfortable. None of these mean that your sex life is over, if you do not wish it to be. Suggestions later in the book show how you can adapt your love life to these conditions.

SEX – THE PHYSICAL FACTS

Whatever your variations in preferences and sexual needs, one thing doesn't vary – and that is the physical changes and stages that take place in your bodies during sex. Everyone needs to know these basic biological facts, because understanding them is what gives the lie to some of the unhelpful myths.

THE MALE GENITALS

This is an unaroused penis. In most men it is roughly three to four inches long, though some are smaller or larger. Except during sexual excitement, the penis is soft and floppy. The head of the penis, the glans, is the most sensitive part. It corresponds to the clitoris in women. When a baby is growing in the womb, this is the part of the genitals that develops first, before it can be seen whether the baby will be a boy or a girl. In a boy it becomes the glans, in a girl it becomes the clitoris.

The glans is covered with a skin, called the foreskin, which can be removed (circumcision). In the unaroused state this completely covers the glans, except for an opening through which urine passes.

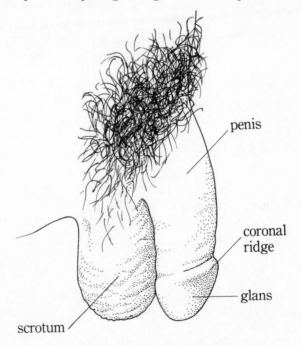

penis

coronal ridge

glans

scrotum

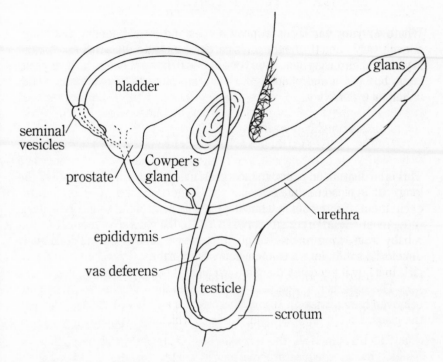

The scrotum is a 'bag' of skin which contains the two testicles, or 'balls'. In an unaroused state, the skin is loose and wrinkly, and it hangs slightly, holding the testicles away from the body. Usually one hangs slightly lower than the other.

Inside each of these testicles sperm are produced – and they are being produced all the time. They need a cooler than body temperature to be produced, which is why the testicles hang outside the body. The manufactured sperm are stored in the epididymis until they are required.

Leading up from each testicle is the vas deferens. This is the tube that is cut or tied when a man has a vasectomy, so that the sperm can travel no further and no longer fertilise his partner.

The vas deferens takes the sperm into the seminal vesicle. It is here that most of the fluid that surrounds the sperm is made – the ejaculate. The rest of the fluid is produced by the prostate gland.

The two Cowper's glands also produce fluid during arousal. Unlike the cloudy ejaculate, this is a clear and slightly sticky fluid, which lubricates the urethra in readiness for ejaculation, and perhaps neutralises any acid that remains there from previous passage of urine. It is this that produces the droplet of fluid that appears at the tip of an aroused penis.

The man's arousal

There are four stages to the sexual experience.

- **Excitement.** This can happen in a few seconds; a sexy thought or touch, or the sight of an attractive person starts the process. Almost instantly there is an increased flow of blood to the pelvic area. The penis is largely composed of spongy tissue, which starts to fill up with blood. As a consequence it becomes larger, firmer and erect. Smaller penises increase proportionately more than larger ones, which is why erect penis size is roughly the same for most men.

At the same time, the testicles are drawn up further into the body. The skin of the scrotum starts to thicken, and it feels more leathery and firmer. The colour becomes more intense and darker because of the increase in blood to the area.

If the man becomes distracted at this point or loses interest, or is not in a situation where sex is possible (it might be a sexy thought he has on the train!) the process will go into reverse. The blood will drain away and the genitals return to their unaroused state.

- **Plateau.** If nothing happens to halt the process, he moves on to the plateau phase, when there are other discernible changes. The testicles have been elevated as high as possible and are at their tightest. The coronal ridge becomes swollen and engorged and darker in colour. If the man is uncircumcised, the foreskin rolls right back, fully exposing the glans. Inside, the urethra marginally dilates to help the passage of seminal fluid.

Again, if something should happen to distract the man, even if he is in the middle of sex with his partner, this stage can be reversed. If the phone rings, or the baby cries, or he suddenly remembers a problem at work, or begins to get over-anxious about his performance, the excitement can subside. He might return to the last stage, or go right the way back to the unaroused state.

When this happens, some people believe that is the end of sex. But it is like a ladder on the side of a house, you can go up and down as many times as you like. A man can become re-aroused to this stage again frequently.

- **Orgasm.** This phase has two stages for men. During the first stage, the vas deferens starts to contract and the sperm is packaged in the fluid in the seminal vesicles. With experience a man can recognize the sensations this creates and know that if he is excited any more he will reach the point of 'ejaculatory inevitability'. (This is the equivalent to the ladder being kicked away when you step off the top on to the roof – there is no going back.) At this point, however, if stimulation stops he can go back a stage or two and delay ejaculation.

At the second stage this is no longer possible. This is the moment of ejaculation. The sperm arrive in the urethra, and the man will feel contractions in the whole of his penis which will cause the seminal fluid to be ejected. In a young man this can be very forceful. Usually ejaculation is accompanied by the intense, pleasurable feelings of orgasm, but not always. The contractions start at intervals of 0.8 seconds and continue for a few seconds. The female orgasm involves contractions of exactly the same rate.

● **Resolution.** After ejaculation the man passes into the resolution phase. Gradually all the changes in the genital area go into reverse. The penis goes back to its usual size and becomes soft, the testicles descend and the scrotum becomes softer and looser. For a time no stimulation can re-arouse him. In a teenager this refractory period can be short – a few minutes – but it becomes longer with age, when it can be hours before he is ready to become aroused again.

THE FEMALE GENITALS

Unlike the male genitals, the female genitals are hidden from sight, and you will have only seen the view over the page if you have looked. Some women have never looked at their own genital area, and some men have also avoided the sight. As with male genitals, there are variations. Just as all faces look different, though they have two eyes, a nose and a mouth, so do genitals – and this is just one picture.

The labia majora are the outer lips, these vary in fleshiness from woman to woman. Inside is another fold of fleshy tissue, the labia minora or inner lips. This is a continuous fold of flesh, often quite uneven, so that one side might be bigger than the other. Sometimes these lips protrude so that they are always visible, sometimes they are hidden by the outer lips. Enfolded in the upper area is the clitoris, a very important focus for female sexual pleasure. It is covered by the clitoral hood. Many delicate nerve-endings are in the clitoris, and most women will get a lot of pleasure from touching it directly or indirectly, just as the man gets pleasure from stimulation to the glans.

Below this is the opening from the urethra, through which you pass urine. Next to this is the vagina. Unaroused, the walls of the vagina lie close together, not like an open tunnel. A comparison is two sheets lying flat on a bed: there is no space between them – but if you slip between them there is plenty of room.

Inside, at the end of the vagina, is the cervix, the mouth of the uterus or womb. It is completely closed except for a tiny hole through

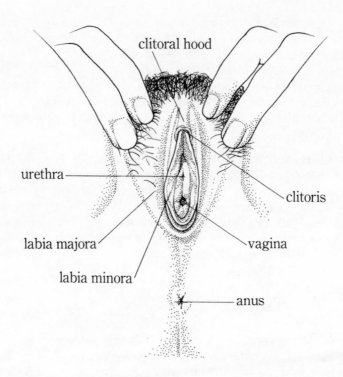

which menstrual blood passes. You can feel the cervix with your finger: it is rather like a small nose with a dimple in it. Leading from the womb are the two Fallopian tubes and ovaries. From one of these ovaries an egg is released each month, approximately fourteen days after menstruation starts. This egg will be passed along the nearest Fallopian tube until it comes to the uterus. This takes about two days. The uterus prepares for a fertilised egg (which will grow into a baby) by thickening its lining. If, when the egg arrives, it has not been fertilised, the lining of the uterus will shed itself through the vagina – which is the menstrual period.

The G-Spot, which is on the front wall of the vagina, roughly in the same place that the man has his prostate gland, is another sensitive area, which gives some women pleasure when it is stimulated.

A woman's arousal
There are also four stages of arousal for women.

● **Excitement.** As in men, the changes of this phase happen in a few seconds. Sexy thoughts, romantic songs, and especially the right touch, start the process immediately. Blood flows to the pelvic region, and the walls of the vagina start to open up. The walls of the vagina start to

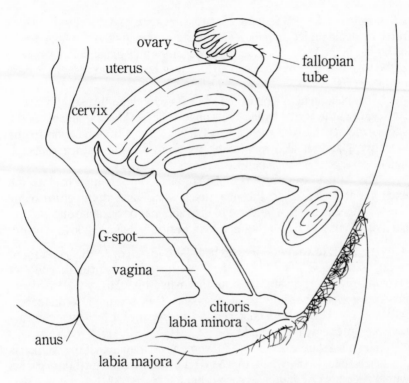

sweat, causing them to become smooth and lubricated. This lubrication starts to creep out and moisten the lips. The lips themselves become fuller and swell, and the colour will darken. At this stage the clitoris becomes much firmer and might emerge from within the clitoral hood. Like the penis, it swells in size, but is rarely larger than a small pearl.

The uterus starts to tip slightly, and the cervix exerts a pull on the top of the vagina. This causes the vagina to lengthen and, near the cervix, it starts to balloon out.

Most women will also experience nipple erection. As the arousal process continues, the area around the nipple swells slightly so the nipple can appear less erect.

As with men, this stage can go into reverse if the touching stops, or there is some distraction, or the woman is not able to have sex. A woman can remain in this phase throughout love-making, never reaching the plateau phase or going on to orgasm.

● **Plateau.** If excitement continues, the woman reaches the plateau phase, where there are further physical changes. The outer and inner lips continue to increase in size, becoming more full and visibly deepening in colour. As the blood supply increases, the lips open out like a flower, to make for easier access to the vagina and the clitoris, which retreats again under its hood. The uterus continues to tilt, being drawn up higher in the body, and the vagina becomes fully expanded, ballooning at the top so as to provide a 'cup' to hold the seminal fluid and sperm next to the cervix.

This ballooning is one of the reasons why deep thrusting is not as satisfying as the myths would lead you to believe. The opening out of the vagina means that the man doesn't have so much stimulation to the sensitive glans. It also means the woman's sensations are reduced, however large the man's penis.

The woman can reach the plateau phase and then go back to the excitement phase or to the unaroused state, and then return many times. This can happen because of distractions, or because she and her partner choose to take rests in a long period of leisurely love-making.

● **Orgasm.** In women, orgasm has just one stage. At this point there is no going back. The outer third of the vagina starts to contract involuntarily, at the same rate as the man's ejaculatory contractions, producing peak sensations of orgasm. The uterus also contracts rhythmically. Unlike birth contractions, these smaller muscular contractions are intensely pleasurable.

The main difference between women and men is that the woman is physically able, if she wants to, to go on to experience further orgasms within seconds or minutes of each other.

● **Resolution.** After the orgasm is over, the woman's genitals gradually return to their unaroused state if there is no further stimulation. Some women reach the plateau phase of intense arousal but do not go on to have an orgasm. In certain cases, this can lead to pelvic pain, because the 'trigger' of orgasm does not release the congested blood that has flowed to the genitals. Without orgasm, the resolution phase is much slower. The blood eventually flows back, but it takes longer.

These stages are usually experienced by all men and women during love-making. It is remarkable that this process is identical, when individual experiences of sex are so different. It shows, once again, that the mind and the emotions are as important to sex as the physical act itself. That is why your relationship with your partner needs examining if you are to understand why and how sex works for you. In the next chapter you will take a closer look at your own relationship, and whether the sex is satisfactory for you both.

4

YOUR SEX LIFE NOW

This chapter is for all couples who are in a stable, loving relationship, who want to take a closer look at their sex lives together. It is appropriate if you are married, living together, heterosexual or homosexual, and whatever age you are.

Perhaps your relationship is quite new and you are happy about your sex life. This chapter will help you talk about why it is good, so that you have a better chance of keeping it so. But, as we saw in the last chapter, the longer you are together, the more likely it is that your sex life will change for many reasons, and you might be going through a patch when it is not so good. If so, this chapter aims to help you isolate what might have gone wrong and decide together what to do about it. There might be more serious problems or difficulties in your sex life; again, by the end of this chapter you should be able to identify what needs to change, and use the information in later chapters to help yourselves.

Above all, this chapter is designed to get you talking about your relationship – something few couples ever set aside time to do once they have been together for a while.

The concentration here is on the physical side of your relationship – after all, that is what sex is. But your sex life is an integrated part of your lives together, and it is affected by other matters. In the next chapter, 'Is It Really a Sexual Problem?', you look at the other elements that might be getting in the way of satisfaction in your sex life.

HOW WAS IT FOR YOU?

First of all, be honest with yourself. What do you feel about your sex life? Does it suit you? Do the following quiz. This is one that you can do alone, especially if you are not ready to talk about such matters. At some point you must talk – and that can come later – but being clear about your own feelings will help when you are ready to do so.

? _____ **Quiz** _____

State of love-play

- Are you happy with the amount of sex you have?
  YES/NO

- Do you enjoy the sex you do have?
  YES/NO/SOMETIMES

- Can you remember a time when you enjoyed it more with your
  partner?
  YES/NO

_____ **?**

The answers you give to this quiz raise complicated issues, which will be
dealt with one by one. The important thing is to acknowledge whether
you are content. It's not what your partner feels that counts at this point,
or what other people do, or what they find satisfying. If you are not
content, then something is wrong. If you are happy, then you have a
strong foundation on which to build. Knowing where you stand, even in
general terms, is where you start.

_____ YOUR FEELINGS ABOUT YOUR BODY _____

As we saw in Chapter One, your sexuality is unique, and much of it
involves how you feel about your body. Broadly, if you are not happy
with your body, it is hard to build a good sex life, however much you love
or fancy your partner. The ideal is to become comfortable with your
body. That means appreciating its good points and accepting the less-
than-perfect aspects that can't be changed. This is a constant process.
As you know, your body changes through life, and you have to continue
to 'make friends' with it.

    During sex therapy, couples are often shown pictures of normal
men and women unclothed. This is when many couples betray anxieties
about their own bodies. Some people worry that they might not be
normally formed, when in fact they are. Others have previously
compared themselves to the air-brushed, carefully posed pictures of
young people at the peak of physical perfection – and only a tiny number
of people have bodies like that.

    When you accept your body two main things happen. The first is that whatever your shape or your looks you become more attractive. People who are comfortable with themselves move differently, clothed or unclothed. They sit, stand and walk in such a way as to say, 'I like being me'. This is a strong message. Other people are drawn to them because they feel comfortable round them. Sometimes the message is so powerful that other people literally see them differently. People who have gained in confidence might be believed to have lost weight, done something to make themselves look younger, bought new clothes or had a new hairstyle, when everything about them is just the same as before. You might have noticed the effects yourself when your partner was first in love with you, which made you feel good about yourself. If you don't accept your own body or worry that it is not good enough, it is hard to think that anyone else will accept or like it – and that misery communicates itself, too.

The second main effect of feeling comfortable with your body is that sex itself is better. If you worry about how you look, or want to conceal parts of yourself that you think are unattractive, it is hard to let yourself go and enjoy what you are experiencing. Your worry gets in the way of the physical pleasures.

Sex therapists often see this at work. One talked of Hilary, who said that she 'froze' when her breasts were touched. She told her husband, Frank, that she didn't like the sensations this created. As therapy continued it emerged that this was really because she was ashamed of the 'thinness' of her breasts. Later, as therapy worked for them both, Hilary found she actively enjoyed it when Frank paid attention to her breasts.

A counsellor spoke about a gay couple, Jeremy and Henry, who came for counselling about their relationship. One of the problems was that Jeremy was suffering from impotence. There were a number of reasons for this, but one of them was Jeremy's body image, which was poor. He was over-weight, and he said, 'I look at myself all the time. When, during sex I see my tummy wobbling, I lose my erection.' Although they had not come for sex therapy, the counsellor suggested that the couple spent time on the first sensate focus task of non-sexual touching, learning to enjoy being touched, and to enjoy their partner's enjoyment. Through this, Jeremy began to realise that Henry liked him the way he was, and he began to feel better about himself. He reported that one day he went to work wearing bicycling shorts and a T-shirt, instead of the loose and baggy clothes he usually wore to hide his body. He was able to recognise that with his new confidence people looked at him with interest and admiration. 'Maybe I am OK!' he said to the counsellor.

Sometimes it can be harder to change your feelings about your body. Lucy came for sex therapy because she didn't like sex at all. She saw herself as ugly because as a young child she had suffered from a skin condition that affected her entire body. Her mother used to have to cover her in cream from head to foot. Consequently, even when her husband was touching and massaging her during the early sexual exercises, it felt like medical attention to her, rather than a sensual experience.

! ─────────────── *Task* ───────────────

I'm all right!

Make a list of what you do like about your face and body. Forget what you don't like. It can include anything: your toes, your fingernails, the nape of your neck. Spend some time looking at these aspects of yourself, perhaps in the bath, and don't just take them for granted: appreciate them.

!

● **Changing bad feelings about your body.** There are hardly any men or women who feel completely happy with themselves physically. Most women feel anxiety about some aspects of their bodies, especially their breasts (as a therapist said, 'Talking to the women I see, it would seem that breasts come in two sizes – too small or too big!'). Men, too, can be concerned about aspects of their physiques, especially their genitals (the same therapist said, 'You'd think penises came in one size only – too small!').

It can be hard to change bad feelings into good overnight, but the first step is to realise that negative feelings are unhelpful. Stop being proud of your 'modesty' in running yourself down, and decide that the real achievement is in changing your point of view to a more positive one. Sometimes this gives you the impetus to change what you can change – perhaps it is your weight or your general level of fitness that is making you unhappy. What steps can you take to change them? Set yourself realistic goals and a timetable to reach them.

But even more important is coming to terms with those parts of yourself that can't be changed. The following task can help, particularly if you do it over again often, until you have changed your feelings.

!================ *Task* ================

Changing perspective

Tell yourself that every part of you, just the way it is, makes you unique. You are a package not a collection of 'bits'.

Focus on each disliked feature in turn, and imagine it belonging to someone you love. If so, it would not repulse or disturb you. You would feel one of the following: affectionate, amused, warm, tender, endeared.

Each time you feel critical of yourself, consciously try to substitute one of these more appropriate feelings. !

Don't under-value your partner's opinion if he or she likes the 'bad bits' of you. Hear what is said, and believe it. Try to see yourself through your partner's eyes rather than your own. Tell yourself it is self-indulgent to persist in being critical.

Neither is it the end of the world if he or she agrees with you about your 'imperfections'. You can acknowledge that someone is not perfect, but still love them and find them attractive. During sex therapy, Sharon revealed that she never allowed her lover, David, to see her back view in case he was put off by the varicose veins in her legs. During the course of the exercises they were set, it was inevitable that he would see them. At one point, when they were feeling very close and loving, David told Sharon how much he liked her body. Sharon replied, rather awkwardly, '*Not* my varicose veins, though.' David smiled and said, 'Well, they're not my *favourite* part of you.' Sharon reported that this conversation was very liberating. 'He'd seen them, he knew they were there, he didn't pretend that they didn't exist or didn't show, but he *still* fancied me.'

Illness and feelings about your body

Sometimes your feelings about your body change for the worse because of an illness or surgery. Both of these can make you feel temporarily low physically, which means that you are unlikely to be interested in sex for a while. It can also happen that your body is permanently changed; for instance, you have a breast or a testicle removed because of cancer. In these cases you need to review your body and come to terms with it in the ways mentioned above. These changes can affect your partner, too. Perhaps he or she also has difficulty adjusting to your changed body, or is nervous about re-starting sex for fear of hurting you or complicating a physical problem. Sometimes your sex life has to be adapted because of discomfort, and you have to learn, all over again, what works best for you.

When you are committed and loving in other ways, none of these circumstances will cause your sexual feelings to disappear forever. But often it is the person who has been ill who is the hardest to convince. It can be difficult to believe a partner who says, for instance, that he still desires you despite your mastectomy. Again, you must trust your partner's words and actions, or your own desire will not return – or you might act in ways that make your relationship in general more difficult and sex suffers as a consequence.

This was the case with Irene and Bernard. They had been married for twelve years and had three children. They had a fairly happy marriage and a sexual routine that was not particularly exciting but which suited them both. They never talked about sex or touched much except when they were making love. Bernard would signal that he wanted sex by announcing that he was going to bed early, which was about once a month. Irene never touched Bernard when they made love, except to put her arms round him. Bernard would penetrate her after a few minutes of touching. Irene had never had an orgasm, but that didn't bother her. She enjoyed the contact because she felt it was what you did when you were married and loved each other, and it was a sign that Bernard found her attractive and needed her.

This might have continued for many years, but one day Irene had an accident. Irene was cooking when her youngest child wandered into the kitchen and reached for a pan on the stove. Irene, who was getting something from a low cupboard, managed to push the child out of the way, but in the process was badly burned on her face, head and arms by the contents of the pan.

Her face was disfigured and she lost some of her hair. When they came for counselling three years later she had had plastic surgery and was looking much better, but she did not look the same as before. Although Irene had had a lot of medical support, she and Bernard had not talked about the accident once the first crisis was over. They had not had sex since.

Initially Irene had been too ill. Then, when she had improved, Bernard's sexual attentions made her angry. She believed she had lost her looks. Now she didn't feel that Bernard's sexual attentions meant he found her attractive, she thought it just meant he wanted sex. All this was unspoken; Irene would just push Bernard away. Bernard stopped trying to make love to Irene, although he wanted to very much. When he stopped, Irene's worst fears were confirmed, and she felt abandoned and unloved. Over the years Bernard tried once or twice to make love to her, but the tensions that had built up between them made him lose his erection.

Although they never had specific sex therapy, counselling helped them resolve the issues of anger and fear between them. They were encouraged to cuddle and show affection more, so that both of them would feel less rejected. Through this, Irene came to understand that Bernard's love was not lost and that he did desire her.

• **Menstruation.** This, of course, is not an illness, but for some women the monthly bleeding, and the physical and emotional tensions around this time, dominate their feelings about themselves and sex. For some women, it can be so severe that there are very few days in the month when they feel both comfortable and happy enough to have sex. The first step is to see if there are any conventional or alternative medical remedies that can help. If not, it is a problem that needs to be faced by both of you. Some people have as much difficulty discussing menstruation as they do sex, but talking with your partner means he can understand and make allowances for it.

! ——————— *Task* ———————

My time of the month

Keep a menstrual diary for a minimum of four months – more is better. Mark how long your period lasts, and any symptoms before, after and during it. These can be physical symptoms, such as headache, tiredness or pain, and emotional symptoms, such as weepiness, depression, anger or irritability. Also make a note of times in the month when you feel sexy. Sometimes it might be during your period.

Keep your partner informed about what you are writing, and discuss ways in which you can be made to feel better during the bad times. If your 'sexy' times are regular, plan for them by making sure you have the right conditions and time for love-making. Unless either of you have strong personal or religious objections, you can also make love during your period – either without penetration while you wear a tampon, or with penetration while you use a diaphragm (cap) or your partner uses a condom – or neither if pregnancy is not an issue, and you both feel comfortable about it. !

YOUR FEELINGS ABOUT
YOUR PARTNER'S BODY

It is stating an obvious fact that to enjoy sex it helps to find your partner attractive. But it is also true that 'beauty is in the eye of the beholder'. In other words, when you are happy with your partner, and there are good and loving feelings between you, your partner will seem endearing and attractive, too, whatever he or she looks like – and even when you are quite conscious of 'imperfections'.

Some people maintain that their feelings for their partners are wholly positive, but that they don't fancy them. When this is true, it is usually because of the kind of early experiences mentioned in the first chapter, particularly those that made you disturbed or scared by sex. It might have to do with what you learnt about your parents' relationship, and the belief you developed that sex was inappropriate in a long-term relationship. These and other ideas can often be put right by turning the clock back and re-introducing more playfulness, fun and pleasure into your sex life, as described in Chapter Eight, 'Building a Better Sex Life'.

But if you find something physical about your partner actively off-putting it is usually a sign that other things are wrong in your relationship. If you are angry or upset about your general relationship you will find things to annoy you in your partner, physically and otherwise. Similarly, if the problems are rooted in your sexual relationship, which is disappointing or disturbing, you will feel less desire for your partner and find that certain features or qualities put you off. It can be hard to disentangle these issues, but more help is given in Chapter Five, 'Is It Really a Sexual Problem?'

● **Personal hygiene.** Sometimes an exception to this is personal hygiene. There are people who insist that they find everything about their partners attractive except in this area. Perhaps you don't like the smell of breath first thing in the morning, or the feel of a man's stubble, or the smell of cigarettes, or body odour or sweaty feet.

This can be quite simple to deal with by explaining calmly, when you are both feeling friendly, why it gets in the way of your sexual feelings. It is better to do this in a non-sexual situation. Best of all is to explain when the problem is absent: your partner has just taken a bath, or shaved, and you can say positively why you are more turned on by this.

There are two things to watch for here. One is that sometimes these feelings do mask a more general irritation or a more serious problem. For instance, Vera told a counsellor that she couldn't bear her husband, Martin, to touch her because his fingernails were engrained with dirt. In fact, the counsellor said, Martin had a severe drink problem and was occasionally incontinent. He usually smelled of urine. It took many months of counselling before the counsellor judged that Vera and Martin were anywhere near ready to talk about Martin's drinking. Unconsciously, Vera was terrified of even thinking about the problem because it was so big and potentially explosive. It was easier for her to focus on Martin's dirty fingernails.

If matters of personal hygiene never bothered you before, there could well be another reason why you are disturbed now. One way to know this is if the problem is dealt with, but you find yourself settling on something else that turns you off.

The other consideration is that if your partner has only recently started to neglect personal hygiene it can be a sign that something else is bothering him or her. It is often a manifestation of a more important depression when people 'let themselves go'. Clearly, making an issue of cleanliness at this time can make matters worse.

The next talking point is aimed at couples who *do* find their partners attractive. If that is a problem for you, skip it for now. You can return to it when you have taken steps to improve your relationship and are feeling more positively about your partner.

' ——————— Talking point ———————

I love your ...

Think of everything you find attractive about your partner from top to toe. You can make a list if you want. Then tell your partner what you think, one by one explaining what you like – and remember to say *why*. It doesn't matter when you do this – you can be making love or doing the washing up together.

If you genuinely like a feature that your partner is not happy about, explain why it is you like it – it will help your partner feel more positively. For instance, 'I like it just because it's *your* nose', or 'I find fleshy thighs much more exciting', or 'When I see that scar I feel moved, and remember how much I love you'.

Take it in turns to tell each other how you feel.

'

Very occasionally a problem can occur simply because you or your partner are particularly fixated on just one feature. This is usually because you sense that it has nothing to do with your total desirability, or even much to do with you as a person.

This is what happened to Lesley, who came for counselling without her husband, Alan. He was obsessed by Lesley's breasts. He loved to lie and watch her undress, but he never looked at any other part of her. He came with her to choose her bras, and would select which one she was to wear whenever she went out. She found this very oppressive, and it put her off sex. The problem was that he ignored her as a person, and during love-making she began to feel that she just happened to be attached to his real love, her breasts.

Alan didn't see it as a problem, and he didn't care that Lesley was unhappy. All the things that she had initially found attractive about him – that he was a strong, physical man's man – now turned her off. Initially, she had also been flattered that he liked her breasts. The point was that so much else had gone wrong with their relationship that his foible was no longer flattering and even seemed unloving, and Lesley eventually left him.

YOUR SEX LIFE

Before looking at your sex life as it is now, and what you like about it and what you wish to change, it is useful to look back on your sexual relationship in its entirety. This provides the most important clues to what makes sex good for you. It can also pinpoint the time when it started to go wrong, or the conditions that spoil the experience for you.

In the beginning

Your sexual relationship with your partner began when you first started to touch. Contrary to what you might think, the first act of sexual intercourse was *not* the beginning. As you have read, penetration is only one kind of sex, and all the other kissing and fondling you do together is love-making as well. Most people have fond memories of early love-making, and sorting out what made it pleasurable is helpful.

Remembering the good times will help you understand what makes sex good for you. As your memories are likely to show you, the actual love-making is only one part of this. Perhaps you felt most sexy when your partner seemed to desire you very much, or perhaps you liked to feel that you were 'conquering' your partner. It could be that you liked a long, drawn-out courting, with lots of loving chat to get you in the mood, or else you liked to feel that passion made you snatch a few intensely physical moments. Perhaps you were most aroused when there was a lot

=== *Task* ===

I remember...

Pick one specific occasion when you enjoyed love-making at the beginning of your relationship. It can include penetration or not. Take your mind back through it step by step to discover why it was so good. Think about:

- **The conditions.** Where were you? Were you comfortable and relaxed? Was it exciting because you thought you might be disturbed? Were you alone or in company (e.g., at a party)? What time was it? What suited you about the physical surroundings?

- **The love-making.** How long did you spend together (was it a lengthy seduction or hasty)? How did you touch? What was the nicest bit? Were you clothed or unclothed? How aroused were you? Did you have an orgasm? What was most exciting, your sexual feelings or emotional factors? How did you feel after?

- **Your partner.** What did you find most arousing about your partner? What sort of things did your partner say to you? How did your partner look at you? How did your partner react to the love-making? How did your partner behave when love-making had to stop?

There are no right and wrong answers. It might have happened at the start, and your partner was reluctant. Or perhaps the love-making was rushed and urgent. Perhaps one of you behaved without consideration. Or it might have been intensely romantic, perhaps later when you were sure of your partner's love. You might or might not have had an orgasm, but enjoyed the physical sensations you did receive. The point is what *you* felt.

of stroking and petting and love-talk, and less moved when sex became more physical, or when there was penetration. Perhaps penetration felt the best of all to you because you felt 'taken' or as if you were 'taking', or because you liked to feel that your bodies were fused. Later, in Chapter Eight, 'Building a Better Sex Life', you can see how you can use these memories to enhance your sex life now.

It is also useful to talk to your partner about your happiest early memories of sex together. You might remember different incidents that excited you. Sometimes you discover that an occasion that was intensely exciting for one of you was less good for the other. This doesn't matter. It is necessary to accept the differences between you, and understand them, to make your sex life as good as it can be. Knowing that your partner is excited by different things allows you to include them in your love-making, or take it in turns to do what excites you most. If you don't have this information, you might just carry on doing what you like, unaware that your partner is not being turned on in the same way.

❛ ─────────────── Talking point ═══════

It was good for me

Take it in turns to tell each other about the sexual encounter that you remembered for the task I REMEMBER... Settle down comfortably together – hold hands or cuddle. If you are embarrassed, sit on the sofa, the one doing the talking lying with his or her head in the other's lap. Tell your partner all the details that made it good for you. Listen to each other without interruptions, and don't comment on what you have both said. Take time to think about it, and in a few days discuss it again.

This time, tell your partner which of the details in his or her memory were also exciting for you. If anything was actually off-putting, you can mention it. Say, 'It wasn't exciting for me when ...' Explain why, in terms of how *you* felt, not in a critical way. For instance, 'I felt too nervous that someone might come in to relax' or 'I felt that what I wanted was not important' or 'I liked it when we had sex, but felt bored early on'.

❜

Early problems

You might remember some less pleasant memories when you think about the past. Perhaps you didn't enjoy sex at all with your partner in the early days. If this is the case, the problem is most likely to have been rooted in your very early life, as you saw in Chapter One. Or perhaps sex became less enjoyable later. Remembering when this started to happen can also help you identify what turns you off in sex.

For instance, Lisette and Max came for sex therapy saying that Lisette was anorgasmic – she couldn't have orgasms. They were in their forties, had been married for three years, and had both been married before. The therapist quickly established that Lisette was perfectly able to have orgasms – she had had them with Max in the early part of their relationship, but was not able to later.

Lisette had two children from her first marriage. She had never liked contraception, and after her second child was born she and her first husband never had sex. Lisette and Max were agreed that they didn't want any more children, and they decided that Max would have a vasectomy.

It took some months for Max to arrange the operation, and some weeks after that before Max was told that there were no sperm left in his ejaculate and it was safe to have penetrative sex. Until that time, their love-making consisted of 'heavy petting' and mutual masturbation. Both of them found it very arousing, they took their time, and Lisette often had an orgasm.

When Max got the 'all-clear' they agreed it was time to start sex 'properly'. This meant that they dropped most of the love-play they had indulged in before, and would quickly start sexual intercourse. To start, with Max on top, when Lisette was highly aroused she was occasionally able to come to orgasm by continuing to rub herself against Max's penis while it was still in her vagina after he had ejaculated. But neither she nor Max tried any other way to stimulate her. She found herself less able to do this after a while. She found it tiring, uncomfortable, and occasionally painful. He found it boring, and would become irritated.

Lisette soon found their love-making unarousing, and rarely even came close to orgasm. They both agreed that this was mainly Max's problem – he thought he wasn't 'good enough' and she felt he should be able to last longer. By encouraging them to remember when sex was good, and to know when the problems started, the therapist was able to help them see that they needed to put back the petting into their love-play, and to concentrate less on penetration.

For some couples it is the surroundings or circumstances during their early lives together that affected their sex lives. For instance, you might have moved in with your parents. If you had a creaky bed or thin walls, you could have felt inhibited – therefore love-making became rushed, tense and confined to late at night. Something like this can set a pattern in your sex life that it never occurs to you to break – until your dissatisfactions become too great later. Anything that curtails the time and care you give to your love-making at an early stage can have a similar effect.

You might remember that settling down together itself started a problem. As you saw in the last chapter, desire levels inevitably fall after a while. Perhaps when this happened to you it coincided with you establishing a routine for sex that didn't include conditions that you found arousing. Perhaps it always happened on the same nights, or became later and later, something you did when there was nothing else left to do and you were very tired.

!
—————————————— *Task* ——————————————

That's when it happened

Cast your mind back to a time in your relationship when sex became less exciting for you. Compare it with the good time you remembered. What was it about *the conditions, the love-making* or *your partner's reactions* that had changed, or that made it less special for you?

This is useful for you to do alone. But if you both agree, tell each other about it. Choose a time when you are both friendly and relaxed, perhaps taking it in turns to lie with your heads in each other's laps as before. Don't accuse or be critical. Talk in terms of how *you* felt.

!

The birth of a baby

Quite often there is a specific event that changed your sex life. The most common is the birth of a baby. This life-event is such an upheaval in all ways that it would be surprising if it had no effect whatsoever. The complicated issues surrounding this are explored in detail in *The RELATE Guide to Better Relationships*. Here it is appropriate to focus more narrowly on the physical side, including the birth itself.

There is no getting away from the fact that the pattern of sexual activity changes, usually in pregnancy, when certain positions are uncomfortable, and the woman becomes more tired. After the birth it takes time for the woman to be able to have penetrative sex, and both of you will be much tireder than usual and under strain. It is quite normal, after giving birth, for women to go through a period when they lose sexual desire. This is, of course, worrying for both of you, which is why it is important to realize that it happens to most women. It is a biological quirk, which helps the woman focus for a while on bonding with her baby. It is not necessarily a sign that there is anything wrong with your relationship. How long this lasts varies, but if there are no other problems the woman's desire usually returns.

If one or other of you is not ready to resume your sex life yet, you can fall into the mistake of believing that you daren't show physical affection either, in case your partner wants to take it further. This can cause a rift in your relationship generally. It is a time when you both need the reassurance that you are still loved, and that the baby hasn't come between you.

Sometimes the birth itself is traumatic for one or other of you. A woman who has had a difficult labour can find that she is put off sex for a long time because she connects it with pregnancy and birth. Therapists see couples who haven't had sex for many years, and in some cases can trace it back to a difficult labour.

It can also happen that it is the *man* who is put off sex after his wife has had a difficult labour. Very often the man is unable to talk about it or explain what he felt. If he does not do so, and it remains unresolved, the hurt and the horror of the experience can stay with him for years.

One such case was Peter, who came for sex therapy with his wife, Lindsay, two years after the birth of their son. They hadn't had sex since. Lindsay said Peter had made her feel like a whore for wanting sex, and consistently rejected her timid advances. She had given an ultimatum: if he wouldn't agree to try to improve matters through sex therapy, their marriage was over.

Peter was a young, healthy man in his late twenties. He was tall and sporty. There seemed no physical reason for his avoidance of sex. Lindsay was small and pretty, a couple of years younger than Peter. She was feeling 'mumsy' and past it because of Peter's rejection of her.

In separate sessions with the therapist, both of them talked about their lives and the progression of their relationship. When it was Peter's turn he was nonchalant and jokey – until the therapist asked about the birth of his son. Peter went white and couldn't talk about it. When the therapist pressed him he started to weep. Lindsay's labour had been long and agonising. Peter had been with her throughout. At one point she cried out in anger against him. Peter said, 'I hated myself for what I'd done to her – what I'd made her go through. I swore she wouldn't have any more children.'

Peter said he didn't even remember how he got home afterwards, in the middle of the night. He said he had wept and banged his head on the wall. He was deeply ashamed of his lack of control and 'weakness'. He apologised to the therapist for his tears as he spoke.

Peter had never told Lindsay how he had felt. He had never dared admit to anyone that the experience had 'unmanned' him. It had taken him a long time to feel lovingly towards his son, who, he felt, shared the blame with him for making Lindsay suffer.

When the couple next saw the therapist together, she encouraged Peter to tell Lindsay what he had told her. Again, Peter was unable to stop himself crying. Lindsay was moved, and put her arms round him. It made an immediate difference to know that Peter's actions had been out of love for her rather than a rejection of her. Nevertheless, they still needed a period of sex therapy to help them re-start their sexual relationship.

Even if the period around the birth was not so traumatic for you, it can still happen that when your sex life re-starts again it is different from before. You might be happy with the way it is, or you might feel disappointed. Sometimes one or other of you feels differently about the woman's body, occasionally because breastfeeding makes you see it in a different light. Sometimes the woman feels so contented by the physical bond with the baby that she feels less need for sex and intimacy with her husband, which makes him feel excluded.

' ──────────── Talking point ──────────────

Birth of a problem

If you have children between you, discuss the period surrounding the pregnancy, birth and first few months. Share any disturbing memories. If the baby was breastfed, has this affected either of you? Did sex change for you after the baby? Have your feelings about sex changed since?

'

Once you have children, you also have less time for sex. If you were used to a fairly varied sex life, during which you would grab the mood and make love whenever and wherever you liked, you will feel the difference. Now sex might just be relegated to bedtimes and cease to seem so much fun as before.

Another factor that can change the way you feel about sex after the birth of children is that, unconsciously, you identify more closely with your own parents. If they seemed to have little sexual contact, or not to enjoy what they did have, a part of you can believe that it is going to be the same for you from now on. Perhaps you feel you have to behave more 'maturely' now that you are parents, and consequently you believe that your sex life has to be more solemn than before. If you haven't been enjoying sex much up to now, this can provide the excuse you need to avoid it or cut down the frequency. Some people find that they look at their partners in a new way – as a 'mother' or a 'father', rather than – as before – a lover.

! ──────────────── *Task* ────────────────

Banishing Mum and Dad

Look back at Chapter One, and the section on your parents' relationship. If you haven't yet done so, discuss how it appeared to you. What did your parents think about sex? Make a guess at what their sex life was like. Talk about ways you seem to be recreating this, and whether you are happy doing so.

!

These are emotional issues, but they still affect your physical relationship. This is most likely to be the case when you are not in the habit of talking about sexual matters and just think 'what will be, will be'. Chapter Eight, 'Building a Better Sex Life' can help you face these issues and challenge them.

Infertility

If, for a time, you were trying for a baby without success, your sex life is likely to have suffered, too. The longer you were trying, and the further you had to go with physical examinations and intervention, the more likely this is. The trouble is, when you are trying to conceive, your love-making becomes focused on penetration and ejaculation. The more playful side, and the woman's pleasure, reduce in importance. You are likely to see sex as 'work' and perhaps be too tense to enjoy it in the way you did before. Whatever the outcome – whether you went on to have children or not – this can blight your sex life if you did not take steps to recapture the early pleasures. Again, later chapters can help.

Contraception – and whether to have children

For some people the issue that starts to affect sex is contraception. It can be that you don't find any of the methods satisfactory. Barrier methods, such as the condom or the diaphragm, can seem to detract from spontaneity, or you might worry about the health implications of the IUD, the Pill or vasectomy. It is worth switching methods, with the advice of your GP or Family Planning Clinic, to find the method you are both most comfortable with.

If you can't find such a method, this might become an issue that turns you off sex more and more. It helps matters once again to challenge the myth that penetrative sex is the best and most natural way to make love. It is not a question of 'either penetrative sex or nothing at all'. Introducing more varied love-making, which doesn't include penetration yet is still satisfying, is the way to cope with this. If penetration becomes an occasional sex act, rather than the only one, you will mind less using contraception at these times.

But sometimes the issue of contraception masks a different problem. Perhaps one of you is keen to have a child (or more children) and the other isn't. In this case contraception comes to symbolise the difference in your attitudes. One or other of you might have started to withhold sex for these reasons, and your sex life started to go downhill. This again is an emotional issue, and one that allows sex to be used as a battle weapon. When this happens, the all-round health of your relationship is affected, and sex suffers even more. If this heralded the start of problems for you, but you are now reconciled, some of the ways detailed further on in the book can help.

MATURING TOGETHER

As you both grow older, there are certain issues connected with age which can also affect your sex lives. You might find that you need less sex and, if you are enjoying what you do, that is fine. Some of the issues are slightly different for men and women.

Women: the menopause

The menopause is when your periods gradually become further apart and then stop. This process is accompanied by hormonal swings and changes that create physical and emotional symptoms, which some women experience more severely than others. The effects of the menopause can be felt for many years – before your periods stop and afterwards. A few women have severe difficulties. Among other problems, they have incapacitating hot flushes, which makes sleeping difficult, as they wake hot and bathed with sweat. They might feel depressed, suffer from bad headaches, and find that their vaginas don't lubricate in the same way any more, making sex uncomfortable. Fortunately, this is not true for all women, many of whom experience the symptoms much more mildly.

At this time, for one reason or another, some women become less interested in sex. Sometimes this is because of the hormone imbalance at this time. But it can also be because a woman has always associated sexuality with fertility and she does not feel it is appropriate to have sex any more. Often it is because a woman has not been enjoying sex for a long time, and she feels that now she is due a 'break'. While this might make biological sense, sex is much more than making babies. It still means intimacy and closeness. Sadly, in some cases all intimate and affectionate touching stops when sexual intercourse does.

This does not have to be the case, particularly if the woman just feels the need for less frequent sex. Often her partner will feel the same. It does need to be talked about, however, so that you can decide between you how you want to adapt your sex life.

In some cases, it is mainly the effect of the hormone activity that makes a woman feel so bad. In these circumstances, Hormone Replacement Therapy (HRT) is something that should be discussed with a doctor.

One woman who suffered like this was Lynne, who came for

counselling with her husband, Gordon. Lynne was forty-eight and Gordon was fifty. They had four grown-up children. They had had the normal ups and downs of any couple who have been married for twenty-five years. For the last two years, however, their relationship had been stretched to breaking point. Lynne had frequent outbursts of rage and misery, aimed at Gordon. Their sex life had stopped. The counsellor said that during sessions with the couple, Lynne's anger and distress spilled out in quite a frightening way.

They came for a few weeks, while the counsellor helped them explore the reasons for this. Of course, Lynne had some reasons to be angry, but it all seemed quite out of proportion. During one session, they talked about the fact that Lynne was going through the menopause. Some of the symptoms were causing her trouble, so the counsellor suggested that she explored the possibility of HRT with her doctor. He agreed to start Lynne on a course.

Within two weeks the counsellor saw a remarkable change in Lynne: 'She was bubbling – full of the joys of spring.' The issues that had made Lynne upset and angry didn't seem to matter to her any more, and her appetite for sex returned. There were one or two minor issues that Lynne and Gordon both wanted to sort out, and they continued to come for a further month, but the atmosphere in the counselling sessions was positive and optimistic.

Some women are lucky enough to find that the menopause affects them in quite the opposite way: with the fear of pregnancy removed they find themselves able to enjoy sex much more.

Men: erectile and ejaculatory difficulties

As a man grows older he often finds a difference in his sexual functioning. He can find that he has less frequent erections, and that his penis takes longer to become erect. He usually needs more direct physical stimulation of his penis when, previously perhaps, just the sight of his partner's naked body or the start of intimate touching caused an erection. On occasions his erections are less firm than previously.

This can be upsetting and worrying for a man, particularly if his sex life has revolved around penetrative sex. Some men start to avoid sex for fear of failure. If his partner has not been used to touching and stimulating his penis, they might both give up trying to have sex when nothing seems to be happening. His partner might feel that it is a sign that his desire has faded, even though this is not necessarily true.

In fact, of course, if you both still want sex, this does not have to be a problem. It can open up the opportunity for the more varied love-play that you ignored before. It means introducing more 'whole-body' love-making for both of you, and learning that you are equal partners in the sex act. This can make for a very satisfactory sex life, even when the man is not able to get an erection at all.

One therapist commented that when couples come for therapy with this problem, it is often the first time that they really pay attention to the woman's body and needs, and the pleasures of non-penetrative sex. As she said, 'You can see the relief on his face when you tell them that the vast majority of women don't get an orgasm with thrusting – they need manual stimulation. Sometimes it is the first time that either of them realizes the importance of the clitoris.'

If the man is still able to get an erection but needs more time, it is also an opportunity for both of you to pay attention to his penis and find out together what love-play causes an erection. The bonus is that many men find that, when they do have an erection, they can 'last longer' during penetrative sex without ejaculating.

The man can also find that his ejaculatory pattern changes. Perhaps he does not always ejaculate. Sometimes he feels the sensations of orgasm without ejaculating. Occasionally, this is because the fluid goes backwards, into the bladder (which is not dangerous). You know this has happened if, when passing urine after sex, it is cloudier than usual. Even without orgasm or ejaculation the man can still enjoy love-making – just as women can. It is only a problem if you make it one – if one or other of you feels it isn't 'real' sex without a 'product' – the ejaculate.

Giving up on sex

Some people feel that at a certain age sexual activity should stop. In fact, many couples go on being sexually active until the end, thoroughly enjoying the sex they do have because they are open about what they need sexually, and have developed the habit of adapting to each other. Other couples are equally happy to wind down their sex life gradually until it stops altogether. They love each other, enjoy each other's company, but find that other activities are more satisfying than sex. It is an individual preference and you neither 'should' continue sex nor 'should' give it up. A difficulty only arises if you feel differently about this – one of you wants sex and the other doesn't. This can happen at any age, and the solution is always the same: lovingly trying to find a compromise with which you both can live.

Younger people are often (rather arrogantly) surprised to find that older couples still have an active sex life. But RELATE counsellors often see couples who have been together for many years and are still concerned about the quality of their lives together – including their sex lives.

One therapist had two sessions with such a couple. Douglas initially came to see her on his own. He was eighty-three, and since a prostate operation two years previously he had been unable to get an erection. An article he had read had linked the two, saying that some men do have erectile difficulties after such an operation, and had mentioned RELATE as an organization that might help.

Douglas had not told his wife, Joan, that he was going to RELATE. He told the therapist that he had felt a failure as a man for the past two years. Until his operation they had had an active sex life, and he felt that Joan was now upset and frustrated, and took the problem personally.

The counsellor questioned him about their sex life, and was interested to hear how healthy and equal it was. They had experimented thoroughly throughout their lives together, had taken it in turns to initiate sex, and penetration was only one way in which they had made love. But Joan, Douglas said, was now increasingly irritated with him. What could the counsellor suggest to solve the problem?

Douglas was slightly disappointed that the therapist couldn't hand him a 'cure', but she suggested he told Joan that he had been talking to her and that he invite her to come to the next session with him.

When they turned up together, the therapist was struck by what a close, loving couple they were. Joan was eighty-two, beautifully groomed, with a bright red jaunty hat and coat. She was staggered to hear that Douglas had felt that she had been irritated with him for not 'performing' sexually. She admitted that for the last five years she had been much less interested in sex. The year before they had gone to the Canary Islands on holiday. Joan said it had been lovely – it was hot, she felt relaxed and romantic – and sex 'would have been nice'. But, she said, it was the only time for ages that she had felt like that, and it hadn't mattered.

Douglas was flabbergasted and relieved – but he was also puzzled. He asked, in that case, why she had been so irritated with him. It turned out that she was hearing less well than before, and became irritated when he didn't speak up. Douglas said that he, too, had been irritated because of her hearing difficulties. They hadn't talked about this, just snapped at each other instead.

Douglas had so misunderstood Joan, that he had begun to worry that she had taken a lover. A few days before first seeing the counsellor, he said, Joan had gone out in her new red coat and hat without a word to him. This seemed an ominous sign.

Again Joan was taken aback. On that occasion she had been going to meet a friend who was choosing an outfit for a great-grandchild's christening. She had been angry that Douglas hadn't said 'goodbye' to her so she had not said it to him. But Douglas maintained that he had – and Joan had simply not heard him.

What was behind the anger, the counsellor wondered? Joan admitted that really she had felt upset. Throughout the shopping expedition she had started to worry that Douglas might die, and they would not have said their goodbyes.

At that point, the counsellor said, they started to hoot with laughter – their sense of humour got the better of them. They were able to see that they had allowed irritation to get in the way of confronting their real concerns – about ageing and death. 'It just goes to show,' Joan said, 'you're never too old to learn!'

With the irritation out of the way, they were able to talk about the sexual question again. The counsellor suggested that Douglas went back to his surgeon to talk about it. He said that he didn't feel that it was absolutely necessary any more. He felt happier now that he knew he wasn't disappointing Joan. If she was happy, he felt that he could live with the sexual contact they already had, which included lots of affectionate touching, cuddling and body contact. The counsellor said she was moved to see such a good relationship after more than fifty years of marriage. 'They had had their ups and downs, but the core of the relationship was still there and glowing.'

SEX – WHAT YOU ACTUALLY DO

You are now going to look at the specifics of your sex life, whatever age or stage you are at in your relationship. In the first part, you will identify what you actually do, and whether it suits you. In the second part you will identify what you would like to change or add. Homosexual couples can use these questions, too – where there is a 'him and her' response, substitute 'you and your partner'.

Ideally, you should complete the quizzes with your partner, but you might find this difficult. RELATE knows all too well that many people have great difficulty talking about sex, even to a much-loved partner. If there are other problems between you this can be even harder. Neither of you should force the other to complete these questions, and if you find it too awkward, or that it causes difficulty between you, just stop. You might want to come back to the questions later, or leave them altogether. It is up to you.

However, if you find it too difficult, yet are experiencing disappointment with your sex life, you might decide that sex therapy can help. With a trained and dispassionate sex therapist who has 'heard it all before' it can be much easier to talk about sex than when you are alone. It is useful to read through the questions anyway, think about the issues they raise, and whether you feel comfortable with them or not.

! ——————————————— *Task* ———————

What do you call it?

Decide between you what words you are going to use for parts of the body and sex acts. You can use the medical words if you prefer, or slang, or funny, pet words, or 'dirty' words. You can choose to use different words from each other. Agree to choose another word if your partner finds your first choice offensive.

	Her word	*His word*
Penis		
Testicles		
Ejaculate		
Breasts		
Nipples		
Female genitals		
Clitoris		
Cervix		
Anus		
Orgasm		
Masturbation		
Penetration (penis in vagina)		
Fellatio (oral sex performed on man)		
Cunnilingus (oral sex performed on woman)		

When you have decided which words you are going to use, you can look at what usually happens when you make love. Sex therapists sometimes find that couples don't necessarily agree on this. When the therapist talks to the couple separately, they give different descriptions of what happens and when. You can answer the questions on separate pieces of paper and then look at what each other has written. Or, if you feel confident, answer them together, out loud, taking it in turns to say what you think.

!

? _____ **Quiz** _____

What we do

1. We make love _____ times a month.
   a) This suits me/doesn't suit me.
   b) This suits my partner/doesn't suit my partner.

2. We usually make love (say where this is and at what time, or if it varies): _____
   a) This suits me/doesn't suit me.
   b) This suits my partner/doesn't suit my partner.

3. The lighting is off/on/low/varies.
   a) This suits me/doesn't suit me.
   b) This suits my partner/doesn't suit my partner.

4. We are usually nude/in nightwear/in erotic clothing.
   a) This suits me/doesn't suit me.
   b) This suits my partner/doesn't suit my partner.

5. I initiate sex/my partner initiates sex/it varies.
   a) This suits me/doesn't suit me.
   b) This suits my partner/doesn't suit my partner.

6. The person who initiates sex does so by (explain whether this is by word, touch, implication): _____
   a) This suits me/doesn't suit me.
   b) This suits my partner/doesn't suit my partner.

7. Do you make love in silence? Yes/No/Varies.
   a) This suits me/doesn't suit me.
   b) This suits my partner/doesn't suit my partner.

8. Do you kiss while making love? Yes/No/Sometimes.
   a) This suits me/doesn't suit me.
   b) This suits my partner/doesn't suit my partner.

9. Love-making usually lasts for _____ minutes/hours.
   a) This suits me/doesn't suit me.
   b) This suits my partner/doesn't suit my partner.

10. Does sex always end in penetration? Yes/No.
    a) This suits me/doesn't suit me.
    b) This suits my partner/doesn't suit my partner.

11. When we have penetrative sex we use one position/alternate two or three positions/try more different positions.
    a) This suits me/doesn't suit me.
    b) This suits my partner/doesn't suit my partner.

12. Love-making before or without penetration usually lasts for _____ minutes/hours.
    a) This suits me/doesn't suit me.
    b) This suits my partner/doesn't suit my partner.

13. Do you have an orgasm/ejaculate when you make love? Never/ Sometimes/Always/Don't know.
    a) This suits me/doesn't suit me.
    b) This suits my partner/doesn't suit my partner.

14. Does your partner have an orgasm/ejaculate when you make love? Never/Sometimes/Always/Don't know.
    a) This suits me/doesn't suit me.
    b) This suits my partner/doesn't suit my partner.

15. The parts of my body I like to be touched are _____
    a) This suits my partner/doesn't suit my partner.

16. The parts of my body I don't like to be touched are _____ (if none, say so).
    a) This suits my partner/doesn't suit my partner.

17. My partner likes me to touch the following parts _____
    a) This suits me/doesn't suit me.

18. My partner doesn't like me to touch the following parts _____
    a) This suits me/doesn't suit me.

19. I find it hard to become aroused if _____
    a) This suits my partner/doesn't suit my partner.

20. My partner finds it hard to become aroused if _____
    a) This suits me/doesn't suit me.

21. What I like to happen after love-making _____
    a) This suits my partner/doesn't suit my partner.

22. What my partner likes to happen after love-making _____
    a) This suits me/doesn't suit me.

_____**?**

As with all the quizzes and tasks in this book, there are no right answers to these questions. If you answer them honestly and find yourselves in agreement about what suits you, then you have developed a love life that is right for you. You might be content to leave it as it is, or you might want to develop it further. If, however, you find that a lot of what you do doesn't suit you, or you find from your partner's response that what you thought was fine for him or her is not, then your sex life needs further discussion and experimentation to improve.

Whether you are happy or not with your sex-life, it is interesting to consider whether there is anything you would like to add to your love-making routine. Perhaps there is something that you used to do, but have stopped, or something you have often wanted to try but have never got round to.

Complete the following quiz – separately, if you prefer. You can go on to discuss the variations that you have liked or would like to try with your partner. If you both like the idea, fine – you can arrange to try it together. Similarly, you can also do so if one of you is neutral about it but prepared to try. However, if one of you has strong reservations, leave it for now. You might want to come back to your list at a later date and see if feelings have changed.

?   Quiz

Sexual variations

	Have tried	Liked	Didn't like	Want to try	Don't want to try
Different positions					
Massaging your partner					
Being massaged by your partner					
Cunnilingus					
Fellatio					
Masturbating partner					
Having partner masturbate you					
Watching partner masturbate					
Being watched while you masturbate					

	Have tried	Liked	Didn't like	Want to try	Don't want to try
Visual stimuli (porn magazines/ videos)					
Verbal stimuli ('dirty' talk)					
Anal stimulation					
Fantasy and erotic imagery/day dreams					
Sharing fantasies with partner					
Vibrator					
Dressing up					
Others that you have tried and liked or want to try: (list)					

?

WHAT YOU WANT FROM YOUR SEX LIFE

If you have completed these quizzes together you will now know whether you want to make any changes to your sex life. To do so, you can make a Better Sex Plan of agreed aims and changes. However, if there is a physical reason for your disappointment, such as pain with sex, the woman unable to be penetrated, a difficulty with orgasm, or the man having trouble with getting or maintaining an erection, or ejaculatory difficulties, you should first read Chapter Six, 'Overcoming Sexual Difficulties', which deals with these and other problems. It contains suggestions which you might want to include in your plan. You might also find it useful to read the last two chapters, in the section 'Improving Your Sex Life'.

Achievable aims

When sex therapists work with couples to set their goals for changing their sex lives, they usually have to help them decide what is achievable or not. You should do the same when drawing up your own plan.

● **Is it physically possible?** For instance, many couples say that they want to achieve simultaneous orgasm through penetration and thrusting alone. As has been emphasized throughout this book, this is a rare occurrence. What *is* usually achievable is for both partners to have an orgasm – but it won't necessarily happen at the same time, and the woman will usually need some other stimulation of her clitoris as well. Similarly, if the woman has a higher sex drive than her partner, she might have as a goal for him to increase his sex drive and have penetrative sex with her as often as she likes. Again, this is not an achievable goal. He *can* satisfy her in other ways, bringing her to orgasm with his hand or his mouth, or he can lovingly participate while she masturbates herself.

● **Do you both agree?** Therapists point out that the preferences of each partner must be taken into account when setting goals. If one of you wants to include a variation that disgusts, frightens or turns off your partner then this will not do your general sex life much good, even if you find it temporarily exciting. For instance, Sandra and Bruce worked with a sex therapist for a while on their relationship. Sandra found their sex life off-putting. The worst of it was that Bruce used to cut pictures of sexy women out of magazines and put them on the pillow when they made love. Sandra didn't mind the pictures, but she felt that Bruce was making love to the other women rather than to her. They agreed that they would look at the pictures together, before making love, and that Bruce would then put them away. Alongside other negotiated changes, this improved sex for Sandra.

If one of you wants sex much more than the other you will also have to compromise. A woman *can* just 'lie back and think of England' without any sexual pleasure, and a man *can* masturbate a woman to orgasm as often as she likes even if he would rather be doing something else. But having sex as often as the partner with the higher sex drive wants creates bad feeling, and eventually turns the other off more. A better balance is achieved by agreeing to have sex less often, during which time the partner with the lower sex drive agrees to participate with whole-hearted willingness.

An example of this was Geraldine and Roland. They came for sex therapy because Geraldine had lost all interest. Roland, on the other hand, said, 'I love her. I want her all the time. I'm always thinking about sex with her.'

Geraldine dressed primly, and was cold to Roland in an effort to put him off sex. Her strict upbringing had given her the idea that sexual feelings were wrong and dirty, and she had never explored her own. Roland went on a business trip for a few months, and during this time the counsellor put Geraldine on a self-focus programme in which she learnt about her own body feelings, and how to masturbate without guilt. Geraldine found herself able to enjoy the sensations, and to feel good about herself altogether. When Roland returned, he agreed to having sex less often and not to badger Geraldine the rest of the time. She became softer towards him and enjoyed their love-making. She felt warmer because he didn't pester her, and sometimes she initiated sex. Roland found that now she was more affectionate and responsive when they *did* make love, he stopped thinking about it so much. By the end of therapy they were enjoying good sex twice a month, and both were content with that.

●   **Be specific.** It is important to be specific when setting your goals. To say that you want sex to be 'more exciting' or 'romantic' or 'wonderful' is not especially helpful. What specific touches, acts, or words would bring your sex life closer to matching up to these descriptions? If you want 'more sex' you must also be specific. In a busy life, this means agreeing on dates and making sure you both keep them free. Similarly if you want to give your sex life 'more time', how are you going to do this?

●   **Be flexible.** You might agree to something and then find that in practice you don't like it, or in some way it doesn't work. Rather than giving up, you should both be prepared to think again. More positively, you might find that it works so well that you decide to make a new plan, including other factors.

This was the case with Jenny and Humphrey. Jenny loved him very much, but sex left her cold. Their goal was for Jenny to enjoy it more. She wasn't bothered about having an orgasm, she just wanted to find sex pleasurable. To this end, the therapist recommended the sensual, but non-sexual massaging exercises of the sensate focus programme (in Chapter Six, 'Overcoming Sexual Difficulties'). This worked so well, that they changed their goal. Now Jenny wanted to be able to experience orgasm, which she eventually did.

YOUR BETTER SEX PLAN

The idea is to draw up a plan for a month at a time. At the end of the month, discuss how you felt about it and whether you want to continue with the same plan for another month, or make a new one.

Don't be too ambitious. If you have chosen to do the sensate focus exercises in Chapter Six, start with the first one, and continue it all month – don't move on to the second until you have reviewed the month and both decided that you want to. Similarly, if one of you has a sexual difficulty, such as premature ejaculation or inability to have an orgasm, don't expect to cure it – aim to make your love-making more relaxed and fun during the month, preparing to tackle the difficulty in future months.

Part of your plan is to include one aspect of love-making that you would like your partner to do for you and one that you agree to do for your partner. This can be as simple as talking lovingly to you or kissing you, or it can include more time concentrating on a specific part of your body, a sexual caress or sexual variation. Remember to make this a request that your partner feels comfortable with.

- Our goal this month is _____
- To reach this we have agreed to _____
- This month we will make love _____ times.
- These are the dates and times we will do so _____
- We will make love for _____ hours (minimum one hour)
- The setting we have agreed is (include place, clothing, lighting, heating, music or silence) _____
- To ensure we are undisturbed we will _____
- What I have agreed to do for my partner _____
- What my partner has agreed to do for me _____

Note: Don't be too disappointed if you can't stick to what you agreed – or if it doesn't make matters better or you uncover further anxieties. It could be that you decided to do too much too fast. Make a new plan with smaller and less disturbing changes. Above all, don't regard it as a failure – instead recognize that you have learnt even more about your sexuality. Building a better sex life means understanding each other's anxieties and making allowances for them.

Remember, you have taken the most important step – you have talked about your sex life and agreed that you want to make it better. A positive next step would be to seek sex therapy. Many couples who find that they can't improve their sex lives on their own find that it is much easier under the guidance of the therapist. The trained therapist has the experience to know at what pace the couple should go, and is a helpful sounding-board to talk through any problems or anxieties that arise.

IT WON'T WORK...

After reading this chapter you might have decided that there is nothing that you could do that would make you enjoy sex with your partner. Perhaps you have felt angry, upset or anxious. Thinking about this most intimate area of your life, particularly if there are problems associated with it, can churn up these feelings. What this is likely to mean, however, is that the sexual difficulties are connected to more general problems in your relationship. Sometimes these surface through sex, particularly if you have avoided dealing with them.

An example of this is Jane and Angus, who had been married for twenty-five years and came for therapy because Jane had gone off sex. She said Angus was 'dirty' (he did, in fact, have a physically dirty job) and that she couldn't bear him touching her. Angus agreed to clean up for the sexual programme they were set. They worked well through the first non-sexual exercises, but as soon as they moved on to the sexual programme Jane started cancelling the report-back appointments. They turned up intermittently, and eventually told the therapist that Jane 'liked it now' and they wanted to stop therapy.

A month later Angus was on the phone, telling the therapist that Jane had lost interest again. The therapist invited them in for a one-off talk. She said, 'I've given you most of the help and advice I can – you've tried almost everything. There is a little more I can suggest if you are really committed this time.'

Jane took charge of the session. No, she said. She didn't want any more sex therapy – she just wanted Angus to leave. She didn't love him any more, and she felt they had nothing in common. Angus's response was, 'Why the hell didn't you say that earlier instead of blaming sex? I've wasted three years of my life when I could have been facing facts.'

Doing the therapy had forced Jane to conclude that it was much more than sex that was wrong. With the children grown up and gone away she could see no more point in staying with Angus. Angus, in fact, was equally fed up, and ultimately he was relieved that Jane had taken the initiative.

This was a rather dramatic end to the therapy. If you suspect that other problems are getting in the way of your sexual feelings, it doesn't have to mean that you should break up with your partner. The next chapter shows you how to confront them in a more helpful way.

Part Three
PROBLEMS

5

IS IT REALLY A SEXUAL PROBLEM?

When sex is disappointing or worse, you start to look closely at your sex life to see what has gone wrong. In fact, many couples who come to RELATE never get as far as sex therapy, because it becomes clear that their problems are more complicated. Sex going wrong is a symptom. In many cases, when these other problems are sorted out, sex becomes better – or ceases to be an area of conflict.

This was the experience of Terry and Liz. Terry dragged Liz along to sex therapy after eighteen years of marriage, because their sex life was so barren. Throughout their married life Liz had only 'allowed' Terry sex once every few months. If he had been especially helpful around the house she would instigate sex that night. She would lie still thinking about the chores for the next day, and periodically say, 'Haven't you finished yet?' Terry was now forty-eight and he couldn't bear to think that their life together would always be the same. They had one child.

It was not appropriate to put this couple into sex therapy. Liz wasn't ready. She thought sex was a waste of time, had no desire for Terry, and couldn't contemplate any sort of gentle touching, clothed or nude. Instead, the counsellor concentrated on their relationship. Liz was in charge of everything, yet was disappointed that Terry was so ineffectual – he was her other child. Terry resented Liz for being controlling, yet wanted her to make all the decisions for them both; he hid behind her. The breakthrough came when they realised that both of them contributed to a balance of power that made neither of them happy.

Over the next few emotional months they were able to make quite radical changes in the way they related. They were surprised and delighted that in consequence Liz felt more sexual towards Terry. She started to participate in love-making, and felt close to him. The counsellor said, 'They didn't "swing from the chandeliers" – but neither of them wanted that. Sex was more frequent and satisfying to them both.'

YOUR GENERAL RELATIONSHIP NOW

Take a considered look at your relationship. If sex is not good, are you aware of other problems too? It is a rare couple that has *no* problems, but it is the balance that matters. In a good enough relationship you feel, on balance, more loving than not, and like your partner more often than not. When the balance swings the other way your sex life is a casualty of the resulting unhappiness. Do the following quiz on your own. Each issue has a sliding scale of feelings from 1 GOOD to 5 BAD; 3, in the middle, stands for OK. Try to assess where on the scale your feelings lie, and circle the number. It might raise issues that you want to share with your partner later, but for now it should help you focus on your own feelings.

? ———————————— **Quiz** ————————————

How it feels

HOW I FEEL ABOUT...	GOOD		OK		BAD
...myself	1	2	3	4	5
...the amount of time we spend together	1	2	3	4	5
...the amount of time we spend alone	1	2	3	4	5
...how we talk about things	1	2	3	4	5
...how we share responsibility	1	2	3	4	5
...how we share chores	1	2	3	4	5
...how we handle money	1	2	3	4	5
...how my partner understands me	1	2	3	4	5
...how much fun we have together	1	2	3	4	5
...how much affection we show each other	1	2	3	4	5
...the things we have in common	1	2	3	4	5
...how much time we spend on separate interests	1	2	3	4	5
...how we are together in company	1	2	3	4	5
...how much I like my partner	1	2	3	4	5
...how much my partner likes me	1	2	3	4	5
...how much I respect my partner	1	2	3	4	5
...how much my partner respects me	1	2	3	4	5
...my partner's importance to me	1	2	3	4	5
...my importance to my partner	1	2	3	4	5
...how we handle problems	1	2	3	4	5
...how we handle disagreements	1	2	3	4	5
...the future of our relationship	1	2	3	4	5

?

If most of your answers are 1, 2 or 3 then your relationship is in pretty good shape. However, look at the areas where you have marked 4 or 5 and try to identify what it is about them that causes you to feel bad. These are areas that you must talk about with your partner. It is sensible to arrange a time to do so, and see if you can decide together what can be done to improve matters.

Your answer to the first question 'How I feel about myself' is one of the most important. If you don't feel good, then you are likely to feel more negative about the other questions. Sometimes it is *because* your relationship isn't working that you feel bad, but if you have never felt good about yourself then your relationship is bound to suffer, however well it started. Counselling can help here – either relationship counselling with your partner, or one-to-one work.

PROBLEMS BETWEEN YOU

If you circled lots of 4s and 5s to do with your feelings about your partner and your partner's feelings about you, it is fairly certain your sex life isn't happy or satisfying either. These feelings can start early in a relationship. A couple can stay together for a long time, despite disappointments and misery.

An example of this is Linda and Eddie. They grew up in the same village and went to the same comprehensive. Linda became pregnant the first time they made love. Eddie had had one or two fleeting sexual encounters before. There was pressure on them to marry, which they did – two months before their baby was born. They went on to have two more children.

They came for counselling when they were in their mid-twenties. Linda didn't want sex, she had put on weight and didn't care about her appearance. They lived separate lives. Linda was at home with the children. Eddie spent a lot of time at the pub, and had left Linda a few times. He often threatened to do so again, saying it was her fault because of her attitude to sex. They both felt trapped by marriage.

The counsellor found no friendship between them, and nothing in common. On balance, however, they wanted to stay together. Very simple suggestions from the counsellor made a difference to them. They made more time to be together. They made an effort to talk to each other – conversations had been limited to exchanges such as, 'Hello, your tea's on the table.' 'Good.'

They tried sitting together while they watched television, with their arms round each other, and introducing more general affectionate touching. These simple actions made them nervous at the beginning.

They felt embarrassed, but that passed. As far as sex was concerned, the counsellor gave them some basic instruction about how love-making could be pleasurable – none of which they knew.

By the end of the counselling sex was better because they felt more comfortable with each other. Linda started to think there might be something in it for her, and Eddie learnt about consideration. They were both discovering that they could ask things of each other – sexually and in other ways.

- **Anger.** When there are a lot of unresolved issues between you, the result is often anger. Anger can be held inside, making you depressed and miserable. Your motives can be good: 'I didn't want to hurt her', 'I didn't want to have a row', 'I didn't want to make trouble'. But there is trouble and hurt anyway. Your behaviour changes, because you are using a lot of effort containing your feelings.

Anger can also be openly expressed in rows and fights, but unless these are handled well the issues that caused them still remain to fuel more anger later – or they make matters worse.

The result of both ways of dealing with anger is, over time, a reduction in sexual feelings.

This was the case with Mary and Brian, who had been married for twenty years. Their sex life had been all right for many years, but for the last three Brian had usually been unable to make love to Mary. She had insisted they come for counselling about this, despite the fact that she had never particularly enjoyed sex and always felt that he had got more from it than she had. Nevertheless, lack of any sexual contact angered her as she felt it reflected badly on her femininity.

It emerged that Brian, too, was angry, and had been for years. He said that Mary had used sex as currency, to reward him at intervals throughout their lives. Mary, he said, was mean. He had handed his pay packet over to her, and she had always doled out miserly amounts. He said she would count the potatoes that he was allowed – and would have counted the peas if she could. He had always been expected to be the generous one, and he was now fed up with being generous. Anger at Mary had completely sapped his sex drive – not wanting sex had also reduced her 'hold' over him.

If many of your answers to the quiz fell into categories 4 and 5, then it should be clear to you that sex is only one aspect of a more general relationship problem. There are likely to be issues of anger, disappointment, resentment or sorrow to resolve. It would be unhelpful to try to tackle the sexual area until you have worked through some of these and feel better about your relationship as a whole. Counselling can be very helpful if the issues seem too big to tackle by yourself. Later in the chapter you look at constructive ways to talk about these matters.

OUTSIDE PROBLEMS

Problems often arise because of circumstances outside your immediate control, however much you love each other. If you are contending with stressful issues, your sex life can suffer, too. Sexual feelings need the right conditions to flourish, and stress is one of the most powerful inhibitors of your sex drive. A life that is too busy is also stressful – and when you are rushed sex is allocated less time. Sometimes you might lose desire altogether for a while, or find that you are not happy or relaxed enough to enjoy sex the way you normally do. In some cases stress can cause a physical sexual problem to arise, for instance a man might find it difficult to get an erection.

The obvious examples of these kinds of outside problems are pressures at work, money troubles, health problems, the death of someone close, and difficulties with in-laws. Any of these can make you feel stressed and unhappy, and will usually cause tensions between you as well.

One of the most complex issues concerns any children you have living with you – those you have together or step-children. A frequent cause of stress is different attitudes towards the upbringing of children, perhaps because you both brought different ideas about how to do this from your own family experiences. Children also tend to stir up unresolved issues from your own childhood and adolescence. From a practical point of view, children can also have an inhibiting effect on your sex life because you worry that they might hear you making love, or open the door at the wrong moment.

Later on, when they are old enough to go out alone in the evenings you might worry about their safety – listening out for their return once you have gone to bed, rather than concentrating on your partner.

Children can be even more of a worry when they are unhappy themselves, behaving in a difficult way, or have some health or educational problem. Anything that goes on for a long time is likely to cause great stress.

Anne and Jim had this experience. They came for counselling with a sex problem. Their sex life had started off well. They enjoyed it, both took the initiative, and Anne often had orgasms.

The difficulties began with the birth of their first child, who was brain-damaged. By the time they came for counselling she was six years old. They had another child, a son of four, who had no health problems.

The little girl was very difficult to handle. Both Anne and Jim felt guilty about her. They felt hopeless and often unable to cope. All this had affected their sex life.

Ever since their daughter had been born, Anne had been exhausted. The arrival of their son had added to the strain. She resented taking on the whole burden of the two children. She started to avoid sex – it just seemed one more thing to do. Jim, on the other hand, found he became more focused on sex. He needed it for reassurance that love was still there. Sometimes he forced himself on Anne. They were both being seen regularly by their doctor, who had referred them to RELATE.

The counsellor encouraged them to talk about their feelings. She also helped Anne work out ways she could get more support from family and friends to ease the strain. Jim began to see that he needed to back off sexually. They both realized that they needed to spend more time together having fun – going out, and showing each other non-sexual affection. After six months of counselling their lives were much improved and less stressful. Quite naturally, their sex life started to go well again. Jim joked that Anne was now too interested and often took the initiative. The counsellor said, 'They began to have a twinkle in their eyes, and were ready and happy to stop counselling.'

The following quiz can help you isolate whether any issues are causing you problems. Again, choose a number on the sliding scale, from CALM to STRESSED, which most closely corresponds to your feelings about the matter.

? _____ Quiz _____

It worries me

	CALM		OK		STRESSED
HOW I FEEL ABOUT...					
...my health	1	2	3	4	5
...my partner's health	1	2	3	4	5
...my work	1	2	3	4	5
...my partner's work	1	2	3	4	5
...money	1	2	3	4	5
...the amount of time I have to myself	1	2	3	4	5
...the amount of time I spend enjoying myself	1	2	3	4	5
...the amount of sleep I have	1	2	3	4	5
...my family's attitude to my partner	1	2	3	4	5
...my partner's family	1	2	3	4	5
...my relationship with the children	1	2	3	4	5

...my partner's relationship with the children	1	2	3	4	5
...the way we agree or disagree about the children	1	2	3	4	5
...the children's welfare/happiness	1	2	3	4	5
...having sex when the children are in the house	1	2	3	4	5
...where we live	1	2	3	4	5

...Other difficulties
(list; e.g., death of someone close, a
recent house move)

1	2	3	4	5
1	2	3	4	5
1	2	3	4	5
1	2	3	4	5
1	2	3	4	5

?

Choosing a 4 or 5 for any of these could cause enough stress to affect your sexual feelings. The more 4s or 5s you have the more likely this is to be so. This is a quiz you should take it in turns to complete with your partner. It could be that he or she has been feeling anxious about an issue without you being aware. If it is your partner's sex drive or sexual functioning that has been affected, this could help you understand.

When you identify a stress issue, the sexual difficulty is likely to be connected to this. In this case, trying to work on improving your sex life has little chance of immediate success. It is more important to work out ways in which you can help yourselves to cope with the stress and support each other. When it is a practical issue, try to find practical solutions to ease the stress.

It is even more essential at these times to continue to show each other affection, whether you are ready for sex or not. This includes reassuring your partner of your love and being physically close. When the world seems out to get you, it increases your need for cuddling, kissing, hand-holding, face-stroking and other reassuring and friendly gestures.

If you neglect this, your relationship will continue to suffer, sexually and in other ways, even when life becomes calmer.

AFFAIRS

When one of you has an affair it has a number of effects on your relationship, sex is only one area affected.

- **Finding sex elsewhere.** Some people use the excuse of an unsatisfying sexual relationship with their partners for starting an affair with someone else. Your sex life together might be dull and routine or there might be more severe difficulties. Perhaps it is infrequent, or one of you has lost desire for the other. Sometimes your sex life is good enough, but you feel more sexually excited by your lover – as always happens in that early phase of a relationship when desire levels are high.

    This has two main problems. At one level, if you are finding sexual satisfaction elsewhere, you won't be motivated to improve your sex life with your main partner. More problematically, what might have started out as a sexual issue now spreads to the rest of your relationship. The pain caused by a discovered affair introduces new, and far more difficult problems to resolve. A secret affair has a similar effect, by creating distance and loss of intimacy between you and your main partner.

- **Finding emotional satisfaction elsewhere.** Affairs are also started by people who are generally dissatisfied with their relationships with their main partners. Perhaps they feel misunderstood, under-valued, unloved, or that they have little left in common. Again, the affair adds problems rather than solves them. There is little will or opportunity to deal with the fundamental problems in your main relationship, which either remains unsatisfactory, or worsens.

    Whatever the reason for the affair, your sex life together is likely to suffer. Without trust and honesty sex becomes more mechanical and less truly satisfying. Unfortunately, concentrating solely on trying to patch up your sex life stands little chance of success if the other issues are ignored. Jealousy sometimes spices up sex for a while, as fear of loss raises the desire levels. But this doesn't last. Sometimes people say to their partners, 'If you were better at sex (or more enthusiastic, or more willing to try variations, or gave me sex more often) I would stop my affair, or never have another one.' This pressurizing attitude is counter-productive. Sex improves between you when there is caring, generosity and good feelings on both sides. Making demands, even if they are met, creates resentment and further loss of desire.

    If you are committed to staying together, and genuinely want to improve your sex life, your best chance is to work through the other areas of difficulty first. This includes the painful task of sharing each other's emotions of hurt, anger, misery and stored-up resentment.

When this is done to the satisfaction of you both, the result is usually a much increased sense of intimacy. Committed couples who have the courage to open up like this can find the bond between them strengthened. This gives the ideal conditions for improving sex, too. You can use the tasks mentioned later in this chapter to help you, or decide to visit a counsellor.

Counsellors often see couples struggling to rebuild their relationships after an affair. Some are unable to do so, but others go on to make better relationships. This was the case with Michelle and Daniel. They had been married for seventeen years and had two teenage children. Their marriage had been going wrong for some time. Michelle was a loving and efficient woman, who took charge of the family, including Daniel, whom she looked after and babied as if he were one of the children. The consequence of this was that although Daniel loved Michelle he didn't feel much desire for her – she was a mother-figure, rather than a lover. Two years previously Daniel had reached the limit of his career-potential, and facing the fact that others were overtaking him had plunged him into a depression. Michelle pitied him, and he felt her attitude was patronizing.

During this time, Daniel started an affair with a young colleague who thought he was wonderful. Sex was great. Daniel hadn't felt so 'manly' for years. He was no good at subterfuge, and Michelle soon found out. Her reaction was to try and improve their sex life – she bought sexy underwear and frequently tried to seduce Daniel, who wasn't interested.

They came for counselling because Michelle wanted the marriage to continue, but Daniel wasn't sure. Most of the counselling centred around their relationship. Michelle began to understand that although she loved Daniel, she undermined him. Daniel began to see that he acted like a 'naughty boy' (the affair was part of this) and if he wanted to be taken seriously as an adult he had to behave like one.

These insights improved their relationship, which became more equal. As Michelle relinquished being in charge, so she began to show her vulnerability. She had coped with the affair, as she coped with everything, by being practical – in this case by trying to be more sexy. Now she allowed the pain and anger she felt to surface. Daniel was devastated, but it was a positive breakthrough. He felt needed, he could see how much he mattered to Michelle. It brought them much closer.

By the end of counselling, Daniel had broken off his affair and wanted to make his marriage work. Sex between them also improved, and Daniel felt more desire for Michelle than he had done for years.

DEALING WITH GENERAL
RELATIONSHIP PROBLEMS

No relationship problem goes away of its own accord, though that is what many people hope. The reverse is true: if you ignore a problem it worsens. Sometimes the original problem ceases to be an issue, but the way you avoided dealing with it continues to make difficulties between you. If you don't talk about things that matter to you, especially anything that makes you angry and unhappy, you grow apart. It stands to reason that sex will also become less satisfying.

● **Talking.** There is no substitute for talking to your partner about the way you feel. It can be particularly difficult when you fear that talking about something that makes you very angry or miserable will cause more trouble between you. This is why many people keep their feelings inside until they burst out during a row. There are ways that this can be made easier for you. The first is to try to feel closer generally, by having more time together.

!———————————————— *Task* ————————

Getting to know you – again

If you feel that you are growing apart, and there are a number of issues to resolve between you, agree to spend more time together. Make dates with each other for the next month – two a week, if possible. You can choose to spend the evenings or days at home or going out together doing something you enjoy. You can take it in turns to choose what this will be. For now, don't worry about problems.

On your 'dates' try to have fun. Save up things to tell each other, or reminisce about good times. Decide not to watch television – but if you do, pick a programme you both like. Sit close and hold hands or cuddle. When the programme is finished, discuss it.

!

You should continue with this task until you feel more comfortable with each other, and have created some pleasant moments together. You will then be in a better state of mind to deal with some of the problem issues. When you do so, you need to pay attention to the way you say what you are thinking, and how you listen to your partner.

- **The way to talk.** The best way to talk about emotional issues is in a calm and friendly way. When something upsets you this is difficult. It is even more difficult when you feel that your partner is at fault. You have to recognize that it is what the issue makes you *feel* that is important, not what someone else *does*. This means not being critical or accusing. Provocative statements are, 'You made me feel...' or 'You're so unpleasant' or 'I hate it when you...'. If you are blaming, your partner is likely to become resentful and angry, or too upset to take in what you are saying.

It is also better to pick a specific incident that exemplifies what you feel, rather than say, 'You always', or 'You never'.

The ideal way to talk about difficult issues is in three stages. First of all, state without blame the incident you have chosen. Then say what it makes you feel. Finish by stating why this is a problem.

For instance, 'When you carried on reading the newspaper while I was telling you about my day...' [*stating the incident*] '...I felt upset and unimportant...' [*how it made you feel*] '...and that made me irritable, so I wasn't in the mood to talk to you any more' [*why it was a problem*]. It is also appropriate sometimes to use just the first two stages: the incident and what you felt. As this doesn't come naturally at the start, it is worth preparing your words in advance.

- **The way to listen.** Too often we are in the habit of interrupting when someone talks to us. We want to put across our point of view, or say something to change the other person's mind. This can sometimes cause a conversation to turn into an argument. Or it can stop someone fully explaining a point of view.

When difficult emotional issues are being talked about, it is even more important not to do this. The best way to listen is with all your attention and, preferably, not even say anything when the other person pauses. That person's mind is probably still busy with things to say. Wait to be asked by the other person before you speak. Or ask calmly whether he or she has finished yet.

This is particularly hard if what you have been hearing upsets you or makes you angry. Even so, wait your turn – and when it comes, check first that you have properly understood what the other was saying, by repeating it in your own words. This might seem rather artificial, but it is essential to know that you have got the message. For instance, you could say, 'When I was reading the newspaper, you thought it meant I wasn't interested in what you were saying?' Let your partner tell you if you are right or not.

You can go on to use the two or three stages to say how *you* feel. For instance, 'When you say you felt upset and unimportant...' [*the incident*], 'I feel confused, because that's not what I meant...' [*how you feel*], '...and it shows me that sometimes we misunderstand each other' [*why it is a problem*].

These ways of talking and listening don't come easily to many people – it is a knack that needs to be learnt. But if you do learn it, you have a framework for talking about difficult issues without it escalating into a row.

! ———————————————— *Task* ————————————

It's a problem for me

When you are ready to do so, resolve to deal with your problems. Don't aim to tackle them all at once – it won't work and you will be back to square one. Look at your answers to the quizzes, and pick one issue that bothers you. It is probably best to start with the one that is least important.

Agree with your partner to make two dates to talk about what is on your mind. Spend no more than fifteen minutes on this. Prepare what you have to say beforehand, so you can be sure not to accuse. Your partner should not interrupt once during this time. Use the second date to talk about it together, when you have both had a chance to think. When it is appropriate try to arrive at a practical solution together.

After this it is your partner's turn to have two dates to talk about a problem that he or she wants to raise.

!

Sometimes careful talking and generous listening help you arrive at solutions you would have otherwise missed. But if the problems go very deep or there are too many of them, you might not feel equipped to deal with them on your own.

It can't be said too often that counselling can help move you further on, by providing a safe framework in which to discuss difficult matters – with an impartial outsider to help you understand what is going on between you. The RELATE *Guide to Better Relationships*, the companion volume to this book, also goes into all the issues raised in this chapter in much more detail.

After reading this chapter, however, you might have concluded that your general relationship is in good shape. If this is so, but there is a sexual difficulty, the next chapter looks at possible ways of handling it.

6

OVERCOMING SEXUAL DIFFICULTIES

This chapter looks at the most common sexual difficulties and ways that therapists have found helpful to deal with them. If your problem is here, it can give you enough information to start helping yourself. But many people find that they need the professional help of a sex therapist when tackling these difficulties. They have usually developed over a long period of time, and might have caused much anxiety and anguish. For all sorts of reasons this makes it hard to treat them without the report-back sessions with a sensitive therapist, who can help you deal with the emotions that are raised. The therapist also makes practical suggestions and is able to adapt any treatment so that it exactly suits your needs. It is useful to read about possible treatments, but to recognize that you might reach an impasse if you try to carry them out on your own.

Be kind to yourself. A problem with sex, particularly if it has been going on for a while, takes time to improve. As you doubtless appreciate by now, many emotional factors are included in your sexual feelings. The more the problem matters to you and upsets you, the more gentle and careful you need to be when tackling it. When fear is a factor it can take even longer. Fear of intimacy or being vulnerable with your partner can make the most simple-sounding touching exercise seem too threatening in practice. When the fear is of sex itself, or body parts, or of the heights of sexual arousal or orgasm, you need loving patience and the minimum of pressure. Even in sex therapy, dealing with problems takes time, and there is often one step back for each two steps forward. That's why your general relationship needs to be in the best possible shape before you start.

The easiest problems to deal with are those of a practical nature, perhaps a physical difficulty with the minimum of emotional worry attached to it. One such case was Rod, who came for therapy on his own suffering from impotence. The doctor had found no physical reason for this and Rod was able to get erections on his own – it was when he was with a woman that the problem manifested itself.

It did not take long before the therapist identified the problem. Rod, sensibly, was concerned about safe sex and always used a condom. It turned out that Rod had difficulty putting the condom on, and on a number of occasions in the past women had laughed at his fumbling attempts. His worry about whether he would put the condom on smoothly, combined with his worry that he might be laughed at, meant that he usually lost his erection. The therapist suggested that he practised putting the condom on when he masturbated alone until he was confident about it. This simple suggestion made all the difference to Rod, whose erectile problems did not recur.

It is very much harder to deal with a sexual problem that has its roots in childhood experiences, as talked about in Chapter One. Strongly upsetting emotional events in the past can continue to affect sexual functioning.

This was so in the case of Justin and Harriet, who came for therapy after just eighteen months of marriage. Their sex life had been terrific in the beginning – varied and passionate, they had tried everything with great enjoyment on both sides. About six months into marriage Justin switched off. He said he found Harriet demanding and voracious and physically off-putting. Harriet had done everything she could think of to interest Justin again, but it resulted in him becoming colder and more cruel. Harriet was a strikingly attractive woman in her early thirties, but she was rapidly losing her confidence.

Therapy never really got off the ground. Justin talked freely about himself and his childhood. He was bitter with resentment against his mother, who had left his father and embarked on numerous affairs. He thought she had behaved like a slut. Justin himself had been married twice before, each time rapidly falling out of love with his wives as soon as he had found out, he said, 'what they were really like'.

It seemed that Justin had never remained sexually interested in a woman after six months. In that early stage he was filled with desire. When desire cooled he lost interest. If the woman was still keen, she repelled him – she was just like his mother. It seemed impossible for Justin to disentangle his feelings about his mother from his feelings about other women. He didn't care to try. Soon after therapy started he left Harriet for another woman – presumably going on to repeat the same pattern.

There was a much more positive outcome in the case of Owen and his wife, Hannah. They worked with the therapist for a long time before they came close to dealing with Owen's erectile problems. They had been married for eight years, and patently adored each other, despite the fact that Owen was almost totally impotent with Hannah.

It turned out that Owen had been sexually abused by his mother from a young age. She was always inappropriately touching his penis, and on one occasion, when he was a teenager, she goaded him into having sex with her. He left home soon after.

Owen had not connected this with his erectile difficulties. He had been seeing a urologist at the hospital, who had found nothing physically wrong with him, and suggested RELATE.

Over time, talking to the therapist, Owen was able to understand that because of his experiences with his mother he connected sexual feelings with anger, disgust and power. He simply loved Hannah too much to be able to have sex with her. However, they had one child. How had this happened, the therapist wanted to know, if he was always impotent? Owen said, 'Every so often it works, but I don't know why.' The reason turned out to be that he could get an erection when he was angry, so it only happened after they had had a row.

Owen had not told Hannah about the abuse before, but she was marvellously supportive. Owen had to learn to connect sexual feelings with love. During many months of therapy, the couple concentrated on this, by staying with the early sensate focus tasks of intimate and loving touching. This was hard for Owen at the beginning and there was much stopping and starting before he began to feel comfortable. They moved on to trying penetration much later, when Owen was completely ready – and it was a success.

These stories show that when you are tackling a sex problem you need to be realistic and patient. A set-back doesn't mean failure, it means you have learnt a little more about what troubles you.

Above all, your first goal should be to enjoy yourself at whatever stage you are. Don't consider it as hard work leading towards a more long-term goal – that's the opposite of what you need to feel to relax and enjoy love-making. If what you have decided to do is not enjoyable, stop and talk together to try to find out why. Remember: there is no rush. Sexual contact that is pleasurable in itself for both of you is the true aim.

Some common sexual difficulties are now looked at individually. But you can often find that you have a combination of these, and that you aren't sure which is the most relevant. This is another reason why sex therapy is often the best course – to help you identify the problem and arrange the best treatment for it.

LOSS OF DESIRE

Discovering that you don't fancy your partner any more is a common problem. It is quite normal not to feel desire for your partner all the time once you have been together a while, as you saw in Chapter Four, 'Your Sex Life Now'.

This can be disturbing when it happens, particularly if you believe that loving someone means you should be wanting to make love to them all the time. Many people have unrealistic expectations that sex should always be passionate and overwhelming, even with partners they have been with for years. It's not like this for anyone, but feeling it can be so makes for unnecessary disappointment.

This was the worry that brought Celia and Mike into counselling. She was thirty-two and he was a year older; they had been married for a year, after having lived together for seven years. Celia had been depressed since they married, mainly, she said, because she didn't fancy Mike. This was not a problem for Mike, but he agreed to attend counselling to see if Celia's depression could be helped.

Apart from this problem they had a very good relationship. The counsellor worked with them for some time on certain difficulties they had in talking to each other about emotional matters, and she helped them talk about their sex life, which they both found very embarrassing.

Celia's main worry was that she only occasionally found Mike attractive and never felt 'swept away' by desire. The counsellor encouraged Celia to talk about what she felt sex should be like. She was very influenced by the myths of a strong, experienced man who would overwhelm her with passion, and ruthlessly make love to her until she was faint with pleasure.

Mike, on the other hand, was a gentle, courteous man, who had no desire to be aggressive during love-making. Celia felt he should be able to know exactly how to make sex good for her, even though she had no idea herself what she would find pleasurable. She was beginning to think that this was so different from 'normal' that it meant their relationship should end.

The counsellor was first able to help by telling them how normal – and important – it was for a woman to be a full participant in her own sexual pleasure, and that they had to find out together what would make love-making satisfying for Celia. She was able to give them some basic information about how they could set about this.

But what really made the difference for Celia was the counsellor's genuine opinion that they had a very good all-round relationship – better than most couples she saw. Sex was just a part of it, and it could be better, but not like Celia's fantasies. Celia said that she was so relieved. She thought that every other happily married couple were having passionate frequent sex, and the lack of desire to do so meant that their love was somehow inferior.

Celia was able to see that she loved Mike because he was gentle, and he wouldn't be the man she loved if he behaved like her fantasy lover. It was all right to love him but not to think he was perfect. She was also very reassured when the counsellor said that it was fine not to fancy Mike all the time. She should enjoy the occasions when she did, and accept the occasions when she didn't. She needed to accept Mike as *he* was and accept herself as *she* was.

Towards the end of counselling, Celia was able to confide her 'terrible' secret: she often saw men that she fancied more than Mike. Surely that was a sign that she didn't love him enough? Again, Celia was suprised and relieved to find that this, too, was quite normal, and that most people had that experience from time to time. The counsellor pointed out that it didn't mean she had to act on her feelings or see them as a threat to her marriage. By the time they finished counselling Celia's depression had lifted now that she knew that she didn't have to split up with the man she loved because he didn't send her wild with desire.

Partial loss of desire

Celia hadn't lost all desire for Mike, and many other couples find themselves in this situation. If you are enjoying the sex you do have and are quite satisfied with it, then it is not a problem. However sometimes there is more to it than that, and the partial loss of desire is connected to a specific reason. These are some of the more common ones:

● **'I'm not getting very much out of sex'.** If your love-making has become routine and unsatisfying it is natural to begin to feel less desire for your partner. When you start off feeling aroused, but usually end up feeling disappointed, it is logical that over time you will stop becoming aroused in the first place.

To reverse the process, it is also logical that if love-making becomes more enjoyable you will connect it with pleasure and start to want it more. Many couples find their desire levels rise as sex between them becomes better.

Try the sensate focus exercises at the end of this chapter, and also read the last two chapters together. Talk about the suggestions in them and decide together which you would like to try. Paying attention to your sex life might be all you need to make your partner more desirable to you again.

● **'We need different amounts of sex'.** Trouble can start when one of you feels the need for more sex than the other. Usually the partner with the higher sex drive pushes for sex more than the other wants. The result is that the partner with the lower sex drive feels angry or anxious and loses desire even more.

This can start a vicious circle. The partner with the higher sex drive becomes anxious, too, and pushes more – and the other backs further off.

This problem often has two components – the sexual one and an emotional need. In unbalanced relationships like this all kinds of touching become charged with sexual significance. If one partner is trying to avoid sex, he or she might also try to mimimise affectionate contact of all kinds, so as not to give the other one 'ideas'. Both men and women can confuse the need to be physically close and for loving reassurance with the need for sex. Counsellors often find that when a couple become more affectionate and loving, the one who has been pushing for sex finds that it is not so important any more.

! ——————————— *Task* ———————————

Not tonight...

This task is for you if you want sex less than your partner. It is important to say 'no' without your partner feeling rejected.

- Don't push your partner away or become irritated.
- Explain your reasons: 'I'm tired tonight', or 'I'm not in a sexy mood', or 'I'm too anxious about work'.
- Offer an alternative. 'I don't feel like sex, but let's just sit here and cuddle', or 'Saturday afternoon would be better when I'm feeling rested'.
- If you recognise you want sex less because it is not doing much for you, follow the suggestions in the section above.

!

When there is a genuine imbalance in how much sex you both need, it is necessary to compromise. One of the best ways to do this is to agree when you will make love – say, once a week. To make the agreement work, the one with the higher sex drive must undertake not to ask for sex at any other time. The one with the lower sex drive has to agree to participate fully and willingly on the agreed date. Both must concentrate on making the experience good for each other and *themselves*. This breaks the cycle of pursuit and flight, which makes both of you feel better.

- **'I fancy someone else'.** Like Celia, you might be worried because, alongside feeling less desire for your partner, you occasionally find other people more attractive, or perhaps there is one person you particularly fancy. This is quite normal. There are lots of attractive people around – on television and in real-life, and loving someone doesn't blind you to them. An attractive new, unknown person can also seem more exciting than your partner, whom you know so well – faults and all. It is nice to be attracted to someone; it reminds you that you are a sexual being with sexual feelings. Sometimes it jolts you into realizing that you have let your love-making with your partner slide into a routine that is less satisfying that it was. It can be the spur you need to do something about this.

It becomes a problem if you decide you must act on your feelings and start an affair with someone else. This is always a dangerous move, because it has implications for your partnership as well as your sex life, as you saw in the last chapter. If you love your partner and want to stay with him or her, you take a risk when you have an affair. It does not have to end in a break-up, but it might – this is something you have to weigh up. It is also worth reminding yourself that while sex with someone new can be exciting in its way, this excitement will inevitably fade over time.

It can happen, however, that it is when you are very attracted to someone else that you realise that there is more wrong with your relationship than loss of desire. Sometimes people can't or won't deal with problems in their relationships until an alternative partner comes along. In this case, loss of desire is not the main issue, but part of a larger problem.

Absence of desire

It is more complicated if one of you has lost all desire for your partner. This is often the sign of a general relationship problem. If you haven't yet done so, complete the quiz 'How it feels' in the last chapter. If you have a lot of bad feelings surrounding the relationship with your partner it could explain your loss of desire.

Similarly, if you are under stress you can lose all desire for the time being. Again, make sure you do the quiz 'It worries me', in the last chapter, to identify whether an outside worry is affecting your sexual feelings.

If you have a health problem, or a condition that requires medication, this might also be the cause of total lack of desire. Some prescribed drugs have side-effects that inhibit desire. You should talk this over with your doctor before you start looking for other reasons to explain your feelings.

Sex therapists see some people who have never felt desire, or had any interest in sex – usually women. There can be a number of reasons for this. The woman might naturally have a low level of desire, but this is usually reinforced by childhood and adolescent experiences, as shown in Chapter One. Strong anti-sex messages in the past and poor relationships with the opposite sex contribute, as does long-term depression. Therapy might include actively encouraging the woman to have sexual thoughts, as well as the sensate focus exercises, which help increase her enjoyment by the experience of loving sensuality.

PREMATURE EJACULATION

This is a very common problem for men. True premature ejaculation is when a man doesn't sense he will ejaculate until it happens, which means he can't control the time he is erect or thrusting before he 'comes'. For some men this means they ejaculate whenever they become very excited, perhaps before penetration or within seconds of it. The purpose of therapy is for the man to learn to recognize the sensations that occur in his penis just before he is going to ejaculate, so that he can reduce his level of excitement and therefore 'last longer'.

It is *not* premature ejaculation when the woman does not have an orgasm with thrusting alone before the man comes. Some men have perfectly good ejaculatory control, lasting many minutes of thrusting, but believe there is something wrong because the woman does not come during this time. Both men and women sometimes believe that if he could last longer the woman might have an orgasm during intercourse, too. While this might be so in some cases, it is more usually the case that the woman needs additional stimulation to her clitoris for this to happen – before penetration begins, so that she is very highly aroused – and sometimes during intercourse, or after. It is the myth of penetrative sex that causes the problem here, not ejaculatory control.

It is usually suggested that the couple go through the sensate focus programme outlined at the end of this chapter. This helps in two ways. The couple learn together more about the man's reactions and what is necessary for him to learn control over the ejaculatory function. The other benefit is that the couple also learn about the woman's responses and needs, which helps understanding that penetration is not the most important element of love-making.

In sex therapy, specific concentration on the ejaculatory function starts at stage two of the sensate focus programme, when the couple include genitals in their pleasuring of each other.

To help the man concentrate fully on the sensations in his penis, his partner strokes his penis until he is very highly aroused. The aim is for him to recognize the feelings that occur before he ejaculates. When he is able to do so, he lets her know by touch or word, so that she can stop what she is doing until his excitement subsides. This is known as the 'stop-start' technique.

It can also be useful for the man to masturbate while alone, to see if it is easier for him to recognize the sensations before ejaculation without the additional excitement of his partner being around.

It can take many such sessions before the man is able to indicate that his partner should stop. This is why it is important to talk to a therapist between sessions. Many couples fear they have 'failed' when this happens and might decide that it is hopeless. A therapist can help the couple understand that it doesn't matter, sex doesn't have to stop – the pleasuring session can still continue for the whole agreed time.

Once he can recognize these sensations, it is recommended that his partner brings him close to the point of ejaculation three times during the pleasuring session. When he indicates, she should stop until his level of excitement subsides. If the couple likes, they can repeat this for a fourth time, this time carrying on with stimulation until he ejaculates.

After a number of these sessions the man is likely to understand himself well enough to have control some of the time. There are still likely to be occasions when he ejaculates before he realizes it is going to happen, but this is nothing to worry about. It is also important to remember that the pleasuring for his partner should be given equal time during these sessions. The idea is for both to enjoy it – not to 'work' at the ejaculatory difficulty.

Another technique that can help is the 'squeeze' technique. It should only be tried if many sessions have passed without the stop-start technique working.

When the man indicates to his partner that he is highly aroused, she firmly squeezes the head of his penis for fifteen to twenty seconds. This

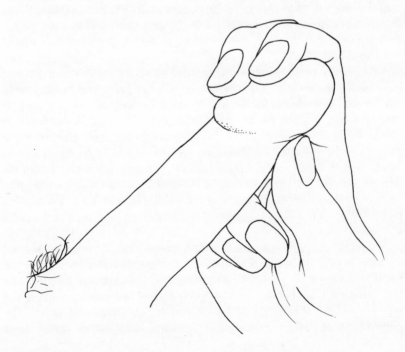

will stop him ejaculating, and he might lose his erection, too. As in the stop-start technique, they should do this three times in a session, his partner re-stimulating him to high excitement before applying the squeeze again. On the fourth time he can ejaculate.

To apply the squeeze, she should have her thumb on the underside of the coronal ridge – on the frenulum, the small piece of skin on the cleft of the glans, and her first and second fingers on the top of the glans. To check how hard she can squeeze, this should be practised when the man has an erection but is not highly aroused. It will take some sessions of practice before both have mastered how to coordinate the technique.

These steps should not be rushed. They can and should be very pleasurable in themselves, and along the way they allow you to develop true, intimate knowledge of each other's bodies. It can take many months before control is better established, and even then there might well be occasions in the future when the man finds he goes through a stage when premature ejaculation occurs. The answer is to go back to these early exercises, relax and enjoy them again, until control is re-established.

When the couple are in sex therapy, and they report that he is able to control ejaculation more often than not, the therapist might suggest that the couple can now start to try penetration again. After arousing each other in the ways they have both learnt work best, it is suggested that the woman takes charge of the penetration. She can do this with the man lying on his back, while she gradually lowers herself on to his penis, or lying side by side, with the woman guiding his penis into her vagina with her hand.

When the penis is in the vagina, neither should move or thrust, just experience the feeling as it is. When he lets her know that he is close to ejaculation, she should lift herself off until his arousal has subsided. It often happens that he finds it difficult to control his ejaculatory function the first few times this happens, but over time he regains control. If the man's erection starts to subside he can move a little until it is strong again. The woman can contract her vaginal muscles if she wants to. These are the pelvic floor muscles, which the woman can identify because one of their functions is to control the flow of urine. Pretending to stop the flow of urine tightens the muscles, bearing down gently relaxes them.

The idea is to remain like this for a few seconds or minutes, but not to have an orgasm in this position. The woman should move so that the penis withdraws after a while, and the couple should continue caressing and pleasuring as before. It is expected that the man's erection will subside during this session, but it can be re-stimulated later. The penetration should be repeated in the same way two or three times during a session. This exercise is a practical demonstration that penetration doesn't have to signal the end of love-making. If his erection goes it can be brought back again later. This makes the love-making pattern more flexible and rewarding. Some sessions later, when control is more certain, the couple can introduce gentle movement with penetration.

These exercises are best carried out in a sex therapy programme when the couple can report back to a therapist. They can seem threatening for couples suffering from ejaculatory difficulties. The couple can be disturbed by the idea that it is now time to 'perform', which raises anxieties that are best talked through with a therapist.

RETARDED EJACULATION

This is a far less common problem. In severe cases the man cannot ejaculate at all, even when he is masturbating. The man should check with his doctor first to see if there is any physical reasons why this happens. In other cases the man can ejaculate on his own, but not during sex with a partner – or not during penetration. What often brings the couple into sex therapy is the desire to have children, or the fact that sex has become painful for the woman.

This was the case with Philippa and Nick. He was able to ejaculate after more than an hour of intercourse, but by that time Philippa was sore and uncomfortable. The problem made both of them tense and Philippa started to dread sex. In their case, the counsellor felt it would be most appropriate to deal with the tensions first and make their sex-play more fun. One of the things she suggested was that they took a bottle of wine to bed together. When they were both nude Philippa was to balance an empty glass on Nick's belly, fill it with wine – and then drink it, with both her hands behind her back. Then Nick was to do the same to her. They reported that they had laughed themselves silly and had felt like two naughty children. Over time, as they both started to relax, Nick found his problem went away.

Often, however, more specific therapy is needed. If the man can't ejaculate at all, he is encouraged to start with a self-focus programme, finding ways to masturbate that will allow him to ejaculate. There has often been guilt about masturbation in the past, and it helps that the therapist is giving 'permission', telling him that it is normal, natural and healthy. This usually happens alongside the sensate focus programme that he carries out with his partner.

When he can masturbate and ejaculate on his own, the couple can move on to the second stage of the sensate focus programme, when genitals are included in the pleasuring. His partner concentrates on stimulating his penis, often with lotion or powder to increase the sensations. During this time, the man concentrates on what he is feeling and relaxing – there should be no pressure to ejaculate.

Over further sessions, his partner should experiment with the speed and firmness of her touch, and try to make him come. If he is unable to, he needs to masturbate in her presence until he is able to ejaculate with her there. When he can do this, she should take over from him, copying what he does, until he feels able to ejaculate at her touch.

At later sessions she should continue to stimulate him manually, but move so that his penis is close to her vagina when he is ready to ejaculate.

When progress has been made, and the man is comfortable, they can try penetration. In these sessions, when the man feels he is close to ejaculating he should insert his penis in her vagina and continue thrusting. It is best in this instance if the man is on top. If penetration causes his excitement to subside, they should go back a stage or two before trying again.

Sex therapists expect this procedure to take time, particularly when ejaculatory difficulties are connected to bad experiences in childhood, or messages about sex being dirty or wrong. The sessions should be fun and pleasurable in themselves if these are to be overcome – and they should always include equal pleasuring for the woman.

ERECTILE PROBLEMS

At some time in their lives, most men will have a problem with getting erections. This is quite normal. It can happen because a man is not aroused enough to have sex, but tries anyway. Anxiety about sexual performance, or general stress can also cause a man to lose his erection or not get one at all, as can general difficulties in his relationship with his partner. Having too much to drink can have the same effect. In most cases these are one-off occurences, or it happens a few times and then seems to right itself.

But sometimes the anxiety this creates can make the problem worse. The man becomes so tense willing himself to have an erection that he finds it more and more difficult to do so. Whenever sex stops being pleasure and becomes duty or work this can happen. This is also the case if the man is suffering from depression, or perhaps has experienced the loss of a previous partner through death or divorce, or the death of someone else close.

In other cases, the problem is a medical one. Some prescribed drugs affect erectile functioning. Circulation problems can also affect erections, as it is the blood supply to the penis that causes it to become erect. There can be damage to the nerves that control the erectile process, or perhaps a change in hormone levels, which do the same. Any man experiencing difficulty with erections should check with his doctor first to see whether there is a physical cause. The erectile process is delicate, and many medical conditions can affect it. If medication is causing erectile difficulties, the doctor can sometimes find an alternative drug that does not have the same side-effect.

If there is no physical cause for erectile problems, and the relationship between the couple is generally good, sex therapy can be the most effective help a couple can seek.

The sensate focus programme is used, with the couple spending as long as necessary on the first stage, non-genital focusing. It is stressed that the purpose of this is to experience the pleasant sensations of being touched by your partner. It is *not* a sexual exercise, and the man should make every effort *not* to get an erection. If by chance he does, this should be ignored. If erections have been a worry it can be quite difficult to relax during these sessions when they start, but they should be continued until both partners find them enjoyable and relaxing in themselves. Sometimes the man finds that he is beginning to get the occasional spontaneous erection during pleasuring.

When they move on to the second stage, where the genitals are included, the man should again concentrate on *not* getting an erection. If he does, the couple should enjoy the fact that it has happened, but not procede to penetration. His partner can use lotion or powder when caressing his penis to increase the sensations. If he is regularly getting strong erections during this stage, his partner should stop stimulating his penis from time to time until the erection subsides – re-stimulating it again later. This shows that a lost erection can be regained.

This stage can be very anxiety-provoking for a man who has had trouble getting erections. Couples who try it on their own can become disheartened if it does not seem to be working. Talking to a sex therapist, however, can help a couple negotiate this stage successfully.

When both are comfortable with this stage, and the man has been regularly getting strong erections, they can move on to try penetration. The woman on top, gently lowers herself on to his erect penis, and stays in that position without either moving. If he loses his erection whenever this happens, they should go back a stage. For the first few times, the woman should lift herself off again after a minute or two.

It was this exercise that Rosemary and Adrian found most difficult.

They had come for therapy because Adrian had been unable to get an erection for a year. They were in their late fifties.

When the therapist first met them she felt they had a good relationship, and seemed committed to making the sexual side work, too. Rosemary was an attractive, sexy woman, and Adrian was rather quiet and reserved. The therapist felt Adrian was rather angry, but he did not admit to it. When she saw him alone to talk about his childhood he answered in monosyllables, and told her he couldn't remember much. However, he did admit at this point to being angry with Rosemary. He said that he often found her pushy and that for years he had felt under pressure from her to have sex. He was prepared to admit this to the therapist, but not to Rosemary. He said sex had been fine until the last year, and he didn't know why it had gone wrong.

When the therapist saw Rosemary alone, she heard a different story. Adrian had had erectile problems for twenty years. They had both ignored it because it was intermittent, though she had sometimes felt disappointed.

Sensate focus went very well to begin with. They loved the exercises, which they carried out without embarrassment and with lots of imagination. They enthusiastically reported back to her how much they were enjoying them. They found great sensual pleasure in simply stroking hands, and Adrian liked it when Rosemary stroked his back with a feather duster.

During the second stage, Adrian was getting strong erections. The therapist had specifically said, 'It doesn't matter whether Adrian gets an erection or not. It's better if he doesn't. This is about a new form of communicating. It's not to arouse you.' Nevertheless, Adrian was becoming aroused and they seemed keen to move on to penetration. When they tried this, Adrian stopped getting erections.

They came back to talk to the therapist once or twice, each time reporting that Adrian couldn't maintain an erection. The therapist said that it didn't matter, they could go back a stage. But before their next appointment Rosemary phoned in to say that they were fine. The therapist knew that this was unlikely to be true. She felt that Adrian's unexpressed anger at Rosemary's sexual needs, and perhaps unresolved issues from his childhood, were getting in his way. Because of this he didn't want to be fully sexual or to penetrate. She suspected that he feared coming back for therapy in case it would mean confronting his anger or hurt.

Other couples have persevered through similar difficulties and have found that they can complete this stage successfully. It is most likely to be successful if the couple are seeing a therapist who can help them talk through the difficult emotions it creates with honesty and loving understanding on both sides.

When the man has been able to maintain his erection while inside the vagina for a number of sessions, the therapist often suggests that the couple try penetration with movement.

While this programme can be very successful, it doesn't work in all cases. Sex therapists are trained to understand what might be hindering the process and are often able to suggest other ways that can help.

But the sensate focus programme also shows the couple that there are many other ways of giving each other pleasure without an erection. If, for some reason, the man's erections do not return reliably, love-making can still be very satisfying without.

Often there are a number of contributory elements in the erectile difficulty, as one counsellor found when she saw a gay couple, Trevor and Alex, about their relationship. There were a number of matters they wanted to sort out with the counsellor, one of them being the fact that Trevor often lost his erection. They were in their twenties, and had been living together for just over a year.

Alex had had a very promiscuous time before meeting Trevor. He said, 'I never thought I was ever going to fall in love.' This was the longest relationship he had ever had, and he wanted it to last.

Trevor, on the other hand, had had a steady sex life. He had been involved with one other man from his early teens until he was twenty-three. When he was sixteen he had tried to have a relationship with a girl, but found he could not feel sexual about her. He said that he would have preferred to be 'straight', but recognised that he couldn't. He had gone back to his man friend, and had hoped they would be together forever. When the man left him, he had first started to have problems getting erections. He had a relationship with another man, which had lasted a year. Then he had met Alex and fallen in love.

There were a number of problems for Trevor. The chief one was that his adored mother had recently died. Alex had been very supportive, but it was about this time that Trevor's erectile difficulties started to worsen. This made him anxious, and the anxiety was compounded by the fact that he knew about Alex's promiscuous past, and thought that if he continued to have sexual problems Alex would be unfaithful, or leave him. Alex, on the other hand, saw the erectile difficulty as a sign that Trevor was going off him.

It was important for both of them to understand that much of Trevor's problem was concerned with depression over loss – first over the loss of his long-term lover, and then over his mother's death. They needed to recognise that the anxiety they were both feeling added to the pressure. The fact that Trevor felt a little guilty about being gay didn't help, neither did his fear that he might lose Alex too.

Both of them felt relieved once these issues were out in the open, and the pressure was taken off Trevor to get an erection. They felt more reassured about each other's love. But they still wanted to see if there was anything that could be done.

The RELATE counsellor felt they would benefit from the first stage of the sensate focus programme. Alex's promiscuous sex life had been fairly brutal and unsensual – he had no idea how to be physically close to someone without a swift sexual conclusion. Trevor, on the other hand, wanted and needed a lot of ordinary physical affection.

The non-sexual touching was a revelation for Alex, who had never known such gentle, sensual pleasure. Trevor felt happy and much more relaxed by the experience. Alex also started to understand that he had chosen to fall in love with someone who wasn't just interested in him for sexual reasons – and although he had said it was a problem, underneath it made him feel more loved.

Over time, Trevor had more control over his erections – but neither of them felt that the issue was so important any more.

VAGINISMUS

This is when the muscles surrounding the vagina contract so tightly that penetration is impossible. Even when the woman very much wants to have sexual intercourse she is unable to control this reflex. Some women have always suffered from vaginismus. In others it occurs after a difficult or painful sexual experience, or perhaps an insensitive internal examination. In some cases emotional reasons are behind it, sometimes because, as a girl, the woman was taught that sex was wrong or caused women pain.

Sex therapists see many women with this difficulty, and find that in most cases therapy can help. The couple often come because they are keen to have children – they are less embarrassed seeing a sex therapist for this reason. It seems more legitimate than asking for therapy to enjoy sex.

The treatment for vaginismus always follows the sensate focus programme. This helps the couple to a greater understanding of their own and each other's bodies.

The woman is also encouraged to get to know her own genitals and feel comfortable with them, by looking at them with a mirror. Over time she inserts the tip of one of her fingers into her vagina, and while it is there she practises using the muscles around her vagina. For instance, she tightens the muscles by imagining that she is trying to stop urinating, and she relaxes them by bearing down as if she were trying to push something out. When she is able to insert one finger easily, she progresses to two fingers, and then three. When this is comfortable, her partner can try inserting one of his fingers during stage two of sensate focusing, perhaps using a lubricant. Gradually they progress to a stage where he too can insert three fingers without this hurting or alarming the woman. Sometimes the therapist recommends 'Stanley Trainers' instead – penis shapes graded in size from very slim to normal width.

When the couple are ready, they can try penetration. When they are both aroused, the man lies on his back, and the woman gradually lowers herself on to his erect penis. It can help if his penis is covered with KY jelly to make penetration easier. The woman can control the speed at which this is done and the depth to which the penis enters. Over time, when the woman is able to do this without fear or discomfort, the couple can try penetration with movement – still with the woman on top, so that she can control the pace. Later, other positions can be tried.

While the treatment stages sound easy, in practice they can be difficult without seeing a therapist between sessions. The emotional elements, the fear, and sometimes the anger, need to be talked through. Without support many couples give up trying.

June and Danny are an example of a couple for whom the support was essential. They were trying sex therapy for the third time. Danny had terminated therapy twice before because he was angry. He thought it was June's problem and she should be sorted out alone. Now they both desperately wanted a baby, so Danny was more prepared to cooperate.

Although many partners of women with vaginismus are understanding, Danny was still angry. He couldn't believe that June wasn't doing it on purpose. When they made love in other ways June always had an orgasm, which seemed a contradiction to him – though this is often the case with vagnismus.

June came from a religious family that never talked about sex. Danny's family was similar, and he had avoided sex till he was married. After this, when penetration was impossible, he felt deprived of his rights. He also felt less of a man.

During the first few weeks of treatment Danny remained angry and thought it was a waste of time concentrating on the intimate sensate focus tasks. The therapist felt it was important to stay at these stages until Danny could see the benefit. In fact, it brought them much closer, so that June was able to tell Danny that his anger at her was making it harder for her to relax. Danny became more understanding, and started to lose some of his anger.

Gradually they moved on to the stage where June could insert her own fingers into her vagina, and when she was comfortable with this, Danny was able to insert his fingers, too. June began to use tampons for the first time – helped by a better knowledge of her own body.

Previously she had thought that when something was inserted it could get lost inside.

When they moved on to Danny penetrating her with his penis, June seized up again. Danny's anger returned in force. For two weeks they made no progress. 'How could she do this to me,' he ranted to the therapist. 'If she really wanted to she could do it!' He had to understand that this reaction petrified June, and he needed to be patient.

On the third week, Danny had control of his anger. He knew he had to allow June to take her own time. On the first session she was able to insert his penis half-way. She couldn't believe it had happened – Danny had to tell her to look. After so many years of dreading what the consequence would be, the reality was almost an anti-climax. They completed the therapy successfully and their whole relationship benefited as a result. Danny's anger was quite gone, and the weeks of increased intimacy developed through the early sensate focus tasks made them feel closer than ever.

As the case of June shows, there can be setbacks, particularly if there is anxiety or anger. The best way to cope with these is to go back a stage until the woman is comfortable again, and take the process more gradually.

Occasionally it can happen that vaginismus is only one of a number of problems between the couple. Sometimes it is when the vaginismus is being treated that other problems come to light. When a woman has had the problem for years, and is in a close and otherwise happy relationship, her partner is usually a gentle type who is not sexually aggressive, and is therefore more easily reconciled to the problem. When the vaginismus is dealt with it occasionally creates problems for him.

This is what happened in the case of Laura and Carl. They had been happily married for twenty years, and were both still virgins. However, they had a marvellous and varied sex life in every other way, which they enjoyed enormously. Neither of them wanted children.

Carl was a highly educated man with a very good job, but a low opinion of himself. He recognized that Laura was much more important to him than he was to her. She was very close to her mother, who always came first in her life.

Laura's mother had had several miscarriages. She had also given birth to three children, including Laura, but this had always involved long stays in hospital. Laura had grown up hearing lurid tales about what childbirth does to women. She believed that having a baby was dangerous and associated it in her mind with death. This was enough to predispose her to difficulties with sex. Her vaginismus had started shortly before she married when she had a painful internal examination. She had been tense and embarrassed, and she felt defiled by the examination. The doctor had made it worse by telling her that she was being ridiculous. Many times she had been on the verge of full intercourse with Carl, but was then unable. She had tried relaxing herself with a few drinks, but that didn't work either.

They came for therapy when Laura's mother died. It was as if while her mother was alive she didn't want to be sexual, but now she was keen.

As therapy progressed successfully, Carl became uneasy. He wondered if he would be able to satisfy Laura once she was able to allow penetration. When they were able to start penetration, he lost his erection. Later, dealing with Carl's erectile difficulties became as important as dealing with Laura's vaginismus.

ORGASMIC DIFFICULTIES

Some women believe that they have a difficulty with orgasm because they don't experience one through penetration and thrusting alone. Therapy for these women and their partners is usually a matter of reassuring them that this is perfectly normal, and encouraging them to include extra stimulation of the clitoris in their love-making. The couple usually go through the sensate focus programme so that they can discover, among other things, what kind of touching the woman likes or needs to experience orgasm.

It is more complicated if the woman has never achieved orgasm, or can only experience one by masturbating alone, but not with her partner. High levels of arousal without the release of orgasm can cause pelvic pain for some women.

Erica was in the first category. She and her husband, John, were in their early thirties and had two small children under five. Erica had read about orgasms, but had never experienced one. She was beginning to feel she was missing out.

In therapy, Erica revealed that she had been sexually abused by her brother for a few years. She had hated this, and had also felt intensely guilty. The guilt had made it difficult for her to allow herself to have sexual feelings. She had never told John about the abuse because she thought he would blame her and think she was dirty and perverted. With the therapist's encouragement she was able to tell John, and she couldn't believe his reaction. His first impulse was to wrap her in his arms. He cried for her, and his anger was directed towards her brother. It was what the therapist had expected, because she had seen what a close and loving relationship they had.

Before any sexual programme began, they talked fully about the abuse. Erica began to understand that she did not need to feel guilty – it was not her fault. It also helped John to know what was behind Erica's difficulty, because he had felt that it was his problem – that he should be able to make her come.

The therapy started with Erica learning about her body on her own. Like many women with a similar problem, she had a fear of 'letting go', and it was easier for her to learn about becoming aroused by herself. She had never masturbated before and it took a lot of talking before she felt able to. She began to get very strong feelings when she started to masturbate, but still found it difficult to reach orgasm. She tended to be thinking, 'How am I doing? Am I nearly there? Will it happen?' When she reported this back to the therapist, she was told to try just to enjoy what she was feeling – to let herself go over the top and not worry about losing control.

The couple also started the sensate focus programme, which both of them enjoyed. Over time, Erica was able to reach orgasm by herself, and occasionally when John stimulated her. Once this had happened, she became much more relaxed. She knew what it was like, she enjoyed it when it happened, but she didn't feel the need to have an orgasm every time they made love.

Penny's case was different. She could come to orgasm within minutes of masturbating, but never with her husband, Oliver. She also never felt aroused enough to have sex with him unless she was under the influence of drugs or drink. Part of the reason she wanted to sort herself out was because she had a young daughter. She felt she couldn't be sure she would bring her up to have healthy attitudes if she had difficulty herself.

Penny's real problem was intimacy. She had been a difficult child in a large family, and she had been the only one put into care. She couldn't really believe that Oliver loved her and this made it hard for her to let go sexually with him. In fact, Oliver adored her. He had helped wean her off the hard drugs she was on when they met. She still occasionally smoked marijuana or drank too much, mainly so that she could feel sexual towards him. Oliver was frustrated; her lack of sexual feelings at other times made him feel 'locked out' and unloved in return.

Therapy was slow and difficult for them. They spent many weeks on the early sensate focus exercises, because Penny found it so difficult. When something felt good she couldn't 'stay with' the feelings. She panicked about lying still and accepting Oliver's caresses. In fact, she found the experience so threatening that she terminated the therapy.

If a woman has never had an orgasm, like Erica she is encouraged to masturbate alone. This involves learning what touches she finds stimulating until she is able to bring herself to orgasm. She is encouraged to let her mind wander into sexual fantasies and to enjoy the experience of giving herself pleasure. Sometimes it is suggested that she use a vibrator so that she can learn what an orgasm feels like. This can make it easier for her to discover how to recreate the sensations with her hand.

Meanwhile, the couple also go through the sensate focus programme. They can then learn together what the woman likes and needs to reach orgasm, and can use the knowledge when they make love in other ways.

PAIN ON INTERCOURSE

Both men and women can experience pain on intercourse, technically known as *dyspareunia*. There may well be a medical reason for this. If the man's foreskin is too tight, it can hurt when he becomes highly aroused. A simple operation to remove the foreskin will solve the problem. Pain on or at ejaculation is very rare, and also has a medical cause. In women, pain can be caused by pelvic infections, internal scarring, or a number of other problems. If either of you suffers pain on intercourse, having a full check-up by your doctor is the first step.

Some women find that intercourse is uncomfortable only in certain positions, perhaps with deep thrusting. A woman can also find that certain positions become uncomfortable or difficult after an operation, such as a hip replacement. In these cases, experimenting with positions to find which are more comfortable is the answer. Some of these are mentioned in Chapter Eight, 'Building A Better Sex Life'.

Sometimes the woman experiences pain on intercourse because she is not sufficiently lubricated. This can happen in later life. If the woman is otherwise aroused, using a lubricant such as KY jelly will often solve the problem.

It is more often the case, however, that the woman is not lubricating because she is not sufficiently aroused. She is saying 'yes' when her body is saying 'no'. In these cases, the sensate programme is most useful. The couple remain on it until they discover what is necessary for the woman to enjoy sexual contact and become aroused.

ILLNESS AND DISABILITY

Sex therapists also help couples who have difficulty in their sex lives after an illness, or who have problems because one or both of them was born with a disability or became disabled later in life. A satisfying sex life is perfectly possible, if both partners want it, although it usually means adapting current sexual practices, or learning about different ways to make love.

As in all sexual functioning, there is a physical and emotional element in these issues, whether you are born with a disabilty (such as cerebral palsy) or develop it later (such as after an operation, a stroke or with the onset of arthritis).

People born with a disability have to struggle against a prevalent attitude that they don't have sexual feelings or shouldn't attempt a sexual relationship. People trying to rebuild a sexual relationship after illness or an operation usually also have to deal with fears that sex itself might be dangerous or impossible. The sex therapist helps by correcting attitudes and by allaying fears, when possible, and making suggestions about comfortable and safe ways to make love. There is not the space to go into the various illness and disabilities in detail, but other books are recommended in 'Further Help', on page 223.

An example of how sex therapy can help is shown by Roger and Prue, a couple in their fifties who were referred by the hospital following Roger's colostomy surgery. This operation involved his excretory system being by-passed, and a bag attached to an opening in the abdominal wall. Roger was worried because he was no longer getting full erections, as well as being disturbed about the presence of the bag. The therapy mainly consisted of helping the couple talk about the difficulties in a free and open way, and to become comfortable talking about sex, which they had never been able to do before. The therapist was also able to suggest ways in which they could extend their repertoire of love-making, which had previously revolved exclusively around penetrative sex.

In fact, penetrative sex was still possible, although Roger's erections weren't as hard as before, but the couple discovered that the other ways of making love were much more satisfying. By the end of the therapy they had resolved their problems – and Prue said to the therapist, 'I'm getting more out of sex than ever before!'

SENSATE FOCUS PROGRAMME

Most couples would find the sensate focus programme fun and pleasurable, even if their sex life is good. For couples who are having problems, or who have never developed satisfactory love-making practices, it is very helpful. In the course of doing it you inevitably learn more about your bodies and what makes sex good for you than you do during usual love-making.

It is also possibly the most intimate thing you can do together – more intimate even than passionate, 'heat-of-the-moment' sex. Lying still while your partner makes love to you, concentrating wholly on your own sensations, is something many people find difficult. Letting your partner know what you are feeling and what you like requires trust and openness, which are features of intimacy. Taking pleasure in caressing your partner, and learning to adapt your touches to your partner's desires, opens up channels of communication between you that might never have been explored. Many people find this very hard. They can have sex, but they find more genuine intimacy difficult. Even if you have been with your partner for many years this can make you feel shy, embarrassed, awkward or anxious.

Sue and Victor found the programme much more demanding than they thought. They came for sex therapy a year after they had married. Sue was uninterested in sex. She had had a strict religious upbringing, and had allowed some petting when they were engaged, but she had started to feel guilty about it and had stopped all touching until the wedding night. She had hated sex then and they were both worried.

They started off on the first stage of the programme, non-sexual touching. They were both uncomfortable with it, but said they would persist. When they reported back to the therapist they often said they hadn't been able to make time for the tasks, or they didn't know whether they were enjoying them or not. Eventually the therapist managed to help them talk about their feelings. Sue was becoming quite depressed and didn't know whether she really wanted to have sexual feelings. Victor revealed that he hadn't been happy about getting married. Sue felt he was angry and Victor felt she was resentful. After this frank talk they both felt very different. The unspoken burden of their fears had stood in the way of the necessary intimacy. Their commitment to the tasks changed and they began to progress with more success.

The fact that these tasks can raise feelings that have remained unsaid before is one of the reasons they are difficult. Although the tasks sound simple, they can be very challenging in practice. Some couples find them too difficult to do without report-back sessions to a therapist, who can help them talk through what was hard to do and why. If you are going to try them for yourself, be prepared for this difficulty. Take them slowly and talk a lot before and afterwards. Start with the first task, and don't move on to the second until you are both enjoying the task for itself and any awkward feelings have gone.

Before you start with each task, talk it through. What do you think you will find hard about it? Is there any way you can make it easier for yourself? Afterwards, chat about how it made you feel and whether it was more difficult than you thought – or more pleasurable.

It is usually recommended that you agree to three sessions a week, of at least an hour in length. It is good if you can vary the time – perhaps one on a weekend afternoon or first thing in the morning. Don't make it last thing at night or you are likely to be too tired or stressed to relax or concentrate. Make sure you won't be interrupted, and prepare the room you choose so that it is warm and inviting. Some people like to have soft music playing or create atmosphere by lighting candles. Spend at least three sessions getting used to the task – and continue for a further three sessions when you are enjoying it before moving on to the next.

Sensate focus 1 – non-sexual touching

This task is to help you become comfortable with your body and its sensual feelings. It helps you to relax with your partner and accustom you to being together, naked and close, without any pressure to perform.

You can touch any part of your partner's body except the genitals or breasts. Penetration is better avoided during the period when you are doing these tasks – either at the end of the session, or at other times until you have moved through the stages of the programme.

The point of this task is to learn to enjoy touching your partner and being touched, but not to be turned on. The idea is that we often miss some of these gentler sensations, which are pleasurable in themselves, because we are pursuing the more intense sexual sensations. If you do become aroused that is fine, but it is not necessary.

You must take it in turns to invite each other to participate in one of these sessions. Toss a coin to see who should make the first invitation. It is important that the initiating is done by both of you, not just one. This task is for mutual benefit.

One partner lies still, while the other partner caresses him or her, using hands and mouth as liked. The caresser should concentrate on taking pleasure in being the active partner, touching in ways that he or she finds enjoyable. The caresser should pay attention to what it feels like to touch the partner. How does the skin feel here? What is nice about the partner's smell, taste, sounds? How does the partner look while this is happening?

The partner who is being caressed should concentrate on what it feels like to be touched in these ways. What is particularly pleasurable? What isn't so nice? This partner only needs to talk if something is disliked, to explain *why* and how it might be better. For instance, the person being touched can say, 'I'm very sensitive there, if you touched more softly it might be better.' However, the person caressing is in charge, and can choose whether or not to respond to these statements. If talking is hard, you can move the partner's hand away from a spot, or indicate by pressure whether you want it more gentle, harder, faster or slower. If nothing is indicated, the caresser presumes that all is well.

The caresser can ask the partner to turn over so that the touching can move to the other side of the body.

Halfway through the agreed time, swap roles – the caresser now lying still to accept the caressing.

If you are shy about being totally naked together, you can keep some clothes on for the first few sessions if you prefer. You can remove them as you become more comfortable at later sessions. Some couples feel more comfortable in the beginning if the caresser sits with his or her back supported, and the person being caressed sits between his or her legs, leaning back against the caresser. This way you are not watching or being watched, just feeling.

After a few sessions you can choose to experiment with creams or powder to see the different sensations these create.

If you do happen to find the sessions very arousing, just enjoy the feelings. Becoming aroused is a pleasure in itself, and doesn't have to lead to orgasm. It is good to learn to enjoy the sensations without feeling that they are a prelude to anything else.

Simply reading these instructions gives you little idea of what the experience will really be like. It might sound boring or easy. In fact, it can be very powerful, as Angie and Bill discovered. They had been married for eleven years, but since Angie had suffered from cystitis, which had made penetration painful, they had not had sex. That was nine years ago. Angie had been depressed for two years, and medication from her doctor hadn't helped.

When the therapist described this task to them the prospect made them nervous. They had been happily married but hadn't touched for nine years. They said they were willing to try it so long as they didn't have to take all their clothes off.

The therapist said this was fine. She also said it was fine if they found that they couldn't do it at all. There was nothing they could do that would be wrong. If they were unable to do the task, it would just give them something to talk through when they next saw the therapist.

When they returned after the first session they reported that it had been the most emotional experience for them. After the session they had wept together in each other's arms. But they were tears of release. They said it was the most intimate thing they had ever done and they felt closer than they had for years.

Sensate focus 2 – genital touching

When you have had a number of sessions on the first task, and are both actively enjoying it, you can move on to this one.

You should continue to take it in turns to invite each other to participate.

This time, the caresser can include the genitals and breasts in the caressing. If you find this difficult because you have been brought up to believe that the genitals are dirty or because a bad experience in the past has caused you to be afraid, take this task gently. You might want to bath first, so that you are reassured that you are both clean. You might prefer to look at and touch your partner's genitals before touching has caused either of you to become aroused. Just handle them gently, and get used to the way they look normally. In later sessions, when you are more comfortable, you can move on to more specifically arousing touching.

The partner who is being caressed can indicate what he or she likes by talking, nodding, smiling or guiding the hand. The caresser can choose to arouse the partner to extreme excitement – but not to orgasm. If the partner being caressed is becoming too aroused, switch focus to a less arousing part of the body. The caresser can bring the partner close to orgasm many times, but it is not the aim of the session to have an orgasm. Don't concentrate exclusively on the genitals or breasts, include the caresses that you learnt your partner likes on other areas of the body. If you are comfortable doing so, you can use your mouth on your partner's genitals, but not if you don't want to.

At the end of the session the caresser can bring the partner to orgasm, but it is not necessary. It is better not to have sexual intercourse during the period you are concentrating on this exercise.

After some sessions you can try caressing each other at the same time. But you should always start by taking it in turns to be active and passive. It is only like this that you can concentrate on the sensations you are giving and receiving. Over the sessions you will discover all the ways that you can give your partner pleasure, and that sex can be highly satisfying, emotionally and physically, without penetration.

This can be a difficult exercise for couples who have anxiety about sex, or for whom a specific sexual problem has caused difficulties. If it is too hard for one of you, it might be wise to return to the first exercise until you are more comfortable.

Like any intimate love-play, this exercise can reveal anxieties or problems that the couple has not previously acknowledged, which is what happened with Charles and Letitia. They were in their sixties, and it was a second marriage for them both. Letitia had been widowed for ten years when she met Charles, whose wife had only died the previous year. They fell in love and had a very good relationship. Charles, who had felt so lost and depressed after his wife died, couldn't believe his luck to have found such an attractive, warm and independent woman, to help him put his life together.

They were very sexually attracted to each other and said that they felt so adolescent – they could hardly keep their hands off each other. This was delightful, but the only problem was that Charles had difficulty getting and maintaining an erection. Charles felt ashamed, and although Letitia wasn't too bothered, she wanted to help him.

Charles had been the son of a powerful mother, and the husband of a strong woman who had always looked after him. Letitia, too, was another strong woman. Although he had been a successful businessman, he had always let the women run his life. During the course of therapy, and the counselling that preceded it, he realized that he also needed to learn to be an equal partner in this new relationship.

The first sensate focus exercise went very well for both of them. With the pressure off, Charles found he became aroused despite himself, and often had strong erections. In the report-back sessions, they continued to talk about the ways in which Charles could develop his sense of self and his ability to stand on his own two feet.

Then they moved on to this second exercise, where genitals are included. Charles's erections continued to be reliable and strong and they were regularly stimulating each other to climax. Suddenly the report-back sessions became more problematical.

Letitia started to say she was becoming bored. She found the sessions too contrived, and was no longer becoming aroused. She preferred and needed her sex life to be more spontaneous.

It was clear to the therapist that Letitia's unease was more complicated than that. She had liked 'looking after' Charles and being the strong one in the relationship. As he was becoming more confident generally she felt panicky. She didn't mind that Charles had trouble with his erections, because she could soothe and comfort him. They told the therapist that they would not continue therapy for the time being, but would re-start later if they needed to.

The therapist was sorry that they weren't continuing, as she thought there was every chance that Charles's sexual functioning would continue to improve. However, she felt that their relationship was good and would continue to thrive – and that what they had learnt sexually would stand them in good stead.

Other couples, who have met similar problems, have coped by dealing with the other issues out of bed. Facing anxieties can bring you closer together, which in turn benefits your sex life.

If you try the sensate focus exercises, and enjoy them, you are likely to find your sex life much improved. But there are other things that can also help make your love-making more pleasurable, which are discussed in the final two chapters.

PART FOUR

IMPROVING YOUR SEX LIFE

7

GOOD IN BED

The concept of being 'good in bed' is one of the most pressurising. The idea is that some people are good at sex and others aren't, and there is a lot of confusion around what is necessary to earn the magic accolade. Before examining what it truly means to be good in bed, and what is unhelpful myth, it is worth looking at two typical examples of the opposite – and what it is that makes them 'bad in bed'.

The first example concentrates on the woman's experience. While her partner makes love to her she lies still, irritable but compliant. Nothing he does seems to arouse her and she does not touch him, impatient for it all to be over. The man's verdict is that she is bad in bed – but why?

On one level, what makes the experience so disappointing for him is her lack of pleasure and enthusiasm. It makes him feel bad, too. If she had enjoyed his attentions, even while remaining passive, he might have felt better about it.

On another level, this is 'bad' because the woman submitted to sex when she clearly had no desire for her partner or sex. It suggests that her sense of self-esteem is so low that she thinks it is of no account what she feels. If he wants it, she'll let him have it – anything for a quiet life or to keep him sweet.

Perhaps, on the other hand, she did feel some desire at the beginning, but his love-making did not arouse her and she felt put off instead. The 'bad' thing in this case is that she did nothing by word or touch to let him know what would make it better for her. Perhaps she didn't know what that might be.

But what many people miss when concentrating on why the woman is 'bad in bed' is the quality of the experience *between* them. There are two people involved here. Her irritation and impatience suggest that not much love is lost between them. She doesn't touch him – probably because she doesn't feel like touching him. What does it say about him, that he will continue the sexual encounter when his partner is clearly uncomfortable and unwilling? Why did he not ask her whether there was anything he could do to make her enjoy herself more? It is the sexual experience itself which is 'bad', and both partners contributed to it.

The second example concentrates on a man, in a different situation. In this instance, he is with a partner who is aroused and wanting to make love. Within a very short time of starting sex the man has moved straight into penetration. After a short time of thrusting he ejaculates, rolls on his side and goes to sleep. The woman feels frustrated and concludes that he is 'bad in bed'.

On one level she feels used. He has behaved almost as if she wasn't there, concentrating on satisfying his desire as quickly as possible, without caring how she feels.

On another level, she believes it shows lack of experience. If he understood women, he would know how to make the sex good for her, too. She thinks he would then 'last longer' and keep pace with her level of arousal.

Again, what is missed here is her own contribution to the sexual experience. At no time does she let him know that he should slow down, or indicate what would make the encounter better for her. She expects him to be a mind-reader and intuitively understand what is expected. Sex *between* them has been 'bad', because she feels disgruntled and he feels he has failed.

These are two extreme examples, but they show that being 'bad in bed' is not a simple matter of one person's responses or actions, but a combination of more subtle issues and a joint responsibility. In exactly the same way, being 'good in bed' is less simple than some people think – but also more achievable than they fear.

WHAT 'GOOD IN BED' ISN'T

There are a number of misleading beliefs around about what makes you good in bed. These can lead you to concentrate misguidedly on elements that are not particularly useful – or can make you believe, wrongly, that you'll never have what it takes. These are the main ones:

Wrong belief: 'You need good looks, good body and youth'
It is easy to see from the above examples that this is wrong. The woman in the first example could have been young, beautiful and sexily built, but the experience would have been no better. The man in the second example could have been a handsome Olympic athlete, but the result would have been the same.

● **What it gives you.** Unquestionably, youth and good looks make you attractive, and can increase your choice of partners, but they have nothing to do with your use of your sexuality. Looking good, so long as you feel good as well, can also make you more confident – but confidence that is dependent on these factors is shaky and easily disrupted.

● **What it can't give you.** Youth and good looks are external qualities, which have nothing to do with the elements that affect your sex life. Sex therapists see many couples who by any standards have everything in terms of looks and success, but who still have sexual problems. Early difficult experiences, as described in the first chapter, can have an effect on anyone, regardless of physical characteristics, and are much more important in shaping your sexuality.

Wrong belief: 'You need a big sexual appetite and staying power'

This belief suggests that if you need a lot of sex you will automatically be good at it. In terms of men, it suggests that men who can maintain erections for a long time will also be better at love-making. However, the desire for sex (a physical appetite) has little bearing on what sort of lover you are, just as a big appetite for food doesn't automatically make you a good cook. Sexual 'staying power' in a man has its uses, but does not make him a better lover if all his energies are concentrated on controlling his ejaculatory function.

● **What it gives you.** A need for frequent sex can mean that you are often in the mood for love-making, or are easily aroused, which can be a good start. Sexual staying power can make the act of penetration and thrusting more rewarding in itself, but has nothing to do with the other, equally important aspects of love-making.

● **What it can't give you.** These factors alone don't give you sensitivity or consideration. Neither do they give you sexual knowledge. Sometimes, a higher sex drive than your partner's can mean the opposite – riding rough-shod over your partner's needs.

Wrong belief: 'Knowing every sexual trick – and applying them'

The belief that knowing about, and introducing, all manner of sexual variations into love-making makes you good in bed is a widespread one. This reduces sex to the level of technique, and its practitioners can give it so much emphasis that they miss out on the more subtle and important elements of sexual satisfaction. If sex is not satisfying they introduce a new position or accessory, rather than looking at more fundamental basics, where satisfaction is rooted.

- **What it gives you.** A willingness to experiment and an openness to new ideas and suggestions is positive and can add to a good sex life. But it is misleading when all sexual difficulties are put down to lack of variety. It can also lead you to think there is something wrong with you or your partner if the tricks don't 'work', or if either of you is uncomfortable with them or repelled.

- **What it can't give you.** Sexual tricks and aids on their own can't give you sexual satisfaction. Neither do they necessarily increase intimacy. Some people, indeed, use technique of various sorts to avoid intimacy. Some men who pride themselves on being 'studs', with a repertoire of sexual variations designed to turn any woman on, can find it humiliating or embarrassing to ask the woman what she really likes and meet her needs. The woman, too, can feel perplexed and at fault if her lover has gone through a complicated routine apparently designed for her benefit, which hasn't 'worked'. Similarly, some women who work at being 'good in bed' by constantly introducing different techniques, can be quite anxious about losing control or taking time for their own pleasures. Technique enhances, but does not create, sexual satisfaction.

Wrong belief: 'Experience with lots of partners is necessary'
This is another common belief. The implication is that having sex with lots of people teaches you all you need to know about love-making with any partner. By extension, it suggests that if you were 'good in bed' with one person you will automatically be good in bed with the next.

- **What it gives you.** Varied sexual experiences can teach you more about your own responses and what makes sex good or bad for you. But this is something you can learn with just one partner as well. Having sex with a number of people can give you a better idea of the kind of partner you want in a long-term relationship, but this is not so for everybody – some people repeat the same mistakes over again. It can also show you, by experience, that sexual feelings change over time, so you are better prepared for this.

None of these guarantee that you will be good in bed.

- **What it can't give you.** Past experience can't tell you about the unique sexual responses of your current partner, or what will make sex between you good for you both. Some people let past experiences get in the way of developing a good sex life with current partners. If what you do 'worked' with someone else you can be irritated if it doesn't with your partner – or else carry on doing what you've always done without reference to your current partner's feelings.

It is a common problem that a fairly experienced man feels he has learnt all he needs to know about sex, so thinks it's unnecessary to do further exploring with his partner. A woman, too, can feel that an experienced man should be able to know exactly what she needs without her intervention.

An example of how experience can have the reverse effect is Gillian, who came for counselling on her own to talk about her difficulties with relationships. She had been twenty-five when she took her first lover, an older married man, with whom she was involved for six years. He had been a sensitive and considerate lover, and between them they had developed a marvellous sex life. They had experimented with what they both liked. For instance, the man liked oral sex but Gillian found it off-putting, so they discontinued it. However, Gillian found anal sex very exciting, and it became an important part of love-making for them. As Gillian turned thirty she became very keen to marry, but her lover was not prepared to leave his wife, so she finished with him. Since then she had had a succession of relationships that broke up very quickly. She was now thirty-seven and wanted to sort out why.

The counsellor soon discovered that Gillian was intent on recreating exactly the same sexual relationship she had with her first lover. Whenever the new relationships turned sexual, sometimes even before, Gillian would announce that she wanted to be made love to anally. The men she had met so far had reacted with startled surprise and sometimes disgust.

The counsellor helped Gillian to see that there was a difference in knowing what you like sexually and demanding it at all costs. She was missing the point that sex with a partner was a *relationship*. How would she have felt if her first lover had insisted early on that as he liked oral sex she must do it for him or he wouldn't be interested? Gillian could see that she would have felt affronted and that her own needs were unimportant. The counsellor reminded her that it had taken time to develop the good relationship she had with her lover, and that it had included adapting his needs to hers. This is how she should approach a future relationship – seeing the man as an individual, and finding out together what worked sexually for them as a couple. In terms of what we are looking at, Gillian was 'good in bed' with her first lover, but not with those that followed.

‘ ——————— Talking point ———————

Not that good

Discuss whether either of you have been influenced by these misguided ideas about what 'good in bed' really means. Have you had experiences that proved to you that they were wrong? ’

__ WHAT 'GOOD IN BED' REALLY INVOLVES __

There are a number of elements that make you 'good in bed' – most of them attainable by anyone, and some of which you might find quite surprising.

Being 'comfortable' with your body

As you read in Chapter Four, 'Your Sex Life Now', it is your attitude to your looks and your body that is important, not how objectively perfect they are. If you are anxious or ashamed about the way you look you can transfer these feelings to your sex life, and feel awkward making love as well. This also involves being comfortable with the most intimate part of your body – your genitals. If you are worried about this area, or think it is dirty or in other ways unpleasant, then sex itself has unfortunate associations.

● **What it gives you.** Feeling comfortable with the way you look gives you confidence, which is attractive in itself. When you have come to terms with your body, imperfections and all, you are able to be more 'free' sexually. You can enjoy yourself without worrying about the effect you are creating. Being able to respond without inhibitions is one of the elements that makes you good in bed.

● **What to do about it.** It can be difficult to change the way you view yourself if you have always been very critical. But it is worth making the effort – you will feel better generally and feel more relaxed about sex. If you haven't yet done so, read *Your Feelings About Your Body*, page 102, and do the two tasks 'I'm all right' and 'Changing perspective'.

   If you feel bad about your genitals it can make sex more awkward. Although many men feel that their penises are 'too small', they are usually more at ease with them, because they are so visible, than some women are with their genital area. If you are a woman, it helps to get to know what you look like 'down there', using a hand-mirror to help you see, and to do this until you feel quite comfortable with the way you are. If you were discouraged from touching yourself as a child, you might feel this is wrong – but it is not only healthy and normal, it is also important in helping you feel relaxed with your sexual feelings.

Understanding your sexual needs

Being a good lover is not just about what you do to and with your partner. Your own sexual enjoyment is an equally important part of love-making. Understanding your needs means knowing what turns you on, what specific sexual behaviour and caresses are arousing, what makes you come to orgasm, and what you like to happen when love-making is over.

- **What it gives you.** It is only when you understand your own sexual needs that you are able to communicate them to your partner, so that sex becomes a mutually satisfying experience. Many people have a better idea of what they don't like than what they do. If this is so with you, communicating about sexual needs becomes wholly negative, 'Don't do that', 'I don't like that', 'That turns me off'. It is much more rewarding to speak in positive terms, 'I like it when you do that', 'Why don't you try...', 'It makes me very excited when...'.

- **What to do about it.** This is something you can do partly on your own. Thinking about situations that have excited you and filled you with desire tells you what turns you on. Masturbation, and the fantasies that accompany it, show you what makes you highly aroused and what sort of touching you need to reach orgasm. Sex therapists often have to explain that masturbation is a normal and healthy part of your sex life, not something you do only when young or when you don't have a partner. It is perfectly normal to masturbate when you are in a relationship – either because you are aroused and your partner isn't, or because you feel the need for sexual release but don't for the moment feel like making love, or concentrating on anyone but yourself.

To complete your understanding of your sexual needs, you also need to share the experience with your partner. The two sensate focus exercises, pages 168 to 173, are ideal to discover the caresses that are most pleasurable or arousing. Showing your partner how you masturbate is also a good way to demonstrate the very specific and individual manner in which you reach orgasm.

Understanding your needs is a continuing process. Your needs can change over time, and they can also be different from one love-making session to the next. The sensate focus exercises, which encourage you to communicate your reactions, as well as experience the sensations, stand you in good stead. Getting into the habit of letting your partner know how you are feeling during love-making, increases the knowledge for both of you. You learn that there isn't only 'one right way', but a variety of conditions and sensations that make sex good.

Learning about your partner's sexuality and needs
To be good in bed with your partner, you need to understand that he or she is different from anyone else with whom you might have made love. Sexual responses are so complicated and individual that every single person is different, just as bodies are formed in all shapes and sizes.

It also means getting to know, and becoming comfortable with, your partner's body – all of it. Some people have sex without ever looking at or touching their partner's genitals. This is such an important element in love-making, that it is hard to develop a fully satisfying sex life without it.

● **What it gives you.** When you learn about your partner's needs you become the best lover it is possible to be. When the guesswork is removed from love-making you are in a position to make sex satisfying every time for you both.

● **What to do about it.** Just as the sensate focus exercises show your partner what you like, so they show you what your partner likes, too. Talking during love-making also helps. You can ask, 'Do you like this?', 'How does this feel?', 'What would you like?' Over time you will discover the variations of mood and sensations that contribute to your partner's sexual responses. If this becomes a habit, you can continue learning all the time, so that adapting to each other's needs as they change is natural.

'Making friends' with your partner's genitals can be hard if your upbringing or unpleasant experiences in the past have made this distasteful to you. Sex therapists often see couples for whom this is a problem – they perceive the genitals as dirty or threatening in some manner. One way to deal with this is to become used to them in a non-sexual situation, for instance when your partner is in the bath, perhaps helping your partner to wash. Also spend plenty of time on the second sensate focus task, where the genitals are included in your exploration of your partner's body, until you are able to feel comfortable.

Developing a sex life that suits you both

As everyone's sexual needs are individual, it would be a miracle if your needs coincided exactly with your partner's. All sorts of variations are possible – the way you like sex, the amount of sex you need, the different moods at different times. Developing a sex life that suits you both takes these variations into account, and depends on flexibility on both sides.

● **What it gives you.** Sexual give and take keeps you feeling good about your sex life. When one partner's wishes predominate, the inevitable result is that the other partner eventually loses interest. Being flexible allows you to adapt to changing needs over the years, which helps keep sex satisfying.

● **What to do about it.** In the first instance, discovering through experimentation what aspects of love-making you both like creates a good basis. It also means being accommodating about each other's needs when they differ – so long as they are not actively disliked. It can also mean compromise about how often you make love, if your needs are very different.

Most importantly, it involves continuing to communicate about your sex life, in whatever way is most comfortable. Sometimes showing your partner through movement or touch what you do or don't like is enough. Talking is the most direct way – and is the most useful when a problem arises, or when your needs have changed. Never expect your partner to read your mind, however long you have been together.

! ═══════════════════════ *Task* ═══════════

Talk to me...

This task is a piece of silly fun, and should be approached in that spirit – it can also help both of you learn about your sexual responses. Agree that on a given occasion when you are making love you will 'rate' every kiss, touch and movement on a scale from 1, pleasant to 5, wonderful. For anything that is 3 or over, explain *why* it is so good. You must both give it a rating before you move on. If something you do is rated lower than you expected, ask what you would need to do to make the rating higher.

!

Being 'good out of bed'

Your sex life is also affected by how you behave together the rest of the time. Being 'good out of bed', means not reserving all your affection, love and physical contact for the times when you are making love.

● **What it gives you.** Showing each other affection, both in the way you talk to each other and the friendly way you touch, makes you feel loved. There is simple pleasure in a non-sexual kiss, a hug, a pat, holding hands, sitting on a knee, which also has a deeper, warming effect. It says, 'I love you for being you', and brings you close. Sex, in this context, becomes a different way of touching, not the only way. Couples who remain physically close also tend to feel more desire for each other.

● **What to do about it.** This is an easy one – just do it! If you are out of the habit, start with what comes easiest. A kiss of greeting and farewell, a thank-you hug, taking your partner's hand when you have something important you want to say. It is a habit that is as simple to get back into as it is to lose.

Loving – and liking – your partner

This might seem obvious, but it is something often missed in a discussion about what makes you 'good in bed'. The more positive feelings you have about your partner, the more responsive you are – and the more desirous you are to give pleasure in return. When these feelings go, sex becomes less satisfying, too, even if no other element seems to have changed.

● **What it gives you.** When your feelings towards your partner are good, you want to spend time together, and you want to touch, sexually and in other ways. You feel generous-spirited and relaxed – and trusting. These are essential ingredients in good sex that satisfies more than the physical appetite.

● **What to do about it.** For these elements to remain, you have to take care of your relationship – all of it, not just the sexual side. It means building on what is good in your general relationship, so that you continue to enjoy each other as people. It also means accepting that problems are bound to crop up as time goes by, and dealing with them in ways that are helpful and uniting, rather than allowing them to push you apart. *The* RELATE *Guide to Better Relationships* is all about how you can do this.

It should also be emphasised that if you love and like your partner your sex life can be satisfying to you, even if some of the other elements mentioned above are missing. There are no rights and wrongs in this very personal area of your life. A couple whose overall relationship is good can find happiness in love-making that does not reach the heights of physical pleasure or that is more restrained – or very infrequent. If it suits you both, it is right.

If, however, it doesn't suit you, the next chapter includes suggestions that might help.

8

BUILDING A BETTER SEX LIFE

This chapter is for couples who have a good general relationship and who both feel motivated to make their sex life even better. The rest of the book will have helped you uncover possible problem areas and give you a more realistic idea of what you can expect from love-making. However, it is sometimes human nature to turn to the 'best bit' first, and you might have decided to start with this chapter. While some of it is relevant to every couple, much of it depends on you having worked through the complexities of your own sexual responses and determining problem areas in your expectations and your relationship. Going straight in to trying to improve your sex life without acknowledging these, can put you on the road to needless failure. When couples see a counsellor or sex therapist these issues are always explored fully before sexual tasks start. The same is true when you are trying to help yourself. By all means read this chapter first – but work through the rest of the book before you put it into practice.

Keep an open mind when you read this chapter, but also remember that some of the suggestions might be wrong for you. The secret of a good sex life is individual tailoring – what other people do doesn't count. Your sex life is private and personal and different from any other couple's. Sometimes what other people do can seem interesting and exciting – but equally it can appear bizarre, dull, comical or disgusting – that is their business. If they are enjoying it and it is satisfactory, then they have got it absolutely right. Included in this chapter are some general tasks, and also some specific ones that worked for other people, under the heading 'It worked for them…'. While some of the suggestions included might appeal to you, others might seem obvious, silly, childish or distasteful. That is fine, too. Regard it as a menu not a prescription. You choose what appeals and ignore what doesn't. Your sex life won't improve if you feel you must include every single sexual possibility whether you like it or not. But if variety is what appeals to you most – try it all, and if you want more, other books recommended in the Further Help section, page 223, might be what you need.

Being realistic

Your sex life can always be improved – but you need to be realistic about what this means. If your upbringing has predisposed you to find certain aspects of sex difficult you might never be able to change these totally – but what you can do is acknowledge them and work around them so that they no longer get in the way of satisfying sex. Daphne and Will are a good example of this. They were a couple in their early thirties, who had been married for six years. They had a good relationship, except for sex. Daphne used to feel threatened and anxious when Will wanted to make love to her, and would avoid it if she could. When they did make love, she usually quite enjoyed it, but would never let Will kiss her on the mouth. He felt rejected, and unsure that she loved him.

Daphne's unhappy past emerged during counselling. She had never known her father and her mother was unloving. Her first sexual experience had been at thirteen, with a much older man, who had used her for sex against her will for many months. She worried that she had let him do this, and felt she was rotten – even physically: she had suffered from a stomach disorder and was often sick. Her mother frequently told Daphne her breath smelt.

The counselling involved helping Daphne feel better about herself. She wrote many letters (which she never sent) to people who had made her feel bad – her mother, her absent father, the abusive man. This exercise freed her from much of the anger and guilt she had been feeling. Will became able to understand that her dislike of kissing was connected to feeling rotten inside, and her fear when he showed he wanted sex was connected to the man with whom she had been involved. By the end of counselling Daphne still couldn't kiss Will, and still dreaded him making the first move, but Will no longer took it personally. He didn't try to kiss her, and he let her initiate sex. As she became more comfortable with herself she enjoyed sex more – she was able to ask Will to do things for her that she liked; before she had felt she had no right. Will's understanding helped Daphne feel more valued and closer to him; sex was no longer a problem.

Being realistic also means understanding what a good sex life is. Some people chase the ultimate orgasm, as described in certain books: a transcendental experience, with the earth moving and other extraordinary phenomena. Orgasm isn't like this. One woman told a sex therapist that she had never quite got over her disappointment that her orgasm wasn't accompanied by the ringing bells and flashing stars one book had promised her. In fact, the first time she had had intercourse she thought it hadn't really happened because the experience was so mundane. She needed reassurance that there was nothing wrong with the fact that her occasional orgasms were very pleasurable, but they never made her lose consciousness. Sometimes, and for some people, the sensations of orgasm are extremely pleasurable and intense. At other times they are just nice – no more, no less. The quality of the orgasm has to be put into the context of the entire sexual experience. A love-making encounter that is truly satisfying is one that includes the element of loving closeness, whether the orgasm was intense or less so – and even when there was no orgasm at all.

Similarly, sex can't be sensational every single time, however satisfying your love-making is. Sex therapists compare it to food. An experience that includes hours of exciting, exquisitely pleasurable love-play, which leaves you physically drained and satisfied and emotionally loving and close, is the sexual equivalent of a gourmet banquet. It is just not possible to have this sort of experience more than very occasionally and without the planning, preparation and sheer time it involves. Neither do you always want it. Just as you would be sickened or weary if you were faced with such a banquet every day, so sex that was always a prolonged, peak experience would eventually become tiresome.

Everyone is subject to moods, and sometimes the sexual 'quickie' that is brief and physical – the sexual equivalent of a sandwich on the run – is just what you want. In between there is the sexual version of a good, plain meal that satisfies the appetite. It's not particularly memorable, but it makes you feel good, cosy and satisfied. Variety is as important in sex as in anything that is not to become boring, and variety of intensity and mood is an element of this.

Being realistic, however, is not the same as being pessimistic. It is realistic to accept that sex can be good for you at whatever age and stage you might be.

Two people on the brink of marrying came for counselling because they were concerned about their future sex life. What made them unusual was that they were in their seventies. They had, in fact, fallen in love when they were very young, but their families had disapproved and they had parted. They had lost touch, and had gone on to marry other people and raise families. Decades later, Arnold noticed in the obituary columns that Margaret's husband had died. His own wife had died eight years previously, and he wrote to Margaret.

When they met again they found that their love re-ignited and, with the blessing of their children and grandchildren, they decided to marry. Their concern was that sex would be a problem. Sex had never been important to Margaret in her first marriage, and her sex life with her husband had ceased many years before he died. She was worried that she was now too old, and possibly too 'dry'. Arnold had not thought about sex since his wife died, and worried that he might not be able to get an erection. Neither of them knew very much about sex, but were very attracted to each other. They held hands in the counselling room and were obviously very much in love.

The counselling mainly took the form of explaining about their bodies and what both might need to become aroused. The counsellor explained the kind of direct physical stimulation that might be necessary for both of them, and ways that they could make love without penetration, if it so suited them. She said, 'They wanted to be reassured that it was OK to have sex at their age, and possible too. What I did was give them information and "permission", and they went away very keen to try.'

It was arranged that they should come back after a month, so that they could talk through any problems. When they returned they said that they were very happy and all was going well. They rarely had full sexual intercourse, but they enjoyed lying in bed together, touching and talking, and the experience was the best that either of them had ever known.

MAKING TIME

The first essential in improving your sex life is making enough time for it. This elementary fact escapes some couples who ask for counselling because their sex lives have become tedious or problematic. Their love-making is often squeezed into the last few waking minutes of a busy day, and they are often resistant to the idea that they can't make it better unless they change this.

! ——————————— *Task* ———————————

Just for us

If you are out of the habit of making time for each other, it can seem odd to make a date for sex. Start by making ordinary dates, when you do things as a couple and enjoy each other's company. Aim for at least one date a week – two is even better – when you will concentrate on having a pleasant time together.

If you have children, find a baby-sitter and go out for a meal, a drink, a walk, a good film – or anything else you enjoy doing.

You can also arrange for your children to stay elsewhere for the night from time to time, so that you have time alone at home without interruptions. Later you can agree to use these dates for love-making.

!

Many people say that there *is* no other time that they can make love. But questioning often reveals that the couple do make time for what they consider important – a sport, a club, a committee meeting, gardening, an evening with a friend. If you look through your diary you are bound to find one or two appointments you have blocked in. If the quality of your sex life is important to you then it is necessary to give it priority as well.

How often?

Couples often want to know how much time they should be setting aside for love-making. Behind this query usually lies a second question – how often is normal? There is no specified number of times that you should make love every week or month. The right amount is whatever suits you as a couple. It is often quoted that the average is two or three times a week – but average isn't the same as normal. Couples can be having dreary and unsatisfying sex twice a week – but that makes them no more or less normal than a couple who have sex once a fortnight and fully enjoy it.

However, if you are trying to improve your sex life it makes sense to step up the number of occasions on which you set aside time for love-making. You don't give yourselves much of a chance if you wait for the mood or only manage to make time once a month. If you are trying to tackle a sex problem, and to deal with the anxieties and conflicting emotions that arise, it is usually recommended that you set aside three occasions every week to do so.

When?

To make the most of the time you spend being sexual together, you need to be alert, relaxed and unstressed. By definition, it means that love-making that is relegated to late at night is unlikely to fit this description. It is important to make some sessions in the morning, afternoon or early evening. This can be at the weekend, or, if you have any flexibility about working hours, during the week. You need to spend at least an hour together, to have the time to explore and enjoy what you are doing. It is even better regularly to make time for a much longer session – if not once a week, then once a fortnight or every month. These give you a chance to build atmosphere and the right conditions, as well as experiment with your love-making.

Of course, you have to take into account other matters that are going on in your life. As has been emphasised already, if you are stressed, tired, or extra busy, your sex life is going to be less important for a while. At these times you might want to plan ahead for a sexually experimental period – later in the year, when you know that things are going to ease up, or on a holiday specifically chosen to be relaxing and give you time alone. But beware of using the excuse of other pressures never to make time. If you are always doing this it either means that improving your sex life is not important to you – or that there are underlying anxieties that you are not acknowledging.

What about the children?

Couples who have children are the most likely to complain that making time is difficult or impossible. The two main reasons given are that children demand so much time and attention that there is no other time left, or that they feel uncomfortable and unrelaxed about their children knowing that they make love.

The hardest period to make time for sex is when you have a small baby. Before babies settle into routines they might need you at any moment, and during this time you are also much more tired than usual, and not in the mood for sex. This is understandable, and if you feel like this, then it is not the moment to concentrate on improving your sex life. However, it *is* essential to talk to each other about what you are feeling at this time. A silent pact not to bother about sex is rarely helpful – usually one of you is less happy about this, and might be imagining all sorts of problems. It can be the on-set of difficulties that become harder to deal with later.

This is one of the occasions on which it helps to plan for an easier period, when the baby is more settled, and to explain how you feel. For instance, you can say, 'I am so tired at the moment and unrelaxed that I can't enjoy sex as I usually do. I'd like to wait until I am feeling different before we start love-making again. How do you feel about that?' If your partner is less happy, discuss together what you can do. Usually you need to show more physical affection at this time, even if it is not sexual.

When the children are older, this particular problem disappears, but others remain. Chief of these is your attitude. You need to recognize that the relationship between you remains important now that you are parents, and that your sex life is part of this. When you accept this, it follows that you teach your children that there are times that you must be alone. Older children can't have access to your undivided attention, and their demands for this can't always be met. Your bedroom, at least, should be out-of-bounds at times. Many parents find this easier if they have a lock on their door.

The other aspect is your own feelings that it is wrong for children to know that their parents have sex, or that you find it embarrassing or awkward to make love when they might be awake. Firstly, it is good for your children's security to know that their parents are happy together. It is also good for their emotional and sexual development to recognize that their parents have a sex life that is important to them. You might be embarrassed, and they might be embarrassed – but ultimately it sends them a good 'message' to know that love-making continues happily and rewardingly in a loving relationship. It means that they are more likely to know how to be happy in their own relationships when they are adults.

But if your own awkwardness gets in the way of you being able to relax and enjoy yourself, you can still be creative about making time for each other. You can schedule sex for times that your children won't be around – perhaps they go to a club on Saturday mornings, or someone will take them off to the zoo or a film for the afternoon. You can also arrange for them to stay elsewhere overnight or over a weekend. Your family might help, or you can make reciprocal arrangements with other parents, who might be delighted if you have their children to stay at other times. If you can afford it, you can also book in to a hotel for an evening when you have a baby-sitter – which can also be fun in its own right, re-creating some of the sense of daring illicitness that you might remember from early days together.

Children were a problem for Andrew and Miranda, who came for counselling because she had gone off sex. Their three-year-old son was very demanding. Miranda had to stay with him, sometimes for hours, before he went to sleep. When he was awake he took up all her attention with tantrums, which left her exhausted. Unsurprisingly, she never had any time to spend with Andrew. When they did try to have sex, Miranda was worried that their ten-year-old daughter would walk in on them. Consequently she never enjoyed it, and was always asking Andrew to hurry up.

During counselling, the counsellor helped them look at ways they could deal with these problems.

Disciplining the three-year-old effectively was the first of these: They had tried smacking, but that used to make it worse. He knew his tantrums were a good way of getting attention, even if it wasn't very enjoyable. They tried a new system of making him stand outside the room with the door closed if he misbehaved badly. This worked very well. He learnt that bad behaviour lost him attention, rather than gained him any. Miranda also gradually cut down on the time she stayed with him to settle him at night.

Andrew was encouraged to put a lock on their bedroom door so that they could be sure they would not be disturbed. They also agreed to spend some more time together, alone as a couple. Miranda didn't like leaving the youngest with a baby-sitter at night, but was happy to leave both children with her mother on a Saturday afternoon. By the end of counselling their sex life had improved without specific sexual tasks. They were getting on better and Miranda was more receptive to the idea of sex. Locking the bedroom door improved matters enormously; they also sometimes made love in the living room in the evening with a chair wedged against the door handle. They developed the habit of making love on the Saturday afternoons that the children were with Miranda's mother. Both of them enjoyed these novelties and were getting renewed pleasure from their sex life.

Whatever happened to spontaneity?

The objections that some people raise to making time for sex is that it sounds so contrived. Sex, they believe, should be about spontaneous passion – being overtaken by desire and deciding to make love there and then. Of course, this is great when it happens – as it sometimes does at the beginning of a relationship. But it becomes increasingly unlikely – you feel overwhelmed by desire, but the situation makes love-making impossible. Or you suddenly feel very aroused, but your partner doesn't. If you wait for the spontaneous burst of passion to hit you both at the same moment, at a time when you can take advantage of it, you can wait a very long time.

That is the practical reason for making time for sex. But there are better reasons, too. Spontaneity as the trigger for sex is sometimes over-rated. Yes, it is one exciting way to start sex, but anticipation and planning is another way, which can be equally arousing and sometimes more exciting.

Think back to the early days, perhaps when sex seemed totally spontaneous. Was it? Many couples often realize that they expected and looked forward to some sort of sexual contact with each other when they were first together. They would think about their partners off and on for hours – how they looked, what it was like being with them and touching them, perhaps imagining what was going to happen when they got together. They usually made efforts to look their best beforehand, wanting to feel good about themselves. Perhaps they chatted affectionately on the phone beforehand. All this was preparation. It set up a sexy mood of anticipation. The 'spontaneous' love-making that followed later was actually a culmination of hours of mental 'foreplay'.

These are the kinds of feelings that can be re-created when you make dates for sex with your long-term partner. Planning them, working out what the right conditions are, getting yourself ready – all of these things can put you in the mood for love-making. It is a much more creative version of the sexually numbing, 'It's Saturday night, when we always do it, so let's get on with it.'

What if we don't feel sexy?

It doesn't always work out the way you hoped. Your date for sex might arrive and, for one reason or another, you are not feeling sexy. This doesn't matter. Setting aside time for love-making does not require you to feel passionate and lustful. Good, satisfying sex, after all, is also about intimacy and the gentler experience of being close and touching in any way that suits your mood. Don't cancel your date because you are now tired or not especially interested in sex. Discuss how you both feel, and adapt your plans to accommodate your current mood. Perhaps all you want to do is lie close and cuddle, or kiss and stroke gently. It is fine to do just that. Chat about your feelings, allow yourself to relax, and continue to do whatever feels most comfortable for the entire agreed time. Sometimes your feelings might change. Touching in this way might begin to put you in the mood for sex. If so, you can always change your mind. If not, don't worry. This is love-making, too – an important variation that increases the intimacy necessary for improving your sex life.

CREATING THE RIGHT CONDITIONS

Feeling sexy is also dependent on the right conditions. You have probably had quite a lot of experience of the wrong conditions if you have been together for some time. One has already been mentioned – late-night love-making in bed, when you are worn out, or knowing that this is the day and time you always do it. The right conditions are as individual as any other aspect of your love-making, and sometimes they might be different for both of you. Finding out what they are, discussing them, and putting them into practice goes a long way to improving your love-making.

Turning on – and off

The questionnaire in Chapter Four, 'Your love life now', which concentrated on the specifics of how and when you make love, included the sections, *'I find it hard to become aroused if…'* and, *'My partner finds it hard to become aroused if…'*. Be sure to complete this questionnaire if you haven't yet done so, and pay particular attention to your answers to these. Knowing what inhibits your arousal is something you should share with your partner when aiming to create the best conditions for love-making. For instance, one woman told a sex therapist she found it very off-putting when her husband came up behind her and grabbed her breasts. A man said that it was difficult for him to become aroused if his wife put rollers in her hair and a heavy night-cream on her face before coming to bed. Situations that make you feel uncomfortable, unrelaxed and unconfident are also likely to be the opposite of arousing. It can help to talk about these. In the same chapter, the task 'That's When It Happened' encourages you to think about sexual situations with your partner where this was the case. If you talk about them you both know what not to do.

It is just as important, and more fun, to consider what you find exciting and arousing when you are preparing the right conditions for love-making. You usually have some idea what these are, but rarely think it is necessary to tell your partner. In fact, because we are all so different, your partner might find it surprising and revealing

! ─────────────────── *Task* ───────────────
.

It turns me on...

Describe to each other what turns you on. It might be a part of the body, an item of clothing, a particular scent, a non-sexual activity. It could be a way of talking – romantic or 'dirty'. Agree to pay attention to these details, unless one of you finds it off-putting.
                                                                        !

It can be surprising to discover that there are a number of non-sexual things that turn you on – either because they are loving gestures, or because they increase togetherness. These are some of the things that therapists who ask this question have been told: a woman said that she felt turned on when she and her partner cooked together – it was something they both enjoyed and they were always close and happy when they did so. One man said it was when his partner ran him a bath and brought him a drink while he was soaking in it. Another woman said she found she would get into the mood when her husband kept the children away from her for an hour at the end of the day, so that she could relax. Yet another woman liked to be read to, and a further woman said that a quiet time watching television with her husband turned her on – if she was lying with her head on his chest and could feel his heartbeat. One man revealed that he felt most turned on when he and his partner had a 'real' conversation, because it was her wit and insight that was particularly important to him.

More specifically physical or sexual turn-ons are also varied. One man found it very arousing when his partner wore a dress or house-coat with nothing on underneath – especially if it was many hours before they could make love. One woman said she was turned on by the smell of her husband after he had been gardening and 'working up a sweat' in his oldest clothes. Another woman had the opposite experience – she was turned on by her partner when he was in his suit. She liked dining out with him at expensive restaurants *not* because she found the situation romantic, but because she was attracted to the way he looked when dressed up. One man remembered that he used to get most turned on when his partner called him at work to say that she was thinking about sex with him.

Some people also find it arousing to reverse some habitual elements of love-making. For instance, if you usually make love with your night-clothes on, try it without – in the dark or half-light, if that makes you more comfortable to begin with, and sleep together naked afterwards. Similarly, if you are uninhibited about your nakedness and always strip off quickly to make love, consider keeping all or some of your clothes on until some time into love-making or throughout. Any habit loses its flavour after a while, and making a simple switch is exciting in itself.

! ————————————— *Task* —————————————

It worked for them...
...increasing privacy

One couple found that they were turned off simply because they had become too familiar with each other. She said, 'When I'm in the bath and he's sitting on the loo, I just can't see him in a sexual way.' They found that introducing more privacy worked, even preferring to dress and undress when they were alone.

!

Getting ready

Getting yourself ready for a sexual date with your partner is also part of creating the right conditions. It has the effect of focusing your mind on what is to come in a pleasant way. It also helps you feel good about yourself and your body. As we discussed earlier, feeling bad about your body turns *you* off. Feeling attractive, and that you are looking your best, has the opposite effect. If you think you look nice, smell nice and feel nice, it is easier for you to accept loving attention from your partner and believe it is genuine. This is as true for men as it is women – at the beginning of a new relationship in which they are unsure, men prepare for dates just as carefully. Taking a bath or a shower, choosing your clothes carefully, paying attention to your hair and the way you look, all start to build up an atmosphere of pleasurable excitement.

!========================= *Task* ===============

Feeling good

Treat yourself to something that will help you feel good: something for the bath, perfume, after-shave, body-cream, haircut, new underwear – anything that you enjoy and that boosts your ego. **!**

In some cases, getting ready for your date also involves an activity that marks the end of a normal day, and changes your mood. This is particularly the case if your date is for an evening, after you have been working or looking after the children. Moving straight into sex-mode can be difficult until you have wound down, or dismissed the thoughts of the day from your mind. The way you choose to do this is up to you. It suits some people to do something sporty, or go for a walk or a run. Other people like to wind down doing some gardening. Quiet activities, such as listening to music, reading a little, having a drink, taking a nap or a bath can also help. You might either like to do these things together or on your own.

A light meal can help put you in the mood, but a prolonged or heavy meal with lots to drink can have the opposite effect, making you too sleepy or uncomfortable for sex.

!========================= *Task* ===============

It worked for them...
...home health clinic

Ricky and Pauline found that the best way to put themselves in the mood for a love-making session was to re-create the atmosphere of a health clinic. On alternate occasions, one of them would administer to the other. For instance, if it was Ricky's turn, he would take a bath. Pauline would wash his hair for him, and when he was clean and relaxed he would go into the warm bedroom, where Pauline would give him a massage. 'Neither of us know how to give a professional massage,' they reported to the therapist, 'but it doesn't matter. The one massaging pummels and kneads, and tries to work on the other's tense muscles. Afterwards we both feel like making love. It is as relaxing to give the massage as to receive it. And the one "doing the work" knows they'll get their turn next time.' **!**

Where?

You also have to decide where you are going to make love, and prepare the surroundings so that they are welcoming. If you have the place to yourself, you can choose any room you like, or take a different room each time. It doesn't have to be your bedroom, unless that is what you both would prefer or you have no choice. Some people are agreeably surprised to see how different the experience is in another room – perhaps the spare room with a single bed. It makes it harder to 'do what you always do' when the surroundings are different, and can add an excitement quite out of proportion to the actual change. Some people like to switch venues – starting off in the bath or shower, or in the kitchen or on the stairs – and then move somewhere more comfortable.

Wherever you choose, make sure that it is warm and comfortable. Turn the heating up, or bring in an extra fire. This is essential if love-play is going to be prolonged and relaxed – cold makes you tense, warmth is necessary for sexual feelings to develop.

After that, it is up to you what kind of atmosphere you want to create. These are some ideas that have helped other people:

● **Lighting.** It is good to vary the lighting from one occasion to the next. If you are shy, you might prefer to have it as dim as possible on the first few occasions. Sometimes the glow from a fire is enough to allow you to see. Many people like candlelight, whether they are shy or not. It gives a glow that is flattering to skin tones, and is sufficiently different from normal lighting to change the atmosphere of even the most familiar room. Brighter lighting might be better for other occasions, particularly if you have decided that you are going to look carefully at each other's genital areas, and other parts of the body.

● **Background.** It is also interesting to experiment with creating atmosphere in other ways. For instance, you might want to have music playing. To concentrate fully on what you are doing, soft music without vocals is best. Some people also like scent from incense or scented candles.

● **Survey the room.** If there is no bed, where are you going to make love? On the sofa, on a chair, over a table, on the floor? How are you going to feel about this? Do you need to do anything to make it more comfortable? Perhaps you want to protect furnishings with a towel or a sheet. Would you like to bring in extra pillows, or a mattress, or pile more rugs on the floor?

● **Your bedroom.** If your bedroom is the place you most often make love, it is worth making it as ideal for this purpose as possible. Don't let it become a family room, cluttered with anything that is for daily living rather than sex and sleeping. It is best *not* to have a television in there. Train the children to keep out unless specifically invited, and – this can't be emphasised too often – put a lock on the door. Pay attention to the lighting in the room so that you can vary it at will. Consider having a music system for your bedroom. It helps to keep out the noise of the household, and to mask any noise you make yourself.

After lovemaking

Included in the conditions that make sex good for you is what happens after a love-making session. The questionnaire about your sex life in Chapter Four, 'Your Sex Life Now' also had questions about what you and your partner like to happen after love-making. Discuss your feelings, and see how you can incorporate them. If one of you likes to sleep and the other prefers to talk, arrange a compromise. Perhaps you can chat briefly, and then hold your partner while he or she sleeps for a while – resuming your talking later. If you have scheduled sex for an afternoon or an early evening, perhaps you can both sleep – and then go out for a meal afterwards, or eat together at home and talk intimately then.

SEX IN THE MIND

One of the most important elements of your sex life is what goes on in your mind. The negative effects of this have already been explained, by showing how difficult or unpleasant experiences in the past can make sex problematic for you, even when you are physically in perfect working order. Ideas about the rights and wrongs of sex inhibit you, even when your body is giving you a different message.

But the positive side of this is that improvements in your sex life can be affected by changing your ideas about sex. Allowing yourself to think more about sex generally and specifically can also help you to understand your responses better. It can also raise your level of desire and make you more receptive to arousing love-making with your partner.

Just as important as these is being able to talk about sex with your partner. Sometimes there is no substitute for words when it comes to showing your feelings – good or bad. Talking about sex also makes it easier to introduce changes that will improve your sex life. Lastly, talking about sex with your partner can be erotic and arousing in itself – an additional and pleasurable element in your sex life.

Even so, some people find it much harder to talk about sex with their partners than they do to make love. It can seem embarrassing or 'rude'. Sometimes even the most sexually uninhibited people find it difficult, wrongly believing that sex is something that should come naturally without you talking about it. While this might be true to a certain extent for some people, the 'fine-tuning', which makes sex the best it can be, will never happen without talking.

Talking generally

When you are not in the habit of talking about sex at all, you will probably find it difficult to go straight into talking about your sex life. But you can begin to be more comfortable by making sex a topic of conversation on a more general level. For instance, this book has been designed to help you talk about sex. Even if you find it difficult to talk about the more personal issues it raises, you can talk about the general messages it contains – concerning what sex is or isn't, and what it can or can't be. You could also look at some of the case histories and speculate about the couples involved. It can be fascinating to think about other people's sex lives – many newspapers and magazines are sold on the strength of this kind of speculation. Discuss them together, and say what you really think.

! ——————————— *Task* ———————————

Sex on the screen

Watch documentaries that deal with the subject of sex, and talk about them afterwards. When you see a film or a television programme with sex scenes, do the same. What do you think about the sex portrayed? Is it realistic? Did you find any of it exciting – if so which bit? Did it make you feel embarrassed or awkward – if so, why was that? Did you find it offensive – which part? Did it seem silly or ridiculous – why particularly?

!

Talking about yourselves

As sex is part of your lives together, it can seem artificial to try to talk about it in any personal way if you are not in the habit of talking about yourselves generally. Talking about feelings and experiences is a very intimate activity. It makes you feel closer to one another, and also makes it seem more appropriate to talk about intimate matters, such as sex. If you can't talk about the ordinary things that are on your mind, you will find it very hard to talk about your sex life, particularly if you are hoping to make changes.

This is why making time together has been emphasized at different points in this book. If you spend little time alone concentrating your attention on each other, you will rarely talk about anything that is not superficial and practical. No wonder it becomes harder to talk about sex. It is necessary to become used to holding conversations with each other that go beyond the practicalities of daily life. Going out alone is one of the best ways of making sure you have uninterrupted time together. It doesn't have to involve expense. One of the pleasantest ways of talking together is on a walk, perhaps holding hands. You can chat naturally about what you are doing and seeing, as well as more profound matters. Some people find this much easier than a face-to-face talk, which can feel like a confrontation when you have something important to say.

It can also be nice to chat on the phone during the day, if this is practical. The song 'I just called to say I love you' touched a chord with many people because its simple sentiment is so appealing. Do you ever do this? If you think it is silly or unnecessary, think again. Many people reserve the words 'I love you' for passionate or otherwise emotionally highly charged moments. They can be much more touching or powerful at ordinary times.

Talking about your sex life

If you have never been in the habit of talking about the sex you have together, then you must ease yourself into this as well. If love-making has been silent, you will probably find it more comfortable to talk about sex *out* of bed at the beginning. You can talk about it over a meal, washing up – or even on your walk, if you have started to include this in your routine. When these conversations have lost their awkwardness you can continue the dialogue when you are making love, and talk about what you are doing, and what you do and don't like. These conversations should be light-hearted, even if what you ultimately have to say is serious.

'───────── Talking point ─────────

I'm you

A fun way to start talking about sex is to take it in turns to describe one of your usual love-making sessions *as if you are your partner*. Imagine that you are your partner as you talk. Say 'When you do this, I feel…' and 'As I do this to you I am thinking…'. Describe what else might be going through your mind, which sensations you like best, what orgasm is like. At the end, comment on the accuracy of what each other has said.

,

This task is more useful than it looks at first reading. You might never have really thought about your partner's experience before, although you might well have made some assumptions about it. For instance, if you are a man it can be a mind-stretching exercise to imagine that you have breasts and how you feel if your breasts are touched in certain ways. Similarly, imagining how a penis feels when touched, or inside the vagina, can be an interesting imaginative leap for a woman. This task is playful, and any correcting of assumptions should be equally playful. Even so, it can be educational to hear your partner say, 'No, what it *really* feels like is...'

Another playful task involves talking about a *future* love-making session and what it will be like.

' ══════════════ Talking point ══════════════

And what we'll do is...

The aim is to talk about the next time you are going to make love. Have this conversation in a completely unsexy atmosphere – perhaps over breakfast, or a chore, such as washing the car. Toss a coin to see who starts. That person should begin, 'First I'll...' and describe an initiating move. The partner should respond with 'Then I'll...' and say what comes next. You are allowed to make suggestions to each other if either becomes stuck, saying, 'What about...?' Or you can suggest an alternative touch or move if you prefer – which your partner can accept or reject. Talk through the experience step by step until you have described the entire love-making event. At the end ask, 'How was it for you?'

'

Although the intention is for this conversation to be fun – and you can make your suggestions as silly or realistic as you like – it also has a serious implication. It shows that love-making is a conscious activity, not a purely spontaneous physical interaction. You can also mentally 'try out' actions or techniques that you might not have put into pratice before, and gauge your partner's reactions to them in an unthreatening situation. If you enjoy this conversation, have it more than once – adding more details to stretch the mental love-making session out as far as you can. When the answer to your final question is 'wonderful', you might decide to try out one of your talked-about sessions.

When you can do this task easily and without embarrassment, it is interesting to apply a version of it to an actual love-making session. Again, reserve this task for when you are in a playful mood, perhaps not over-passionate but inclined to make love.

! ———————————— *Task* ————————

Sex talk

On this occasion, make a pact to talk throughout your love-making, explaining to your partner before you make a move what it will be. Say, 'Now I'm going to kiss you' – and do so. 'Now I'm going to stroke your face' – and so on. Sometimes this will make you laugh – that's part of the experience.

One of the rules is that when you particularly like what you are doing you should say so, and when you like something your partner does to you, you should also say so, and why. You can ask your partner to repeat, or carry on, with anything that is specially pleasurable. For the moment, ignore anything that you don't particularly like.

!

This task can show up an imbalance in your sexual interaction. If one of you is making all the moves, it becomes more obvious, because that person will be talking about it. But like all the tasks mentioned so far, there is only real point to this if you both find it enjoyable. If it makes either of you feel awkward or anxious, then it is not right for you, and you don't have to continue with it.

If you find it relatively easy to integrate these talking tasks into your sexual relationship, then you are in a very good position to talk about any problems or changes that you might want to make in your love-making.

Making changes

For love-making to remain good between you, it follows that you will make many changes over time. Change doesn't have to be the result of a problem, it can be for its own sake. Routines are boring and variety is enlivening. You might go through phases when what you need from sex is different – a time when it is important for you that it be tender and love-affirming, or another time when you are feeling out-going and energetic, and this is reflected in your sexuality with a need for more frivolity or passion. You can also discover in yourself a desire to try some sexual variation you never considered before. While these different needs can be partly expressed by your manner and actions, straight-talking is more direct and effective.

At other times changes need to be made to resolve problems or dissatisfaction in your love life. These can happen to the most sexually well-suited people. They are also inevitable if you have been together for some time and have never talked about sex.

Your answers to the questionnaire about your sex life now will have identified if there are aspects of your love-making that don't suit you or your partner. These are matters that you are going to have to tackle, particularly if you are going to draw up your own 'Better Sex Plan', as suggested on page 129.

Dealing with asking – and not getting

Feeling free to ask your partner to do something for you supposes the freedom for your partner to decline. This is what many people find most difficult. If it has been hard to voice your wish, a 'no' can make you feel it would have been better to keep quiet. You can also experience it as hurtful when your partner reveals to you that something you have always done is not pleasurable or is actively unpleasant. Coping with these tensions needs you both to accept that there are bound to be differences in your sexual desires and that uncovering these transcends personal feelings in a move towards better sex.

Nevertheless, these are delicate issues, and they need to be handled with sensitivity and a desire to help, rather than hurt. It is useful to talk about how you are going to deal with comments or requests from your partner that are distasteful to you or hurtful. This should be a conversation about generalities, rather than specifics. Ask each other, 'How are we going to deal with it when we ask for something the other doesn't like?' and 'How will we cope if we hear that we have been doing something that doesn't suit the other?'

One of the ways is to agree that a 'no' is given without attacking your partner. It is unhelpful to say, 'That is disgusting!' or 'How could you think something like that?' A 'no' should be given in personal terms. For instance, 'I find that off-putting/frightening/worrying', or 'It reminds me of [*a specific unpleasant incident in the past*] which is hurtful/ distasteful/anxiety-creating'.

If you are not sure what your reaction would be to trying something new sexually, you can also decide to have a go – with the proviso that if it is disturbing you stop.

You might also agree to take small steps towards an unfavoured activity to see if your feelings about it change. For instance, one woman wanted her partner to perform oral sex on her. He didn't like the idea and wasn't sure if he would be able to, but he agreed, in the first instance, to use his mouth on the inside of her thighs – which she discovered she loved.

!

================================ *Task* ================================

Do it for me

Before starting love-making you should agree to ask each other to
do one thing for you – no more. It can be a touch, a kiss, or sexual
act. Say, 'This time I would like you to...' Be quite specific in terms
of exactly what you want and how long for. An example is, 'This
time I would like to spend at least five minutes just kissing', or 'This
time I would like you to stimulate me to orgasm with your hand'.
Your partner is free to decline to do what you ask, using the
suggested formula. But, if so, you should choose something else.
Make these requests a regular feature of your love-making. You
can change your request each time, or make the same one often, if
you prefer.

!

The same care needs to be paid to telling your partner that you want
a certain aspect of love-making to change. You must bear in mind that the
issue is *your* feelings, not what your partner has done. The responsibility
is joint – if you have put up with something you don't like for a long time,
you must accept that you contributed to the state of affairs by not
mentioning it before. Perhaps it was something you used to like, but no
longer. Even so, the issue is that your feelings have changed.
Therefore, it is also unhelpful to attack with comments such as, 'I hate it
when you...'.

It is also your responsibility to help your partner understand what
would be better. For instance you can say, 'I would prefer [*make a
suggestion*] to [*whatever the unarousing aspect is*]'. Examples are, 'I
would prefer it if we spent longer on touching before sexual intercourse.
I will be more aroused', or 'I would prefer it you would make the first
move sometimes, rather than wait for me to initiate', or 'I would prefer it
if you kissed me and paid me some attention after sex, rather than
turning away immediately'.

These new ways of talking often need some practice. It is wise,
therefore, not to try to revolutionize your sex life in one go. If there are a
number of areas of dissatisfaction, take them one at a time – certainly no
more than one a week. It is best to start with the aspect that is least
important, and gradually work up to the others that cause you more
distress, as you see some improvement, and trust and ease are
established. Honesty about your feelings is what is most important – and
that includes acknowledging any awkwardness you feel. It is quite
legitimate to say, 'This is very embarrassing for me', or 'I find this very
hard to say.'

! ——————————————— *Task* ═══════

Make love to me

This task supposes that your basic sexual relationship and the way you communicate is good. The idea is that one person is the active partner throughout a love-making session of at least an hour, and that the other makes no moves at all. For the first half hour, the active partner should make love to the other in whatever way he or she wants to. During that time, the passive partner should say what he or she feels, and why something is particularly nice. The passive partner can also comment on anything that is not enjoyable, but only in such a way as to suggest what would make it better: transferring attention to another part of the body, gentler or firmer touches, and so on.

After half an hour, the passive partner, while remaining passive, should direct the other's love-making, with suggestions as to what he or she should do next. Remember that the directions should include all actions, from kissing and gentle sensual touches to more specific sexual acts. The active partner should follow the instructions *unless* he or she finds a suggestion distasteful, says why this is so, and asks for a new instruction.

At the next session, switch roles.

!

If you can carry out this task happily, it shows that you are very well placed to deal with any difficulties in your sex life. Telling your partner how to make love to you is the positive side. Being able to express what you find off-putting or unarousing is also positive, because you can then adapt your love-making so that these elements go.

Fantasy

For many people 'sex in the mind' means fantasy. Some people say that they never have sexual fantasies, as if it is something to be proud of. In fact, fantasies are not only natural, they can be an important element in your sex life – alone or shared. Perhaps it helps you to think of them as 'sexual thoughts', which is what they are.

Your sexual fantasies show you what you find arousing. They often include things you would never want to put into practice, but they reveal what you find erotic. Day-dreaming about erotic matters, or imagining a sexual fantasy while you masturbate, also raises your level of desire. If you never have sexual thoughts or fantasies it is likely to mean that you are rarely in the mood for sex. Some therapists specifically encourage people to develop fantasies if their interest in sex has dropped away. It is healthy to cultivate sexy thoughts. They can also enliven a boring train journey, or make the washing up pass more quickly! They are particularly useful for women who are learning to masturbate because they have never had an orgasm. These therapists occasionally encourage individuals or couples to read books on sexual fantasies if they have difficulty imagining any for themselves.

Your fantasies are your own business. You don't have to share them. In the privacy of your mind, they can be as X-rated as you like. You might have a range of fantasies – for many people their sexual thoughts are about their partners and what they have done or might do together. It is also common to have sexual thoughts that only last a few seconds – perhaps yourself in a sexual situation, or passing 'naughty' thoughts about people you see or know, or a famous person. There are also full-blown dramas that would make a good porn movie. Some people feel that they are being disloyal if fantasies include sex with people other than their partners – but fantasizing isn't the same as putting it into practice. If it is fun and arousing for you, that is good enough.

Sex therapists often see couples for whom fantasy is a problem. This is usually the case when one of them says that they never have sexual thoughts at all. Sometimes this is because they feel that fantasies are wrong in some way and might have deliberately suppressed them over the years. The therapist usually points out that allowing yourself to think sexually is important in creating sexual 'appetite' – in a similar way that looking at glossy pictures of delicious recipes stimulates your appetite for food. Just as looking at a perfect chocolate cake might create a hunger that is satisfied by a piece of toast and honey, so thinking sexual thoughts can increase your desire for your partner, even if the thoughts were unconnected to him or her.

Less often sex therapists see the reverse problem – someone who is fixated on a particular fantasy, without which it is impossible to become aroused, or if one of them wants to put a disturbing fantasy into practice. These fantasies are 'distancing'. They block intimacy with your real-life partner, and they also inhibit real appreciation of the physical sensations of love-making. Fantasy can put you in the mood, but satisfying sex involves becoming more aware of your body and its reactions to touch. This is one of the reasons why, although fantasy-generated orgasms through masturbation are sometimes more intense than those in love-making with a partner, the all-round sexual experience is more fully satisfying.

Fantasy should not be confused with reality. Day-dreaming about sexual acts with your partner can be turned into a real-life happening, but some sexual thoughts are better seen for what they are – arousing fantasies that have no part in real sex, although some people find talking about them with their partners very erotic.

Sharing fantasies with your partner should be handled with the same sensitivity as any talking you do about sex. Your partner can be offended if you reveal a fantasy that you are having in the middle of sex – particularly if it involves someone other than your partner. But talking about fantasies before sex and at other times can be fun and stimulating, if you want to. To do so, you need to have a sense of your partner's ideas and feelings about sex, and his or her readiness to hear what you have to say. If you are in the habit of talking about sex generally and specifically you will know this quite naturally, and probably have little difficulty doing so. Otherwise, you will probably want to take it gradually and see how each of you reacts to a moderate fantasy before deciding whether it is something you enjoy sharing.

Sex therapists are also aware that it can be important to you to keep your fantasies private. Some people find that for the fantasies to 'work' they need to be secret, and they are spoilt if they are talked about.

‘ ═══════════════ Talking point ═══════════════

It's only make-believe

If you enjoy doing so, describe to each other a sexual fantasy you have had, now or in the past. Discuss whether you find each other's fantasies erotic. Have fun making up a fantasy together – one person starts and the other adds the next bit. Take it in turns until the fantasy is complete.

’

Some people like going one step further and play-acting their fantasies. For instance, some women and men enjoy it if the woman pretends to be an experienced prostitute, who 'takes care' of the man, or if the man pretends to be a forceful stranger. Some couples happily incorporate these sorts of games into love-making, and enjoy dressing up to make the fantasies even more real.

MAKING IT FUN

Sex is not a deadly serious activity. Its implications are serious – making babies, showing love – but if you approach it too reverently you are in danger of boring yourselves. Many people make the mistake of thinking that long-term sex should be serious and 'mature', and therefore lose the elements of fun that are exciting in themselves. Of course, one person's idea of fun is another's idea of crassness. Sense of humour is individual and ranges from banana-skin slapstick to sophisticated wit. Only you know what is fun for you.

It would be impossible to cover everything that might appeal to you here – and it might all seem too silly for words. Silliness, however, is tension-breaking, and most people benefit from letting go from time to time. Talk about devising your own humorous approach to sex if nothing here appeals.

'———— Talking point ————

No-one's looking!

Some people feel constrained sexually because they imagine what someone else might think if they saw them. A common problem is to watch yourself mentally – 'spectatoring' as sex therapists call it – worrying that you might look stupid, unattractive or not be performing correctly. To enjoy sex fully, you need to turn off this mental switch, and also recognise that no one else can see you.

During sex therapy people often reveal that it is the idea of what their parents might think, or a religious figure, or their children, that inhibits them when they are making love. Discuss whether this is something of which either of you are aware.

'

One sex therapist routinely suggests that couples with problems make their sex life fun. She said that when they were dealing with a difficulty that was causing anxiety, a couple sometimes dreaded the more specific sexual tasks – feeling that they would 'fail' or be otherwise disappointing to their partner. Having a laugh, however, was perfectly possible – and took much of the strain out of therapy.

For instance, she encouraged one couple to take a picnic to bed, and eat it in the nude. She suggested that they included a bottle of sparkling wine. They had to find a place on their partner's body to balance the glass, and deal with any over-flow by licking it up. This couple had a good and happy general relationship, but were over earnest about their sex life.

This task freed them to tackle the man's premature ejaculation in a more positive way.

! ———————————— *Task* ————————————

It worked for them...
...mock fights

Catherine and Tony started sex therapy to deal with Tony's erectile difficulties. They were in their late fifties. To ease some of the tensions between them, the therapist suggested a task from the book *How to Make Love to the Same Person for the Rest of your Life* – a fight in the nude with ping-pong balls. They can't hurt, but can be aimed with accuracy.

Catherine and Tony were amused by the idea. They went together to buy the ping-pong balls, and the fun started then. They felt 'naughty' buying a 'sex aid'. They found they could buy different colours, and giggled over the choice. During their first fight, one of Catherine's balls got lost, and they found themselves crawling round the floor stark naked trying to find it. They laughed throughout – and also found it erotic. Some days later one of their grandchildren found the lost ball. Catherine remembers blushing, and snatching it off him, saying, 'You can't have that. It's mine!'

Incidentally, Tony's erectile difficulty disappeared.

!

One of the reasons this task worked for Catherine and Tony, and can work for other couples, is that it is more than just fun. Anger and aggression are physically arousing – the body goes through changes similar to the changes of sexual arousal. That's why 'kissing and making up' after a fight can sometimes lead to good sex. A mock-fight is stimulating for a similar reason – and so is other physical activity, such as sport, which gets the system racing as well as reducing tension. Playing a sport together that requires energy and stimulates adrenalin, puts your body in a state of readiness.

Other couples have discovered that playing gentler games together helps create an affectionate rapport between them. Even if these are played in a non-sexual situation the feelings spill over. Silly card games that require no skill, such as 'Snap', or building a tower of cards or non-competitive children's games, like trying to keep a feather in the air by blowing it, or 'hunt the thimble' where you hide something and your partner has to locate it with the instructions 'hot', 'warm' or 'cold' are two examples. Some couples use this last one as a sexual game, rating touches to the parts of the body between 'cold' and 'hot'.

! ———————————————— *Task* ————————————————

It worked for them...
...home entertainment

One couple improved their sex life, by taking it in turn to choose videos to watch before sex. She usually preferred ordinary films with sex in a romantic context, he liked more obvious 'blue' movies. They would discuss the films as they watched, and talked about anything they would like to try.

!

Films can put you in the mood – but some people find hard-core blue movies offensive or off-putting. Be sure to take each other's feeling into account over these. Similarly, some people find looking at sex magazines together stimulating, and it is perfectly all right to do this. On the other hand, some women, especially, find this a turn-off, so it best not to force them on an unwilling partner.

Enjoying your sensuality

Sensual sex – an awareness of all your senses when making love – heightens the pleasures of the sexual experience. Part of the aim of the sensate focus exercises in Chapter Six is to help you become aware of sensations you might otherwise have missed. Doing this can, and should, be fun as well.

If you are out of the habit of noticing how things look, feel, smell, taste and touch, it can take practice to develop your awareness. One sex therapist often suggests that a couple go home via a department store after a session talking to her, and wander around it sharing the experiences of their senses. She suggests going into the perfume department, trying out the scents, and discussing which they like. They then move on to the fabric department, to feel different textures, and appreciate the colours. They end up in the food hall – looking, sniffing, and eventually deciding on a food to buy and share. This might seem to have nothing to do with sex, but anything that stimulates the senses, and is fun, helps.

Another sex therapist encourages couples to prepare for a sensate focus session by going around their home finding objects of different textures to touch each other with. The more the better – they can be scratchy, soft, shiny, slippery. The aim is not necessarily to find the most erotically pleasurable, just a variety. She suggests that they try them out on themselves first, to see their own reactions, and then to find out whether their partners feel the same or differently about them. She talked about one couple who found this enormous fun. On one occasion, the man prepared well in advance, and had put his chosen objects on his bedside table. When they started the sensate focus exercise, he suddenly felt a familiar sensation. 'You're using *my* brush!' he accused his wife. 'No, I'm not,' she insisted, 'it was just lying around!' They had a spirited argument, and ended up laughing. The therapist said, 'It might seem unrelated to sex, but this couple had never been able to talk while making love, and sex had become problematic and boring. It was, in fact, a breakthrough for them generally.'

The good old days

Many people remember the early days of their relationship with affection and sometimes regret. Quite often sex seemed more exciting and satisfying then as well. Sex therapists usually encourage couples to remember what it was about sex then that made it special, to see whether there are any elements that have been forgotten or simply allowed to lapse. In Chapter Four, 'Your Sex Life Now' there were some tasks to help you do this. 'I remember...' on page 111, encouraged you to remember a specific occasion when sex was very exciting with your partner, and 'It was good for me' on page 112, encouraged you to tell your partner about this.

Sex therapists often suggest that couples quite consciously re-create early sexual encounters with each other. Some of the things are simple, and have been mentioned already – making more time for love-making and planning it, as perhaps you used to do. Other elements might strike you as more strange. For instance, you might remember that you used to be very aroused petting in your parents' living room. You kissed for ages – you didn't dare remove any clothes, in case someone came in, but you managed to stimulate each other to high excitement, perhaps even to orgasm this way. Now, of course, you don't have to do such a thing – you are perfectly entitled to go to bed, strip off and have 'sanctioned' sex. But why not try a session on the sofa, as you used to have? It's fun, it's childish – but you might find it as arousing now as you did then. Other couples have found re-creating other early sexual situations exciting – 'snogging' in the cinema, the awkward gymnastics of trying to make love in a car, touching each other in public – perhaps under the table at a pub or restaurant. It can be surprising how enjoyable these staged reconstructions of early love-making can be. Look back at 'I remember...' and decide, just for fun, to live that occasion all over again.

When you look at the conditions that made this early occasion arousing for you, it includes how your partner behaved, talked, looked at you. It is play-acting, but include these elements, too. For instance, some couples remember that part of the excitement of early sex involved some form of loving coercion. The woman might remember that she was nervous of letting her partner go 'all the way', or of appearing to want sex. To change her mind, he might have spent a lot of time trying to put her in the mood, which she secretly found very exciting. He too might have found it exciting to turn her on gradually, so that she then became a willing participant. Similarly, other couples remember that love-making used to take up a whole evening – not all of it specifically sexual. For instance, kissing, hand-holding and petting might have been interspersed with talking – about each other and life generally, creating a warm intimacy that made sex special.

!―――――――――――――――― *Task* ――――――

It worked for them...
...acting like strangers

One couple, who first met in a wine-bar, found that it was exciting to re-create the tensions and flirting of that first meeting. Occasionally they would arrange to meet at a wine-bar in the evening, but then act as if they didn't know each other. He would 'pick her up', insist on buying her a drink and on sitting down at her table. They would flirt for a few hours, until he had 'persuaded' her to take him home.

!

In remembering those early days, some couples realize that it was the surprising newness of their partners that was also arousing. This is something that you can't re-create, and it is not even desirable – the more profound benefits of knowing the person you love very well far outweighs this transient excitement. Even so, it has the effect of making some people realize that perhaps their togetherness is too complete. Couples who learn to spend some time apart, in activities that they enjoy alone, or in seeing friends separately, often bring back a freshness into their relationship. The healthiest relationships thrive on a measure of independence where each person sees the other as an individual rather than as the 'other half'.

! ———————————— *Task* ————————————

> ## It worked for them...
> ## ...separate rooms
>
> A couple who fought a lot came for counselling and sex therapy. Their habit was for the husband to take to the spare room whenever they had an argument. Sometimes she would go home to her mother.
>
> It was suggested that for a period of a month, the husband slept in the spare room, even if they were getting on perfectly well. When they were ready for sexual tasks, the therapist suggested that they took it in turns to invite each other into their separate rooms. At night they could choose to sleep apart, or one of them could invite the other to share a bed.
>
> At the end of this time, they decided to continue the arrangement for a while. The husband decorated the room to suit his tastes. They were sleeping together most nights out of choice, and love-making had improved. Both found inviting and being invited an extra erotic element. They also realized that their arguments had been their way of creating 'personal space', and with their own rooms they found they argued less.
>
> **!**

Separate rooms might seem a radical solution to you, but there are other, less drastic ways of creating healthy distance. Apart from occasionally going out without your partner, it also helps to give each other some time alone at home. Many people appreciate a quiet period at the end of a busy day, and if you have children it is helpful to take it in turns to keep them occupied while your partner winds down.

INTRODUCING VARIETY

When sex is going wrong, many people believe that variety for variety's sake is the answer. In fact, variety in the sense of new sex acts, positions or sex aids is the least important of all the things you can do to improve your sex life. The other elements should be tried first, which is why this section is the last in this chapter, and the last in the book.

It is not unimportant, however, and for some people variety, and the newness it creates, is a very exciting part of sex. If this is so for you, then other books will give you many more details and ideas. This simply outlines some possibilities.

Positions

There is a large variety of possible positions for penetration, some of them subtle variations of the basic positions, others that require gymnastic ability and strength. Five of the most basic positions are listed here, with some of their advantages noted. For many people five positions are more than enough – and many are happy alternating two or three. But you don't have to feel limited by what is described. Sex is also about using your imagination, and it is possible to try your own variations without a book to help you.

- **Man on top.** In this position, the man lies on top of the woman, who spreads her legs so that his penis can enter her vagina. He can either lie with his weight fully on top of her, or lift himself up on to his elbows or use his hands to support his weight. The woman can lie with her legs straight, bent, or wrapped around his body. There are many other ways that this position can be varied, and you can find your own favoured way by experimenting.

  This is still a favourite position for many couples who have experimented with other positions. It is good for face-to-face contact – kissing, talking, looking into each other's eyes. The woman's movements are more restricted in this position, and the man is more in charge of the experience. For some people this is an advantage, particularly if the woman likes to feel she is 'being made love to' or 'taken'. Sometimes it is harder for the man to control ejaculation in this position, so is often best for men who have trouble 'coming'. It is a good position for deep thrusting, and the best position for couples who are trying to become pregnant.

- **Woman on top.** The easiest way for a woman to get into this position is to kneel or squat over her lover and gently lower herself onto his erect penis. Two of the ways this can be varied is by the woman lying on top of the man, or facing away from him before she lets him enter her.

This position allows the woman to control the pace and depth of penetration, and is particularly good if her partner is heavy. It can be very arousing for a man to feel that he is 'being made love to', and that the woman is actively taking her pleasure. It gives the man good access to the woman's breasts, and easier access to her genital area, and clitoris. The woman is free to touch the top half of the man's body, and it is easier for her to reach behind and touch his testicles. It is also a good position for men who are tired, or have a heart problem, and it is easier for a man to control ejaculation. It is good for women who find man-on-top positions threatening.

- **Side-by-side – face-to-face.** The easiest way for a couple to get into this position, is for the woman to put her leg over her partner's, and for them to move until their genitals are in contact. It helps if the woman is lying a little higher up than the man, so that he can push his erect penis upwards into her vagina. This position can be varied a number of ways with practice. You can also roll into it from a man- or woman-on-top position.

This is a comfortable and unenergetic position, as thrusting movements are restricted. It allows easy touching access to each other's backs – and you can also pull away to make touching the breasts and

torso easier. It is one of the most 'mutual' of positions, as both partners need to move to help thrusting and no one is in control. This makes it very intimate, and the fact that it is a 'cuddling' position increases this. It is a comfortable position for a man who has had a hip operation, and finds positions that involve spreading his legs uncomfortable.

- **Side-by-side – 'spoons'.** In this position, the woman lies with her back to the man, so that his erect penis can enter her vagina from behind. This is sometimes easier if she draws her legs up slightly.

  This allows the man full access to the front of the woman's body, and is one of the easiest positions for him to touch her clitoris. Because of the angle, penetration is shallower, and the penis presses against the front wall of the vagina, where the 'G' spot is, creating intensely pleasurable sensations for some women. It is a comfortable position for women who are pregnant, as her belly does not get in the way, and for

women who dislike the sensations of their cervix being knocked during intercourse. It is also good for women who have had a hip operation, and who find spreading their legs uncomfortable.

● **T-position.** This is the name given by Dagmar O'Connor in *How to Make Love to the Same Person for the Rest of your Life*, which she also calls 'Too-Tired-For-Sex'. In this position the man lies on his side, and the woman lies on her back at an angle that forms a T, moving so that her

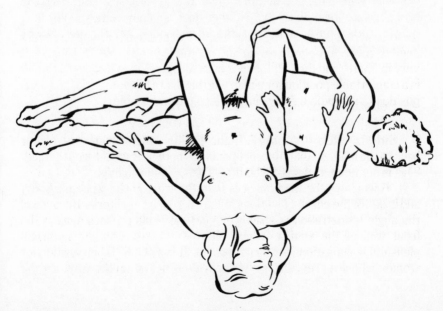

vagina is in contact with his penis, and her legs over his body. In this position, the woman controls the movement by rocking or moving herself by flexing her legs.

As Dagmar O'Connor says, this is comfortable if both of you are tired, or if the woman is pregnant, or the man has a back problem. It is also comfortable if either of you have had a hip operation.

When either of you has a health problem that makes lying down positions difficult, you can adapt these position for that person to sit – on a chair or sofa, supported by cushions, while the other takes active charge of penetration. Sitting positions can be interesting and exciting in themselves, and many couples enjoy the variety they create.

Oral sex

Using your mouth in any way on your partner's body is oral sex, but for many people it means specifically using your mouth on your partner's genitals. This can be highly pleasurable. For many men it causes more interesting and varied sensations for the penis than stimulation by hand or penetration. Some women find it is the best or easiest way to reach orgasm.

However, there are people who find the idea of oral sex unpleasant or repellent. If these feelings are very strong, it is best not to insist on doing it. If your feelings are milder or neutral, then you might like to try and see how you like it. Whether you are performing oral sex on a man or a woman, you can take it by degrees. It is not necessary for a man to ejaculate in his partner's mouth for him to enjoy oral sex – though it can be a pleasure for both of you. Neither does a man have to spend a long time bringing the woman to orgasm with his mouth, it can be one of many ways in which they are making love. Some people like the sensations of mutual oral sex, '69', but most people find it is more powerful to concentrate on the sensations when they take turns.

● **Fellatio.** If you are using your mouth on your partner's penis, you can do it in whatever way pleases you and your partner. You don't have to take the penis entirely into your mouth. You can kiss and lick the penis and the testicles, and the 'seam' of skin that runs down from the testicles. You can suck on your partner's penis, using your tongue around the sensitive head, flicking the frenulum – the little piece of skin on the underside of the glans.

Your partner should not attempt to thrust, but if you worry that he might do so, you can hold the shaft of the penis with your hand, and can stimulate it like this while you lick and suck. If you take the penis deeper into your mouth, you should either cover your teeth with your lips, so that there is no danger of scratching, or open your mouth wide. If this is tiring, you can continue love-making in other ways, and return to oral sex later. Some men like their testicles gently sucked, too, although others find the sensations too strong. Your partner should let you know what feels good.

If you want to, you can continue using your mouth until your partner comes. It is not dangerous to swallow the ejaculate, and some women find it pleasant-tasting. If your partner finds it difficult to control thrusting at the point of ejaculation, you can hold his penis so that it enters no further than you can comfortably cope with.

● **Cunnilingus.** If you are using your mouth on a woman, you should also experiment with what pleases you and her. It is helpful if you already know what kind of touches she finds exciting, and how much attention she likes being paid to her clitoris. Some people find the taste and smell of a woman very arousing, others prefer to start cunnilingus after some time of love-making, when the woman is already lubricating, as the 'juices' are less definite in taste and smell.

Most women prefer it if you pay attention to the general genital area first, perhaps starting kissing and licking around her inner thighs or her lower belly. Gradually pay more attention to the labia minora, gently sucking and exploring with your tongue. Move on to the clitoris. Some women like quite vigorous sucking, others prefer a more gentle stimulation with your tongue either soft or rigid. It is more exciting if you don't pay all your attention to the clitoris – move away and tease other areas with your tongue. You can also lick around the entrance to the vagina, and thrust your tongue in. She may well like these sensations, but find direct licking on the clitoris more intense.

You can continue to do this until you bring her to orgasm, or choose to make love in other ways. Encourage her to let you know what she likes, and what feels particularly good.

Sex aids

The most commonly used sex aid is a vibrator. Many couples find using this fun. They can produce quick and intense orgasms for most women when used on or near the clitoris, and some women enjoy the sensations of inserting a penis-shaped vibrator. Some women find that they can only reach orgasm with the use of a vibrator, and it is occasionally used by women who have never had an orgasm so that they can learn to identify the sensations of one. The sensations can also be interesting and pleasurable for a man when the vibrator is run up and down his penis, or pressed against his anus, or the area between his anus and testicles.

Some couples like to incorporate the vibrator in love-play together, others find this threatening and prefer to use it alone.

Sex shops and sex catalogues are full of other aids that some people find fun. If you think this might appeal, then browsing through these with your partner and discussing what you think and what you would like to try would probably suit you. But do remember that they can only add fun or interest. Sex aids on their own won't revolutionize your sex life – only you can do that, together.

BUILDING SLOWLY

When you are in a loving and committed relationship, you deserve to have a sex life that is equally good and satisfying. You don't have to rush it – in fact, it is better if you don't. Ironing out problems should be approached with patience, tact and forbearance. They wouldn't be problems if they were easy to tackle. Remember that sex therapists always expect couples to take a step back before moving forward. Loving perseverance is what counts, and not putting too much pressure on yourselves.

Making your sex life the best that it can be is also a continuing process. It is not something you 'get right' once and for all. If sex is fun as well as erotic you can go on enjoying this process endlessly. And if you continue to show each other love and affection in other ways, then difficult times, when sex is less important or otherwise inappropriate, can be managed without unhappiness. You should also remember that you are not alone if you find problems that you can't solve. Sex therapy is a good next step, and RELATE is there to help.

FURTHER HELP

The RELATE *Guide to Better Relationships* by Sarah Litvinoff (Vermilion).
The first book from RELATE, which looks in a practical way at how you can
deal with general relationship problems in a long-term, committed
relationship.

*Becoming Orgasmic – A Sexual and Personal Growth Programme for
Women* by Julia R. Heiman and Joseph LoPiccolo (Piatkus).
A general book about sex, which is particularly useful for women who
have never experienced an orgasm.

The Courage to Heal by Ellen Bass and Laura Davis (Cedar).
This is a comprehensive book to help women who want to begin the
healing process following sexual abuse in childhood.

Cry Hard and Swim by Jacqueline Spring (Virago).
A true story of the childhood and therapy of an incest survivor.

Entitled to Love by Wendy Greengross (from the RELATE bookshop).
A book which focuses on sexuality in people with disability.

How to Make Love to The Same Person for the Rest of Your Life by
Dagmar O'Connor (Bantam).
An amusing and illuminating book for married couples, with practical
suggestions and exercises.

Is There Sex After Marriage? by Dr Theresa Larsen Crenshaw (Exley).
An interesting look at the common sexual problems experienced by
married couples, and their treatment.

It's Up to You by Warwick Williams (Thorsens).
A book for men who want help with overcoming erection difficulties.

The Joy of Sexual Fantasy by Andrew Stanway (Headline).
A well-written and extremely useful book to help you understand sexual
fantasies and achieve an imaginative and stimulating love life.

Living, Loving and Ageing by Wendy and Sally Greengross (Age Concern).
This is a book which challenges the assumptions that sex is just for the younger generation by looking at sexual and personal relationships in later life.

Men and Sex by Bernard Zilbergeld (Fontana).
A reassuring book for men and an eye-opening book for women, about what sex is *really* like for men. It also looks at ways of improving your sex life and dealing with sexual problems.

Not Tonight, Dear by Anthony Pietropinto, MD, and Jacqueline Simenauer (Doubleday).
An intelligent and highly readable book which concentrates on the problem of loss of desire.

Sensual Massage by Nitya Lacroix (Dorling Kindersley).
A lovely guide to the art of touching. It gives intimate, yet practical ideas and advice and is lavishly illustrated.

Sex and Life by Brian Ward (Optima MacDonald).
This is a straightforward and factual account of many aspects of sex in our lives. A book full of practical advice.

Sex Problems – Your Questions Answered by Martin Cole and Wendy Dryden (Optima Macdonald).
A very readable book about sex and sex therapy.

Sexual Happiness for Men and *Sexual Happiness for Women* by Maurice Yaffe and Elizabeth Fenwick (Dorling Kindersley).
Two companion books full of questionnaires, self-analysis and frank illustrations.

Treat Yourself to Sex – A Guide for Good Loving by Paul Brown and Carolyn Faulder (Penguin).
An easy to read, reassuring book, packed with information. Exercises called 'sex pieces' help you learn about your bodies. It also looks in detail at specific sexual problems.

When a Woman's Body Says No to Sex by Linda Valins (Penguin).
This is a sensitively written piece, particularly useful for women who are experiencing vaginismus.

INDEX